Keynote

UPPER INTERMEDIATE
Student's Book with the Spark platform

NGL.Cengage.com/Keynote
PASSWORD keynoteStdt#

Helen Stephenson
Lewis Lansford
Paul Dummett

Australia • Brazil • Canada • Mexico • Singapore • United Kingdom • United States

Contents

UNIT	TED TALK	GRAMMAR	VOCABULARY
1 Identity 8–17	**404, the story of a page not found** Renny Gleeson AUTHENTIC LISTENING SKILL Recognizing key terms CRITICAL THINKING Relevant examples PRESENTATION SKILL Giving examples	Present tenses: active and passive	Tasks and interests
2 Careers 18–27	**Keep your goals to yourself** Derek Sivers AUTHENTIC LISTENING SKILL Listening for signposts CRITICAL THINKING Using appropriate evidence PRESENTATION SKILL Thinking about your audience	Future forms and uses	Career collocations

REVIEW 1 (UNITS 1 AND 2) | **About Balance** 28

UNIT	TED TALK	GRAMMAR	VOCABULARY
3 Growth and development 30–39	**Global population growth, box by box** Hans Rosling AUTHENTIC LISTENING SKILL Focused listening CRITICAL THINKING Supporting the main argument PRESENTATION SKILL Using props	Present perfect simple and continuous	Personal growth: abstract nouns
4 Success and failure 40–49	**Success is a continuous journey** Richard St. John AUTHENTIC LISTENING SKILL Collaborative listening CRITICAL THINKING Challenging assumptions PRESENTATION SKILL Repeating key phrases	Narrative tenses *used to* and *would*	Success and failure Countable and uncountable nouns

REVIEW 2 (UNITS 3 AND 4) | **Krochet Kids** 50

UNIT	TED TALK	GRAMMAR	VOCABULARY
5 Exercise 52–61	**Got a meeting? Take a walk** Nilofer Merchant AUTHENTIC LISTENING SKILL Rising intonation CRITICAL THINKING Reflecting on experiences PRESENTATION SKILL Beginning with a strong statement	Modals and related verbs: past forms (1)	Finance
6 Values 62–71	**Please, please, people. Let's put the 'awe' back in 'awesome'** Jill Shargaa AUTHENTIC LISTENING SKILL Listening for gist CRITICAL THINKING Reading between the lines PRESENTATION SKILL Being authentic	Zero, first and second conditionals	Consumerism: phrasal verbs

REVIEW 3 (UNITS 5 AND 6) | **FooARage Skateboard Company** 72

PRONUNCIATION	READING	LISTENING	SPEAKING	WRITING
Word stress Using intonation to ask a question	A personal view on personal branding	Networking	The Internet and me Personal branding Making an impression (Meeting people)	An online profile Writing skill: symbols and notes
Elision Elided /d/	Jobs for the future	Little people, big plans Applying for a job	Future goals Learning skills for the future Planning to meet up (Arranging to help someone)	A career goals statement Writing skill: formal language
Intonation in requests	What do you need?	Market research	Popular brands Are you satisfied? Leaving voicemails	Making notes from voicemails Writing skill: abbreviations
Elision of consonants *t* and *d* Intonation and meaning	Lessons for life	Reviewing an event	Old habits Passing on lessons learned Making and responding to suggestions	Minutes (1) Writing skill: bullet points
Word stress in ellipsis	What's in a name?	Young entrepreneurs	Getting motivated A sponsored event Ellipsis: omitting information when the meaning is clear (Asking questions)	An email (1) Writing skill: questions
Words beginning with *u*	Ethical consumption	Sales talk	Consumerism and the economy Ethical awareness Requesting and giving clarification (Consumer to consumer)	A consumer review Writing skill: intensifiers

UNIT	TED TALK	GRAMMAR	VOCABULARY
7 Innovation and technology 74–83	**The sore problem of prosthetic limbs** David Sengeh **AUTHENTIC LISTENING SKILL** Dealing with accents **CRITICAL THINKING** Asking significant questions **PRESENTATION SKILL** Taking the audience on a journey	Passives	Innovation: verbs Online operations
8 Balance 84–93	**How to make work–life balance work** Nigel Marsh **AUTHENTIC LISTENING SKILL** Elision: dropped vowels **CRITICAL THINKING** Convincing the listener **PRESENTATION SKILL** Pace and emphasis	Verb patterns with -ing and infinitive	Relaxation

REVIEW 4 (UNITS 7 AND 8) | **Enova** 94

UNIT	TED TALK	GRAMMAR	VOCABULARY
9 Creative thinking 96–105	**Doodlers, unite!** Sunni Brown **AUTHENTIC LISTENING SKILL** Understanding fast speech **CRITICAL THINKING** Supporting arguments **PRESENTATION SKILL** Supporting key points with slides	Relative clauses	Personality adjectives (1)
10 Connections 106–115	**5 ways to listen better** Julian Treasure **AUTHENTIC LISTENING SKILL** Dealing with unknown vocabulary **CRITICAL THINKING** Identifying problems and solutions **PRESENTATION SKILL** Body movement and gesture	Reported speech	Customer service

REVIEW 5 (UNITS 9 AND 10) | **Alpha Communication** 116

UNIT	TED TALK	GRAMMAR	VOCABULARY
11 Resources 118–127	**Cloudy with a chance of joy** Gavin Pretor-Pinney **AUTHENTIC LISTENING SKILL** Vowels: sounds and spelling /aʊ/ and /əʊ/ **CRITICAL THINKING** Identifying the 'take away' message **PRESENTATION SKILL** Being enthusiastic	Articles Quantifiers	Resources Quantities
12 Change 128–137	**Dare to disagree** Margaret Heffernan **AUTHENTIC LISTENING SKILL** Grammatical chunks **CRITICAL THINKING** Relevant background information **PRESENTATION SKILL** Using pauses	Third conditional Mixed conditional sentences Extension: *wish*	Personality adjectives (2)

REVIEW 6 (UNITS 11 AND 12) | **GiveMeTap** 138

Grammar summaries   140 | Communication activities   164

PRONUNCIATION	READING	LISTENING	SPEAKING	WRITING
Linking with /w/	The real value of digital tools	New ways of doing things	Technology in everyday life New ideas for unexpected problems Asking and talking about how something works	A formal online message Writing skill: being clear and precise
Stress in expressions	Leisure time around the world	Adjusting the balance Taking a break	Making the most of your time Giving advice Discussing options (A day off)	An email (2) Writing skill: linking expressions
Stress and meaning	The left brain – right brain debate	Launching a new product	Are you persuaded? Boosting your creativity Co-operating in a discussion: turn-taking (Organizing a campaign)	A personal account Writing skill: informal language
Sounds and meaning	Cross-cultural awareness	Two sides to every story Helplines	Two sides to every story Leaving tips Taking part in a meeting: RASA (Comparing experiences)	Minutes (2) Writing skill: reporting verbs
Linking with /r/	Life in the slow lane	Making enquiries	How much is too much? Making a difference Making and responding to enquiries (Finding out about a club)	Short emails Writing skill: fixed expressions
Tone and meaning	A letter to my younger self	Managing change	What if … ? Never again! Being assertive (Tricky situations)	Letter of complaint Writing skill: past modals (2)

Audioscripts   165 | TED Talk transcripts   174

Featured TED Talks

Unit 1
404, the story of a page not found
Renny Gleeson

Unit 2
Keep your goals to yourself
Derek Sivers

Unit 3
Global population growth, box by box
Hans Rosling

Unit 4
Success is a continuous journey
Richard St. John

Unit 5
Got a meeting? Take a walk
Nilofer Merchant

Unit 6
Please, please, people. Let's put the 'awe' back in 'awesome'
Jill Shargaa

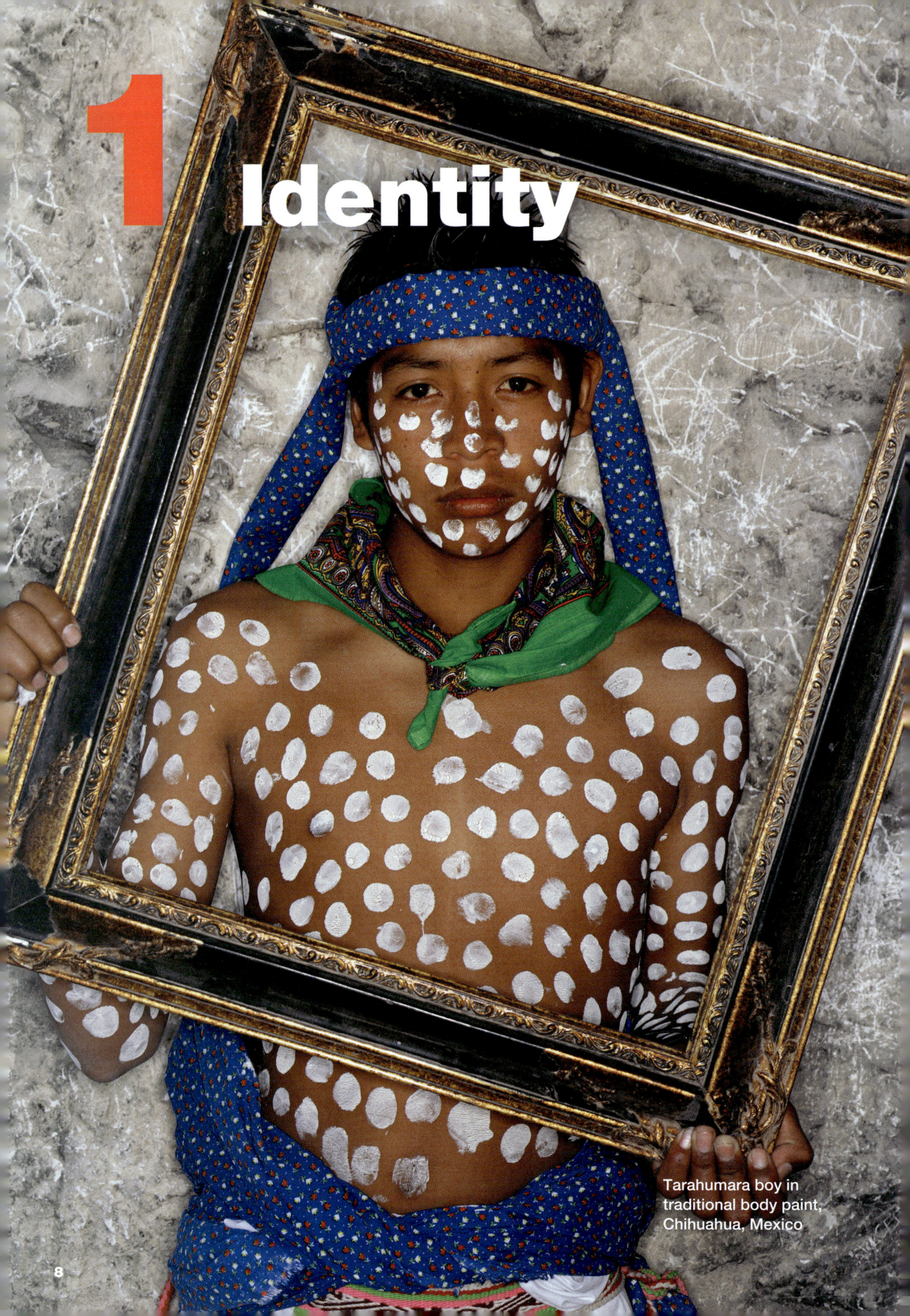

1 Identity

Tarahumara boy in traditional body paint, Chihuahua, Mexico

TEDTALKS

RENNY GLEESON works with companies to help them to use new media to promote their companies. He originally worked in game design, before moving into marketing and advertising.

Renny Gleeson's idea worth spreading is that even the errors that we make can be opportunities to build better relationships with our customers.

BACKGROUND

1 You are going to watch an edited version of a TED Talk by Renny Gleeson called *404, the story of a page not found*. Read the text about the speaker and the talk. Then work in pairs and discuss the questions.

1. The 404 page is one of the most recognizable pages users can find on the web. When would you see this page on a website?
2. Have you seen any funny 404 pages? What did they show?
3. Renny Gleeson works in 'new media'. Can you give any examples of new media?

KEY WORDS

2 Read the sentences (1–6). The words in bold are used in the TED Talk. First guess the meaning of the words. Then match the words with their definitions (a–f).

1. As director of ICT development, I **head up** the whole department in my company.
2. I am looking for people to invest in my **startup**. It's a computer repair shop.
3. Do you know how to **embed** a video from the Internet into an email?
4. We always get the same **sitters** for our cats when we go on holiday.
5. Apple is one of the earliest and most well-known computer **brands**.
6. When I turn on my computer, I get an **error** message and then nothing happens.

a a new company at an early stage of development
b to manage or run a business or part of a business
c the identities associated with particular products or companies
d to insert something, e.g. software or a web address, into another programme
e something that is wrong or done incorrectly, a mistake
f people who look after your child, pet or house temporarily

AUTHENTIC LISTENING SKILLS
Recognizing key terms

When you aren't sure about the pronunciation of key terms – especially numbers, abbreviations and jargon – this influences how much you understand when you are listening to someone speak. You can make a note of terms that are used in your area of work or study and learn the pronunciation. If the English terms are used in your language, learn how they are pronounced by native speakers.

3a Look at the Authentic listening skills box. Then look at these terms from the TED Talk. How do you say the terms?

| $404   4.04   default   sites   URL |

3b 🎧 **1** Listen and complete the sentences with the terms from Exercise 3a.

1. At _____ the next day, we gave out _____ in cash.
2. But these things [404 pages] are everywhere. They're on _____ big, they're on _____ small.
3. The 404 page is that. It's that broken experience on the Web. It's effectively the _____ page when you ask a website for something and it can't find it.
4. You can type in an _____ and put in 404 and these [webpages] will pop.

3c 🎧 **1** Listen again and check your answers. Did you pronounce the terms in Exercise 3a correctly? Then work in pairs. Read out the sentences and practise saying the terms.

1.1 404, the story of a page not found

TEDTALKS

1 ▶ 1.1 Watch the edited version of the TED Talk. In which order (1–3) does Renny Gleeson do these things (a–c)?

   a He tells a story about a 404 page competition.
   b He explains what a 404 page is.
   c He suggests that 404 pages are usually a negative experience.

2 ▶ 1.1 Watch the first part (0.00–1.28) of the talk again. Are the sentences true (T) or false (F)?

   1 404 pages are standardized around the world and on different websites.
   2 Most 404 pages are interesting.
   3 Finding a 404 page is a negative experience compared to our normal experiences on the Internet.

3 ▶ 1.1 Watch the second part (1.28 to the end) of the talk again. Choose the correct option to complete the sentences.

   1 Renny Gleeson helps *startups / established companies*.
   2 Athletepath *made / found* a video that illustrated the '404 feeling'.
   3 The contest Renny Gleeson organized lasted *24 hours / four hours*.
   4 The contest helped the businesses to think carefully about their *websites / identity*.

▶ learned **N AM ENG**
▶ learned, learnt **BR ENG**
▶ mobile phone /ˈmoʊbəl foʊn/ **N AM ENG**
▶ mobile phone /ˈməʊbaɪl fəʊn/ **BR ENG**
▶ head up **N AM ENG**
▶ run **BR ENG**

4 Work in pairs. Read what Renny Gleeson says about what the startups learned. Discuss the questions.

'And what they learned was that those little things, done right, actually matter, and that well-designed moments can build brands.'

1 How did the 404 contest help the startups to build their brands?
2 Why are brands so important to companies?
3 What have you learned from watching this talk?

VOCABULARY IN CONTEXT

5 ▶ 1.2 Watch the clips from the TED Talk. Choose the correct meaning of the words.

6 Work in pairs. Complete the sentences in your own words.

1 Before my holiday, I made a list of things to … , but a couple of things fell through the cracks.
2 When my friend told me … , it felt like a slap in the face.
3 I was no good at … at school and I never really figured it out.

CRITICAL THINKING Relevant examples

7 Renny Gleeson showed examples of 404 pages that helped the startups to build their brand. Work in pairs and discuss the questions.

1 Can you remember what kinds of companies these 404 pages were from?
2 Do you agree with Renny Gleeson that they were well-designed for their brands?
3 How well did these examples support Renny Gleeson's main idea / idea worth spreading?

8 Read these comments* about the TED Talk. Which viewer(s) do you think give(s) a good example of what Renny Gleeson explained? Write a reply to one of the comments.

Viewers' comments

H **Hans** – Enjoyed this! It's just like the new Nokia ad running on TV at the moment – humour always sells.

B **Brooke** – Yeah, but I think he's talking more about clever design moments – like those Google doodles that change for important dates. The Nokia ad is good, but it's just a standard advertising campaign.

G **Greta** – Yes, it's like the way they write your name on your cup in the Starbucks I go to. It's just a great detail.

*The comments were created for this activity.

PRESENTATION SKILLS Giving examples

TIPS

Giving examples in the form of stories or visuals (slides, objects, videos, etc.) can help your audience to understand your message. Here are some tips to help you to use examples effectively.

- Your examples should clearly support the points you are making.
- If your example is a story, it should be easy to understand quickly.
- If your example is a visual, it should be simple and have a strong visual impact.
- Choose examples that your audience might be able to relate to personally.
- Try to choose examples that link your arguments with the audience's own.

9 ▶ 1.3 Look at the Presentation tips box. Then watch the clip from the TED Talk. What examples do you see of these things? Do you think these examples follow the techniques in the box?

- a global experience
- a good experience
- a bad experience

10 Work in pairs. Decide whether you would use a story or a visual to give an example of each of these items. Then choose one item and decide what you would say and/or show an audience. Use the techniques in the Presentation tips box and practise presenting your example.

- a brand name
- a viral video
- social media

11 Work with a new partner. Give your presentation. How well does the example work?

▶ URL /ɜːl/ **N AM ENG**
▶ URL /u r l/ **BR ENG**
▶ opportunity /ɑpərˈtunəti/ **N AM ENG**
▶ opportunity /ɒpəˈtjuːnəti/ **BR ENG**
▶ figure out **N AM ENG**
▶ work out **BR ENG**

1.2 Building identity

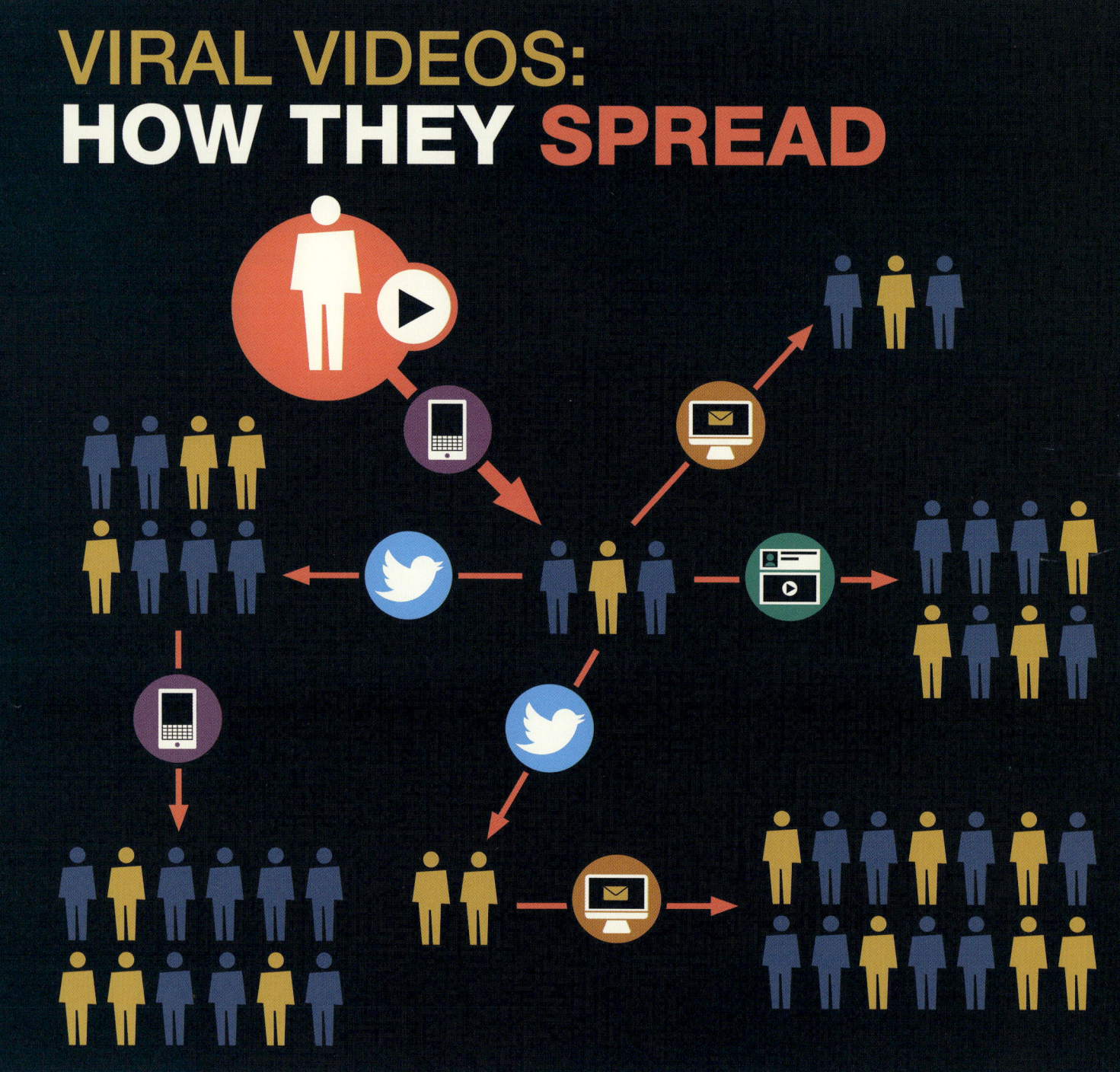

VIRAL VIDEOS: HOW THEY SPREAD

GRAMMAR Present tenses: active and passive

1 Work in pairs. Have you ever been sent a link to a video of any of these things? Tell your partner about some viral videos you have seen.

> an astronaut   cats   people dancing   songs

2 Look at the infographic. Explain how a viral video spreads.

3 🎧 2 Listen to part of a radio programme about viral videos and answer the questions.

1 Why are people studying the phenomenon of viral videos?
2 What are the differences between how people watch traditional media and content online?
3 Do people earn money from viral videos? If so, how?

4 Read the sentences in the Grammar box. Answer the questions (1–2).

PRESENT TENSES: ACTIVE AND PASSIVE

Present simple: active and passive

Millions of people **watch** mass media every day.
Millions of videos **are uploaded** to the Internet.

Present continuous: active and passive

More people than ever **are posting** videos online.
The whole phenomenon **is being studied** closely.

1 Which tense describes routines, facts, and general truths?
2 Which tense describes temporary situations, activities in progress, and trends?

Check your answers on page 140 and do Exercises 1–6.

5 Choose the correct option to complete the sentences.

1 On the Youtubing 101 course, students *are teaching / are taught* how to make videos.
2 People *are making / are made* videos all the time.
3 Some music videos *receive / are being received* over a billion hits.
4 Most online videos *are streaming / are streamed*, although people also *download / are downloaded* a copy to their devices.
5 Increasingly, people *are informing / are being informed* by online news.
6 The influence of the Internet on broadcasting *is growing / is grown* every year.

6 Complete the questions and answers from a podcast about viral videos and businesses. Use the present simple and present continuous active and passive form of the verbs.

Q: So, ¹ __do__ a lot of businesses __use__ viral videos? (use)
A: Oh yes. They ² _____ their brand to a massive number of potential customers. (bring)
Q: And so how ³ _____ you _____ a video go viral? (make)
A: Well, Quentin, that's a question lots of companies ⁴ _____ right now. (ask)
Q: And how ⁵ _____ a business _____ how many people are viewing the video at any given moment? (know)
A: Well, every view, or 'hit' ⁶ _____ by very sophisticated software. (register)
Q: And how ⁷ _____ that information _____ by a company? (use)
A: Basically, this data ⁸ _____ the business to track what's popular. (allow)

7 Complete the text with the active and passive form of the verbs.

Videos Go Viral — VOTE NOW in the annual Videos Go Viral Award!

This competition ¹ _____ (hold) every year to celebrate creativity and originality in short videos. Voting ² _____ (take) place online and the winners ³ _____ (decide) by the number of votes. The short-listed videos ⁴ _____ (host) here. This year we ⁵ _____ (not accept) professional videos: only amateur video-makers can enter. Vote as many times as you ⁶ _____ (like).

8 Write sentences about online videos. Use the nouns, and the active and passive form of the verbs. Compare your sentences with your group.

Online videos give information about a range of different things.

information	people	rules	statistics
produce	update	upload	view

Pronunciation Word stress

9a 🎧 3 Listen to the sentences and underline the part of the word that is stressed. Then listen again and say if the word is being used as a noun, a verb, an adjective or an adverb.

1 a <u>down</u>load   b download   3 a update   b update
2 a online   b online   4 a upload   b upload

9b Work in pairs. Take turns to use each word in a sentence of your own. Check that your partner has stressed the correct part of the word.

SPEAKING The Internet and me

10 **21st CENTURY OUTCOMES**

Work in pairs. Look at the profiles of Internet users on page 164. Then use the ideas to complete the questions for a quiz 'The Internet and me'. Add two questions of your own.

The Internet and me	
TIME ONLINE	how often? / for how long?
VIEWING	live? / download for later?
SHARING	how often upload or download?
ONLINE COMMUNITIES	belong? / post? / host?
WEBSITE OR BLOG	own? / write?
PASSWORDS	how many? / how often update?

11 Work with a new partner. Ask and answer the quiz questions. Then decide which profile on page 164 fits your partner.

21st CENTURY OUTCOMES **ICT LITERACY** Use technology as a tool to evaluate and communicate information

1.3 Who am I?

READING A personal view on personal branding

1 Work in pairs. Discuss the questions.

 1 Do you read any blogs regularly? What are they about?
 2 Why do you think people write blogs?
 3 Do you write a blog or anything similar?

2 Read the blog post by an acupuncture therapist. What is the writer's purpose (a–c)? What helps you to decide?

 a to sell products connected to personal branding
 b to give a personal perspective on personal branding
 c to explain why personal branding is important

3 Read the blog post again. Match the headings (1–5) with the paragraphs (A–E) in the blog post.

 1 Clothing with a message
 2 Defining my personal brand
 3 Promoting myself
 4 Something to think about
 5 Why is personal branding important?

4 Choose the best option (a–c) according to the information in the blog post.

 1 The T-shirts the writer talks about are printed with … .
  a a sports brand logo
  b information about you
  c your photograph
 2 The writer's blog is read … .
  a around most of the world
  b because her brand is well-known
  c by a lot of people
 3 The writer says … describe herself in a few words.
  a it's impossible to
  b most people know how she would
  c she'll think about how to

5 Work in pairs. Find these terms in the blog post. Is the writer negative or positive about these aspects of her 'personal brand'?

 1 presence (line 12)
 2 communicating (line 13)
 3 profile (line 15)
 4 email address (line 16)
 5 self-promotion (line 19)
 6 brand (line 20)
 7 stand out (line 21)
 8 passionate (line 22)
 9 distinct (line 26)
 10 benefit (line 26)
 11 reputation (line 27)
 12 self-image (line 28)

6 Work in pairs. Discuss the questions.

 1 Do you agree with the statement 'These days you are nobody unless you have a personal brand identity'?
 2 What advantages does personal branding give? How do you think it helps someone professionally?
 3 What would you put on your own brand T-shirt?

VOCABULARY Tasks and interests

7 Match the words in bold in the sentences with these words.

assists	committed to	concentrate on	
fascinated by	give	handle	
is responsible for	lead	loves	makes

 1 I **head up** a technology company.
 2 My boss **is passionate about** what she does.
 3 We **focus on** the customer experience.
 4 My colleague **helps** people with their queries.
 5 They **offer** a service to elderly people.
 6 Our designer **creates** amazing works of art.
 7 I'm **interested in** how things work.
 8 My manager **co-ordinates** all aspects of our work.
 9 We **deal with** financial matters every day.
 10 Our secretary is **involved in** local sports events.

8 Use the expressions in Exercise 7 to write ten sentences that are true for you. Then work in pairs and compare your sentences with your partner. Ask follow-up questions for at least five sentences.

A: I'm passionate about animals.
B: Oh? Does your job involve working with any animals?

SPEAKING Personal branding

9 **21st CENTURY OUTCOMES**

Work in pairs. Think of three people you both know professionally or by reputation. Discuss the questions. Try to use some of the words from the blog on page 15.

 1 How successfully do they promote themselves?
 2 Do you think they have a personal brand? How would you describe it?

AT EASE With Acupuncture

A Personal View on Personal Branding

About Me

About This Site

Acupuncture

Reflexology

Therapeutic Massage

Homeopathy

Hypnosis

Complementary Medicine

Archived Posts

At Ease With Acupuncture

A Personal View on Personal Branding

A   A clothing company in Canada will sell you a T-shirt printed with your vision of yourself for the modest price of $20. It's a new twist on the concept of personal branding – why promote a multinational sportswear brand by wearing their logo when you can promote yourself instead? And it got me thinking. First, what kind of thing do people come up with for their T-shirt design? And second, what exactly does wearing a self-branded T-shirt say about you?

B   Apparently, these days, you are nobody unless you have a personal brand identity. We're sending out signals about ourselves all the time, so we should make sure they are the right signals – or so the argument goes. So I decided to look more closely at how well I'm developing my own personal brand. And this is what I found out.

C   Firstly, just by writing this blog, I'm building my brand. It gives me a presence on social media and a way of communicating with the world. And my blog is read by a healthy number of people. So that's good. But I'm not doing so well when it comes to my profile: my details are minimal and I haven't joined any of those networking sites for professionals. Worse still, my email address says nothing about me! The ideal email address is something like *firstname.lastname@ …* , not the name of your favourite superhero with a few numbers added in, like mine (*Storm 376*). So far, then, I'm giving myself 4/10 for self-promotion.

D   The next thing to look at, apparently, is the brand itself. Who am I? What do I stand for? What makes me stand out from my colleagues? Now here, I'm happy to say, I think I score a bit higher. I know what I'm passionate about (and so do you if you're a regular visitor to this blog).

E   People often use words like 'empathy', 'expertise' and 'supportive' when they talk about my approach to acupuncture – and in fact that's exactly what I try to bring to my sessions. So I know what makes me distinct and the benefit that I offer my clients. I have a reputation for quality (almost all of my new clients are sent by previous clients) that fits with my self-image. I reckon I can award myself 8/10 for brand identity. But can I sum that up in ten to fifteen words? And that brings me to the all-important question – what would I put on my T-shirt? Well, let me give it some thought, and I'll reveal all in my next post …

21st CENTURY OUTCOMES   **CRITICAL THINKING**   Effectively analyse and evaluate evidence, claims and beliefs

1.4 I don't think we've met

LISTENING Networking

1 Work in pairs. What do you talk about with people who you meet in these situations?

- in the lift on the way to your workplace
- during a company-wide workshop
- after a meeting of your neighbourhood association
- in a break during a work-related conference
- when travelling for work: for example, on a plane

2 Work in pairs. Discuss the questions.

1 Which situations in Exercise 1 are useful for networking?
2 How would you try to follow up your conversation and stay in touch with the person? Would you use email, social media, a text message or a phone call?

3 🎧 4 Listen to three conversations and decide on the relationship between the speakers. You can tick (✓) more than one relationship for each conversation.

	1	2	3
they haven't met before	✓		
they don't work in the same field			
they work for different companies			
they live in the same area			
they are connected by a mutual acquaintance			

4 Look at the expressions in the Useful language box. Match the groups of expressions (1–3) with these techniques for making a good impression (a–c). Can you add any more techniques?

a they show you are a good listener
b they give you an opportunity to introduce yourself
c they give the other person a chance to talk about themselves

MAKING AN IMPRESSION

1 Starting a conversation

I don't think we've met, I'm …
Do you mind if I join you?
I believe you live near … ?

2 Open-ended questions

How are you finding the conference?
What was that like?
So how do you like living here?
What kind of things does that involve?

3 Reflecting comments

So things are going well, then?
Really?
Digital Strategies?
That sounds interesting.

5 🎧 4 In each conversation, one of the two speakers tries to make a good impression by using the expressions in the Useful language box. Listen again. Say which person uses expressions from the box.

1 conversation 1: Paul / Rowan
2 conversation 2: Joan / Nikolai
3 conversation 3: Roger / Elise

Pronunciation Using intonation to ask a question

6a 🎧 5 Listen to five questions from the conversations in Exercise 3. Only one question has a grammatical question form. Which one?

6b 🎧 6 Listen and repeat the other four questions, focusing on your intonation.

SPEAKING Meeting people

7 Work in groups. Imagine you are attending a social event between several English schools. You can be a teacher or a student. Introduce yourself to at least three people and use the expressions in the Useful language box to help you in your conversations.

A: Hi, how are you finding your course so far?
B: Oh, you know – it's a bit tough at the beginning. Which class are you in?

8 Work in pairs. Tell your partner about the people you spoke to, which one(s) you will contact again and why.

WRITING An online profile

9 Work in pairs. Read the profile from a networking website for IT professionals. Does it cover the same or different areas from other online profiles you have seen?

ROGER KENNEDY
GLOBAL DIRECTOR OF INTERACTIVE STRATEGIES AT LYNNE ROBSON JONES

Summary

I began my career as a game developer, but moved into digital advertising for Gold & Hartford. From there, I was recruited by PowerSkool, where I led the marketing team and created online platforms.

Currently, I am the Global Director of Interactive Strategies for Lynne Robson Jones, handling international clients. I also write a blog on new media.

Biodata	email: rog@kennedy.com skype: rokennedy twitter: @roken, #sunnysites instagram: rokennedy wechat: ro_k blog: www.kennedy.com/blog
Languages	English, Italian
Areas of expertise	Web technologies, video games, human technology
Areas of special interest	Startups, fuzzy interface, open source, learning, teaching, vintage motorcycles
Universities	Yale University, University of Pennsylvania
Other interests	Gaming, growing orchids, painting, renovating vintage motorcycles, Italian cookery

10 Look at the information under *Biodata*. Match the symbols with the words.

1. at
2. dot
3. forward slash
4. hashtag
5. underscore

Writing skill Symbols and notes

11a We often use more concise forms of writing, such as omitting pronouns, when filling in standard formats like online profiles. Decide how you would give this information in a conversation.

1. but moved into digital advertising
2. and created online platforms
3. handling international clients
4. skype: rokennedy
5. twitter: @roken
6. Languages: English, Italian
7. Areas of expertise: Web technologies
8. Yale University, University of Pennsylvania

11b Write this profile information as full sentences.

1. Education: London School of Economics 1999–2002
2. Experience: software development, five years
3. email: amelia@cruz.com
4. areas of expertise: customer care, online client support
5. joined Gaming Inc 2009, created new online format
6. currently assistant manager, B&T Ltd
7. interests: marathon running, theatre group
8. previous posts: personal assistant Greenly Foods; office manager Dairy International

11c Write this information in note form.

1. My email address is c underscore trott at revlon dot com.
2. My skype name is ClaraTrott.
3. I speak German and Spanish.
4. I work primarily in accounts management.
5. I've got ten years' experience in financial planning.
6. I'm involved in various children's charities.
7. I left that post and I set up my own company.
8. I head up a research department and direct new projects.

12 **21st CENTURY OUTCOMES**

Complete the sections of the website profile for yourself.

13 Work in pairs. Exchange profiles with your partner. Read the profile and ask some follow-up questions about the things that interest you both professionally and non-professionally.

21st CENTURY OUTCOMES PRODUCTIVITY AND ACCOUNTABILITY Present yourself professionally and in the accepted way

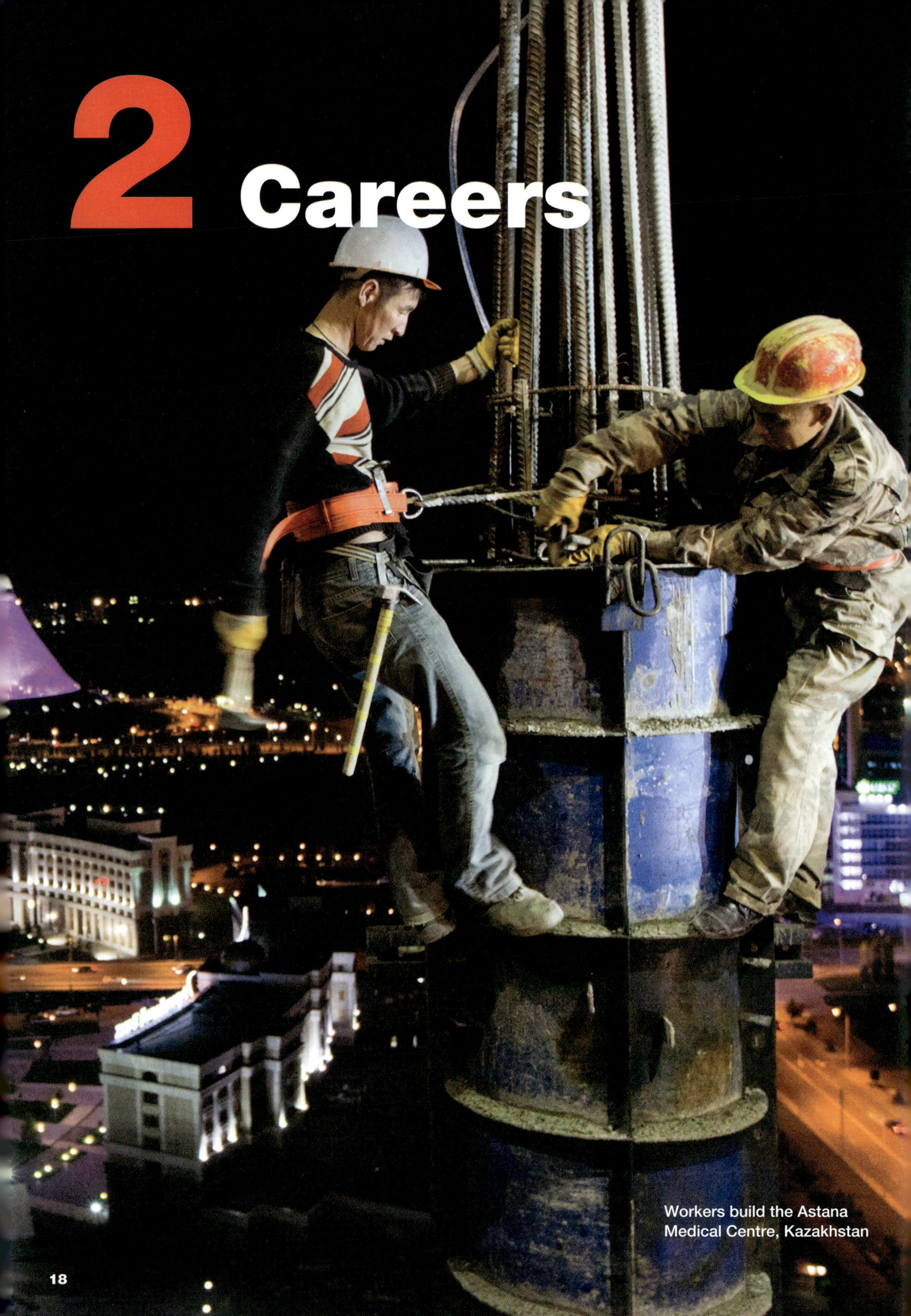

2 Careers

Workers build the Astana Medical Centre, Kazakhstan

TEDTALKS

DEREK SIVERS was originally a professional musician and circus clown. He is best known as the founder of CD Baby, a company he started in 1998. It became the largest seller of independent music online. In 2008, Derek sold CD Baby for $22 million, giving the proceeds to a charitable trust for music education. In this talk, he explores what happens when we discuss our goals.

Derek Sivers' idea worth spreading is that telling someone what you want to achieve can actually make it less likely to happen.

BACKGROUND

1 You are going to watch a TED Talk by Derek Sivers called *Keep your goals to yourself.* Read the text about the speaker and the talk. Then work in pairs and discuss the questions.

1 Do you like to plan ahead for things you want to do in your life? If so, what kinds of things?
2 Do you tend to tell other people about your plans and goals for the future?
3 Do you think Derek Sivers originally had specific plans for his career? Why? / Why not?

KEY WORDS

2 Read the sentences (1–6). The words in bold are used in the TED Talk. First guess the meaning of the words. Then match the words with their definitions (a–f).

1 I have to **acknowledge** that I had help from colleagues with this project.
2 He's really **motivated** to pass his exam because he's had a great job offer.
3 **Conventional wisdom** says that hard work is more important than luck in achieving our goals, but is it?
4 She's a very creative person. Her **mind** is always full of ideas.
5 My employees show great **commitment** by working late at busy times.
6 People who can **delay gratification** are often more successful at losing weight.

a to wait for some time before expecting satisfaction
b ideas that most people agree are correct
c to show you recognize something
d the brain or imagination
e a promise or dedication to something
f enthusiastic and determined to succeed

AUTHENTIC LISTENING SKILLS Listening for signposts

Signposts are sentences or phrases that speakers use to begin a new section of their talk. They usually give the listener some idea of the things that the speaker is going to say next. For example, a speaker might say, 'So let's look at what we've learned here,' and then go on to summarize what he or she has just said.

3a ⌂ **7** Look at the Authentic listening skills box. Derek Sivers uses the first sentence of his talk as a signpost. Put the first four sentences from his talk in order (1–4). Then listen and check your answers.

a Take a few seconds and think of your personal biggest goal, OK?
b You've got to feel this to learn it.
c For real – you can take a second.
d Everyone, please think of your biggest personal goal.

3b Here are four other signpost sentences (1–4) from the talk. Match the signpost sentences with what Derek Sivers says next (a–d).

1 Well, bad news:
2 So, let's look at the proof.
3 It goes like this:
4 So, if this is true, what can we do?

a 163 people across four separate tests – everyone wrote down their personal goal.
b 1926, Kurt Lewin, founder of social psychology, called this 'substitution'.
c Well, you could resist the temptation to announce your goal.
d you should have kept your mouth shut …

3c ⌂ **8** Listen and check your answers.

2.1 Keep your goals to yourself

TEDTALKS

1 ▶ 2.1 Complete the summary of the TED Talk with these words. Then watch the talk and check your answers.

| plans proves secret suggestions tests |

Derek Sivers says it's better to keep our goals
¹ _____ . He claims that telling people our
² _____ tricks our minds so that we think we have already achieved our goal. He describes an experiment that
³ _____ this claim, which compared two groups of people doing some ⁴ _____ . He concludes by making a few ⁵ _____ to help us to achieve our goals.

2 ▶ 2.1 Watch the first part (0.00–1.28) of the talk again. Choose the correct option to complete the sentences.

1 Psychology tests have proven that telling someone your goal makes it *less / more* likely to happen.
2 Because you feel satisfaction after telling someone, you're *less / more* motivated to do the hard work necessary.
3 Conventional wisdom tells us that we *should / shouldn't* share our goals.

▶ for real **N AM ENG**
▶ really **BR ENG**

▶ proven **N AM ENG**
▶ proven, proved **BR ENG**

▶ any time **N AM ENG**
▶ whenever **BR ENG**

3 ▶ 2.1 Read these sentences (a–e) about the 2009 psychology test. Then watch the second part (1.28–2.26) of the talk again. Which sentence is not true?

   a 163 people wrote down a personal goal.
   b Half of them announced their commitment to this goal to the others, and half didn't.
   c Everyone was given tasks to help them towards their goal.
   d The people who didn't announce the goal worked for longer than the people who did announce the goal.
   e The people who announced the goal said they didn't feel close to achieving their goal.

4 ▶ 2.1 Watch the third part (2.26 to the end) of the talk again. Tick (✓) the suggestions that Derek Sivers makes.

   If you want to achieve your goal, …
   a announce it to close friends only.
   b understand the tricks that your mind plays on you.
   c share your goal, but ask for help to achieve it.
   d say nothing at all.

5 Work in pairs. Discuss the questions.
   1 What is Derek Sivers' main claim? Does this match your own experiences?
   2 What do you think of Derek Sivers' suggestions?
   3 Have you ever done any of the things he suggests?

VOCABULARY IN CONTEXT

6 ▶ 2.2 Watch the clips from the TED Talk. Choose the correct meaning of the words.

7 Work in pairs. Tell your partner about something unusual you heard recently (a news story or something a friend told you). Use these expressions from the talk.

   | kind of | right | it goes like this |

CRITICAL THINKING Using appropriate evidence

8 Derek Sivers quoted several reports as evidence for his claim and he gave the details of one of them, a 2009 study. Read these comments* about the TED Talk. Do the viewers think Derek Sivers used appropriate evidence?

Viewers' comments

J **Jian** – He mentions a 45-minute study, but I wonder if that's the only evidence there is? Personally, I find sharing my goals does help me.

L **Lianne** – Well, I've read of longer-term studies that found the same effect, but I can't find the references right now. Maybe he just chose this example as it was short and simple?

K **Kevin** – To my mind, he mentions a lot of relevant studies. And he gives an example of how we can talk about goals in more useful ways. Well, I'm going to give it a try, anyway!

*The comments were created for this activity.

9 Work in pairs. Do you think Derek Sivers' evidence was convincing and/or appropriate?

10 Write a short reply to one of the comments, either agreeing or disagreeing and saying why.

PRESENTATION SKILLS Thinking about your audience

TIPS

When you prepare your talk, remember to think about your audience and how you can make them feel more connected to your talk.
- Avoid using technical words that the audience might not understand.
- What might they know about your topic?
- What might get them interested in it?
- Direct your audience to think about their own experiences. (*Have you ever … ? How would you feel … ? Remember when you …*)

11 ▶ 2.3 Look at the Presentation tips box. Then watch the clip from the TED Talk. Which of the techniques does Derek Sivers use? Why is this a good technique for his talk?

12 Work in pairs. You are going to give the introduction to a presentation on some of these topics. Think of things you could ask an audience to do. Write the exact words you would use.

- starting a new job
- moving to a new house
- preparing for a job interview
- making a difficult decision
- giving advice to someone about a problem
- making the right career choice

OK everyone. Now, I want you to imagine that you are walking into the office on the first day of a new job.

13 Work in two pairs within a group of four. Take turns to give your presentations. Which words are most successful in getting the other pair to think about their own experiences?

▶ half /hæf/ **N AM ENG**
▶ half /hɑːf/ **BR ENG**
▶ quit **N AM ENG**
▶ stopped **BR ENG**
▶ marathon /ˈmærəθɑn/ **N AM ENG**
▶ marathon /ˈmærəθən/ **BR ENG**

21

2.2 Are you looking forward to it?

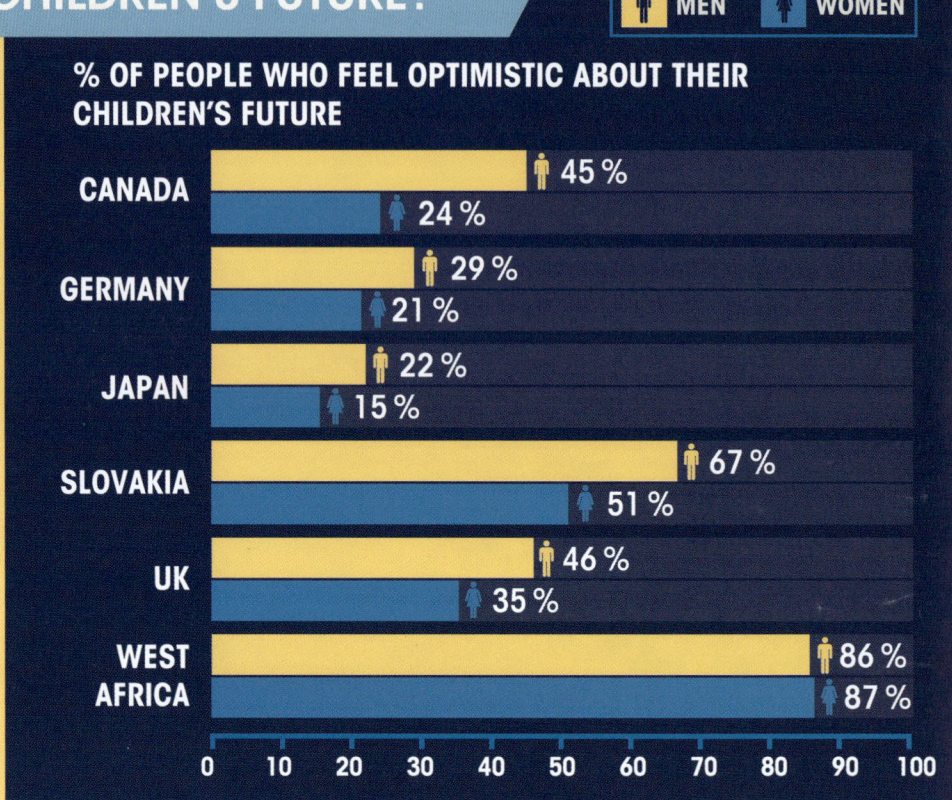

WHERE DO MEN FEEL MORE OPTIMISTIC THAN WOMEN ABOUT THEIR CHILDREN'S FUTURE?

MEN WOMEN

The Barker Research Centre for Global Attitudes conducted **20,000 interviews in 40 countries** to compare how men and women think about the future. Participants were asked if they agreed or disagreed with a series of statements.

'I am confident that my children's education will prepare them for their future.'

'I think my children will be doing things I could never imagine doing.'

'I believe I will have achieved what I set out to do by the time I retire.'

'I am sure that job opportunities for my kids are going to improve.'

% OF PEOPLE WHO FEEL OPTIMISTIC ABOUT THEIR CHILDREN'S FUTURE

Country	Men	Women
CANADA	45%	24%
GERMANY	29%	21%
JAPAN	22%	15%
SLOVAKIA	67%	51%
UK	46%	35%
WEST AFRICA	86%	87%

GRAMMAR Future forms and uses

1. Work in groups. Do you think there are differences in the way men and women think about things like careers, sport, politics, family, travel, etc.? Give evidence or examples to support your opinion.
2. Look at the title of the infographic. What do you think the infographic is about? Read the infographic quickly and check your ideas.
3. Read the statements in the infographic and decide how you would respond to the statements. Would you agree or disagree? Compare your responses in small groups.
4. Look at the graph in the infographic. Do you think the differences it highlights are significant?
5. Read the sentences in the Grammar box. Choose the correct option to complete the rules.

FUTURE FORMS AND USES

will + infinitive, *going to* + infinitive
*I believe that my children **will have** a better life than I have.*
*I believe that my kids **are going to get** better qualifications than I did.*
will be + -ing (future continuous)
*I think that I **will be living** the life I want in ten years' time.*
will have + past participle (future perfect)
*I am sure I **will have saved** enough money to buy a car by the end of next year.*

1. The sentences are about *plans / predictions*.
2. You *can / can't* use *going to* in the first sentence and *will* in the second sentence.
3. We use the *future continuous / future perfect* for actions that will happen before a stated time.
4. We use the *future continuous / future perfect* for activities that will be in progress at a stated time.

Check your answers on page 142 and do Exercises 1–6.

6 Complete the sentences with a future form with *will*.

1 I have more money than my parents did and I'm sure that my kids _____ (be) better off than me.
2 By the time I finish this course, I _____ (spend) 300 hours studying English.
3 I heard that in the future kids _____ (use) computers before they can talk.
4 From what I see in the news, I don't think our economic situation _____ (change) much.
5 I think my parents _____ (support) me financially for another year. Jobs are so hard to find.
6 From what I can see, kids today think that they _____ (appear) on TV before they're 25.

LISTENING Little people, big plans

7 🎧 9 Listen to part of Junior Chef, a TV show. Match the names of the contestants (1–3) with their ambitions (a–c).

1 Giselle   2 Jared   3 Maisie

a I'll have made my name by 22.
b I'll have opened at least four or five places before I'm 21.
c I'm going to run my own restaurant.

8 🎧 9 Listen again. Complete the sentences.

1 Giselle, _____ it to the final of Junior Chef?
2 And what _____ by then, do you think?
3 Hopefully I _____ enough to be a judge on Junior Chef one day.
4 What _____ for us today?
5 Where do you think _____ in ten years' time?
6 Somebody _____ home at the end of today's show, but it's _____ me.

Pronunciation Elision

9a 🎧 10 Listen to these sentences from the TV show again. Notice how the speaker says the words in bold. Which sounds do they not pronounce?

1 Are you **going to** make it to the final?
2 It's a **kind of** ravioli with seafood.
3 I **want to** be famous.
4 I do a **lot of** pasta dishes at home.

9b 🎧 10 Listen again and repeat the sentences. Focus on the elision.

10 Look at the questions in Exercise 8. Then write questions using future forms.

1 in five years' time, / where / you / be / live?
2 at the end of this course, / what / you / have / achieve?
3 by this time next year, / you / be / work?
4 what / you / be / do / this weekend?
5 you / go / use / English / future?
6 you / have / learn / a new skill / by next year?

11 Work in pairs. Ask and answer your questions from Exercise 10.

SPEAKING Future goals

12 21st CENTURY OUTCOMES

Work in pairs. Discuss the questions.

1 Some people like to plan their lives and others prefer to be more spontaneous. What do you think are the advantages or disadvantages of these approaches?
2 In a work situation, it's often important to have targets to work towards. Do you think this applies to everyday life?

A new series of Junior Chef, open to young cooks aged 9–13, starts this week on Tuesdays at 5 pm

21st CENTURY OUTCOMES INITIATIVE AND SELF-DIRECTION Set personal goals with measurable criteria for success

2.3 A job for life?

READING Jobs for the future

1 Work in pairs. Discuss the questions.

1. Do you think people will still be doing the same kinds of jobs as today in ten or twenty years' time?
2. What kinds of new jobs might become more common, and what jobs do you think will disappear?
3. Do you think your job (or a job you'd like to do) will change in the future?

2 You are going to read an article about types of jobs which will grow in the next ten years in the USA. Think of three jobs you think you will read about. Then read the article and check your ideas.

3 Read the article again. Answer the questions.

1. Who produced the study?
2. Which of the eight areas will grow the most?
3. Which job(s) require(s) a degree?
4. Which job(s) doesn't/don't require academic qualifications?
5. Which job(s) require(s) experience?
6. What are the reasons given for growth in these areas?

retail sales	personal care aides
customer service	post-secondary teachers

4 Look at how these words are used in the article. Find other words in the article that have similar meanings.

1. job (line 1)
2. consider (line 3)
3. employment (line 12)
4. occupational areas (line 14)
5. expect (line 20)
6. require (line 21)
7. increase (line 24)
8. opportunity (line 31)

5 Work in pairs. Discuss the questions.

1. Does the article reflect what is happening in your country?
2. How is your local employment situation similar or different from that described in the article?
3. What kinds of changes, if any, would you like to see regarding the jobs available locally?
4. Would you like to stay in the same job all your life? Why? / Why not?

VOCABULARY Career collocations

6 Match words from A and B to make expressions about careers.

A	B
academic	diploma
academic	experience
driving	experience
earn	licence
employment	opportunities
high school	position
job	qualifications
professional	qualifications
professional	a salary
starting	security
workplace	skills

7 Complete the sentences with some of the expressions from Exercise 6. In some sentences, more than one option is possible.

1. I'll be happy to _____ that keeps up with the cost of living.
2. Now that I've got a _____, I can apply for all kinds of transport jobs.
3. The pay for this job is quite low because it's just a _____.
4. Some people spend years in full-time education but forget that _____ is also important when looking for a job.
5. These days with short-term contracts, it's harder to find a position with _____.
6. I didn't have any _____ when I started this job, but I learned what to do very quickly.
7. In my job, you need to study for specialist _____ if you want to earn more money.
8. The new retail park means there are lots of _____ for local people.

SPEAKING Learning skills for the future

8 **21st CENTURY OUTCOMES**

Work in small groups. Discuss the questions.

1. Why are you learning English? What will this enable you to do in your work or life in general?
2. What other languages do you think will be useful to know in the future?
3. Are there skills that you didn't learn at school which might be useful for you in the future? Which ones? Why will they be useful?

A P Wylie

CAREERS & WORK
JOBS for the FUTURE

If you're looking for job security over the next ten years, then you should consider a career in health care, social care or transportation. That's the conclusion you can draw from a recent study into future working patterns that the US Bureau of Labor Statistics has just published. The report focuses on the areas which are increasing in employment opportunities as well as the occupational areas that will begin to decline.

We took a look at the eight job sectors that top the list of jobs for the future.

1 NURSING Along with other healthcare workers and related technical jobs, the demand for nurses is expected to rise by 26 per cent over the next ten years. The minimum qualification required to be a nurse is a two-year degree from a college or university.

2 RETAIL SALES Shopping will never go out of fashion, it seems, even when the economy is suffering. There will be an estimated 16 per cent increase in the number of sales assistants in the next ten years. This is good news for anyone who didn't do very well at high school, as these jobs typically don't ask for academic qualifications.

3 PERSONAL CARE AIDES With our ageing population, more elderly people than ever need part-time or full-time carers. Many of these jobs will be in residential centers and the report predicts that they will need 70 per cent more workers than at the present. Again, these are good employment opportunities for people with fewer academic skills.

4 HOME HEALTH AIDES A similar field to Personal care, with a similar predicted increase, you could be responsible for visiting several people in their own homes to help with basic personal care. A sometimes challenging but often rewarding job which needs no academic qualifications.

5 CUSTOMER SERVICE Businesses are increasing their customer service representatives following the negative reactions that many customers have had to increased automation in things like phone systems. It's still a good area to get into, with a projected 15 per cent rise for the next ten years. You'll need a high school diploma or the equivalent qualification to get a starting position.

6 FOOD PREPARATION AND SERVING As our appetite for fast food gets bigger, people will always find jobs in this sector (projected increase: 14 per cent). While you might not earn a great salary, the food industry gives opportunities to get workplace experience or to combine work and study.

7 TRANSPORTATION: TRUCK DRIVERS Heavy vehicles include tractors and trailers for moving goods around the country. The job can involve spending time on the road away from home. It's fairly easy to find driving courses if you need to upgrade your driving licence. Most companies require a high school diploma too. The study reckons the transportation sector will have grown by 20 per cent by 2020.

8 POST-SECONDARY TEACHERS For people mid-career who are thinking of a change of direction, now could be your chance. Colleges, technical institutes and vocational schools welcome candidates who have professional experience and qualifications in their field. The report says more students than ever will be continuing their education after high school, and predicts 15 per cent more openings for post-secondary teachers.

2.4 A five-year plan

LISTENING Applying for a job

1 Work in groups. Tell your group about the last time you applied for a job.

   1 Did you do any of the things on this list?
   2 Why are these things important?

   To do …

   ___ download application form

   ___ update CV

   ___ fill in form

   ___ ask someone to check form and CV before sending

   ___ change social media settings to private

   ___ find out about the company before interview

   ___ practise for interview

2 🎧 11 Listen to the conversation between two friends, Jill and Andy. Answer the questions.

   1 Why are they going to meet?
   2 When and where are they going to meet?
   3 What will they each bring to the meeting?

3 🎧 11 Listen again. Complete the expressions you hear.

   1 Do you have a _____?
   2 That would be _____.
   3 I'd really _____ that!
   4 Yeah, that's _____ with me.
   5 When are the _____, by the way?
   6 Thanks _____.

PLANNING TO MEET UP

Stating the purpose of the meeting

I was just wondering if you could check my application … ?
And then do you want to meet up and talk about it?
And we could prepare you for the interview too.

Arranging the time and place

When are you free?
I'm not doing anything all week.
Any time is good for me.
I'm working late on Tuesday …
Let's say Thursday at six, then.
I'll come round to your place, if that's OK with you.

Deciding what is needed

So you'll need to do a bit of research.
And will you send the checked form … ?
Yes, either that or I'll print it out …

Pronunciation Elided /d/

4a 🎧 **12** Listen to four sentences from the Useful language box. Notice how the /d/ sound in these words is not pronounced – because it is followed by a consonant.

1 coul**d** check
2 coul**d** prepare
3 goo**d** for
4 roun**d** to

4b 🎧 **13** Listen and repeat these sentences. Don't pronounce the bold /d/.

1 That woul**d** be great.
2 I shoul**d** be able to get away early on Thursday.
3 You'll nee**d** to do a bit of research.
4 Will you sen**d** the checked form back to me?

SPEAKING Arranging to help someone

5 **21st CENTURY OUTCOMES**

Work in pairs. Choose one of these situations. Plan when and where to meet, and what you both need to bring to the meeting. Try to use all of the expressions in the Useful language box.

- you need help with your CV
- you need help with writing a difficult letter
- you want to plan a trip you're both going on

WRITING A career goals statement

6 Read the extracts from four job applications. Answer the questions.

1 What is a career goals statement?
2 Which applicants do you think clearly state their career goal? What are the goals?
3 How will he or she reach this goal?

A

CAREER GOALS: please state your career objectives for the next five-year period.

In the next five years, I **intend** to enhance my leadership skills in more responsible roles and maximize my **strong** organizational skills and planning skills.

B

CAREER GOALS: please state your career objectives for the next five-year period.

My aim is to **obtain** a managerial position in tele-sales with a leading provider.

C

CAREER GOALS: please state your career objectives for the next five-year period.

I have **gained** four years' experience in interacting with existing and potential customers, regularly **achieving** or exceeding all my sales targets.

D

CAREER GOALS: please state your career objectives for the next five-year period.

After five years, I will have **secured a position** where my leadership will improve sales results.

Writing skill Formal language

7a Write the words in bold in the job applications next to their synonyms (1–6). Which of the two sets of words has a more positive impact on the reader?

1 get
2 good
3 got a job
4 had
5 making
6 want

7b Replace the underlined words with these words to make these statements more formal. Use the correct form of the verbs.

be confident	become	complete	effectively
gain	intend	leading	possess
seek	significant		

1 <u>I'd like</u> to become an account executive.
2 I <u>did</u> a three-year course in arts administration.
3 I'm <u>looking for</u> a position in Human Resources.
4 I <u>think</u> I will make a <u>big</u> contribution to your firm.
5 I <u>got</u> extensive experience during my internship.
6 My aim is to <u>really</u> use my experience in customer care.
7 I <u>have</u> skills in mentoring and advising young people.
8 I aim to <u>be</u> the <u>top</u> events manager in the area.

8 A friend who is applying for a similar job to yours has asked you to help them to write a career goals statement. Write a statement which includes two goals.

9 Work in small groups. Compare your statements and check that they use formal language where possible. Work together to see if you can improve the statements.

21st CENTURY OUTCOMES COLLABORATION WITH OTHERS Be flexible and willing to be helpful to reach a common goal

Review 1 | UNITS 1 AND 2

READING

1 Read the article about Balance. How does Balance help people? Choose the correct option (a–c).

a It provides employment.
b It gives financial assistance.
c It offers support services.

2 Read the article again. Are the sentences true (T) or false (F)?

1 A CIC company pays its profits to shareholders.
2 Balance helps people with physical disabilities.
3 You can get confidential help from Balance.
4 Balance doesn't usually have any contact with employers.
5 Balance organized work experience opportunities for Lucy.
6 Lucy is employed by a child-care company.

GRAMMAR

3 Complete the text about Balance with the present simple and present continuous active and passive form of the verbs.

A company like Balance ¹ _____ (provide) a valuable service to employers as well as employees. Many employers ² _____ (need) help in understanding how to deal with staff with health issues and this ³ _____ (give) by such companies. Thanks to them, many more people ⁴ _____ (now / employ) than in the past. The number of people with mental health conditions who have stable jobs ⁵ _____ (grow) all the time. Statistics ⁶ _____ (suggest) that one in four people ⁷ _____ (suffer) from some form of mental health issue at some time in their lives. It is important to make sure this ⁸ _____ (not / have) a negative impact on the individuals and also on business in general.

About BALANCE

The UK company Balance is a community-interest company (CIC) working in the employment sector. A CIC company is defined as a business where profits are reinvested in the company instead of being paid to shareholders.

HELPING PEOPLE

The aim of Balance is to provide services for people who are already in work or who are looking for work. The people they help face particular challenges connected with their health – they have autism or Asperger Syndrome, or they are dealing with stress and anxiety. Some of these health issues are long-term conditions and others are temporary conditions that affect many people at some time in their lives. However, both types of health issue can create barriers that make it more difficult for people to achieve their life goals. Balance concentrates on a number of areas that directly support these people. For example, Balance offers confidential one-to-one support to individuals. It runs courses on managing anxiety at work and building people's self-confidence. For people already in employment, Balance can get involved in talking to employers to find solutions to problems. For people who are looking for work, Balance gives help with preparing CVs, job applications and interview skills.

CASE STUDY: Lucy

One example of how the company works is the case of a young woman, Lucy, who has learning difficulties. She was motivated to work and earn a salary, but wasn't happy in the only work experience she had – childcare – and didn't want a career in that field. Balance helped her to define her work interests and Lucy realized that retail sales appealed to her. A work-experience placement was arranged with two local retailers. Lucy's confidence grew and she felt that she had gained the skills to accept a paid position at the second retailer. She now has a part-time contract and says that she is proud that she is working there.

Lucy is one of many people who Balance is helping, by providing a link between employers and potential employees.

---

autism (n) a condition which means people find it more difficult to interact with others through social and communication skills

Asperger Syndrome (n) a type of autism in which linguistic and cognitive skills are less affected than in other types of autism

4 Choose the correct options to complete the comments about experiences of working with companies like Balance.

Anya, an accountant
'At first, I had problems with anxiety at work and I wanted to leave. But now things are different. [1] *I'll stay / I'm going to stay* in my job and I have new goals for the future. I might have health problems in the future, but I'm sure [2] *I'll deal / I'll be dealing* with them more successfully next time.'

Jim, a young man with Asperger Syndrome
'I couldn't get a job – interviews were a disaster. After training in interview techniques, I think [3] *I'll do / I'll have done* better in the future. I hope that by the end of the year [4] *I'm going to find / I'll have found* a job. I feel confident now.'

PowerLife company spokesperson
'We think that within a couple of years [5] *we're going to hire / we'll be hiring* at least double the number of people with mental health conditions. We've changed our hiring policy since working with Balance, and [6] *we won't be returning / we won't have returned* to our old system.'

VOCABULARY

5 Complete the comments from people who work at a community-interest company with six of the expressions.

committed to create	concentrate on deal with	co-ordinates help
interested in responsible for	involved in	passionate about

1 CIC companies are _____ making a difference in society.
2 Some specialist companies _____ people with particular health conditions, such as autism.
3 In our work, we _____ individuals, businesses and educational centres.
4 We sometimes get _____ solving problems between people and their employers.
5 Our aim is to _____ people to achieve their goals.
6 In my post as training co-ordinator, I'm _____ the course in interview skills.

6 Choose the correct option to complete the collocations.

Getting [1] academic *qualifications / security* can be a big challenge for students with health issues. Sometimes, exams are not adapted for an individual's needs, which makes it difficult to assess their [2] academic *experience / skills*. Once these students have left school, their [3] employment *opportunities / skills* are generally more limited than those of their classmates. Finding a [4] starting *position / salary* in a career that interests them is not easy. Nevertheless, many people with health conditions are able to work and [5] earn a *licence / salary* and become independent. These days, [6] job *position / security* is becoming harder for all employees to find, even if they have years of [7] professional *diploma / experience*.

DISCUSSION

7 Work in pairs. Discuss the questions.

1 Balance states that its goal is to break down the barriers that stop people with health issues from achieving their life goals. What do you think these barriers are?
2 What difficulties do young people in your country face when they leave school and look for a job?
3 Is anything being done to help people get jobs in your country? What kind of thing?

SPEAKING

8 Complete the conversation between two colleagues, Dina and Martin, on a company training course. Use the prompts.

D: Hi, Martin. Do you mind if I join you? That was an interesting session!
M: Yes, it was. Lesley's a good speaker. [1] *How / you / find / the course?*
D: Very good so far. You're leading a session tomorrow, is that right?
M: Yes, after lunch. [2] *I / wonder / you / check / my presentation?*
D: Sure, no problem. When are you free?
M: [3] *Any time / good / me.*
D: Well, it would be better to look at it before tomorrow.
M: [4] *say / tonight / six.*
D: Great, we can get something to eat at the same time.
M: [5] *I / meet / main entrance / OK / you.*

WRITING

9 Read the profile that Julianne Brown has posted on a professional networking site. Improve the profile by using note forms and replacing the underlined sections with appropriate forms of some of these words.

believe	complete	effective	gain
intend	obtain	seek	

Name: Julianne Brown

Contact: My email address is julianne@jpbrown.co.uk or you can reach me on skype at juliannepat.

Languages: I speak both French and Spanish.

Expertise: I <u>did</u> a Masters degree in Organizational Psychology at Manchester University and then I <u>got</u> a job in Human Resources. I've done that for five years.

Career goal: <u>I'd like to find</u> a job in a social enterprise. I <u>think</u> I can make a <u>big</u> contribution to this area.

10 Work in pairs. Exchange profiles with your partner. Did you make the same changes?

3 Growth and development

BACKGROUND

1 You are going to watch an edited version of a TED Talk by Hans Rosling called *Global population growth, box by box*. Read the text about the speaker and the talk. Then work in pairs and discuss the questions.

1 What kind of data do you think Hans Rosling's presentations usually deal with?
2 Do you know what the world population is today? What do you think it was 50 years ago? And in 2010? What do you think it will be in 2050?
3 What are the problems caused by dramatic population growth?

TEDTALKS

HANS ROSLING was a professor of International Health at the Karolinska Institute in Sweden. He co-founded Médecins Sans Frontièrs (Doctors Without Borders) Sweden. He became famous for the creative way he presented data and statistics about global health and economic development.

Hans Rosling's idea worth spreading is that if we want to manage population growth, we must raise the income of the world's poorest billion people.

The city at night, Seoul, South Korea

KEY WORDS

2 Read the sentences (1–6). The words in bold are used in the TED Talk. First guess the meaning of the words. Then match the words with their definitions (a–f).

1 The **developing world** and the industrial world are terms for two types of economy.
2 In many countries, there's an enormous **gap** between the rich and the poor.
3 My parents' **aspiration** was to buy their own home.
4 Investors are usually keen to put money into companies in **emerging economies**.
5 **Child survival** improves when countries invest in primary health care.
6 Spending more money than you earn is not **sustainable** – eventually you will have no money.

a able to be kept at a certain level
b the percentage of children who live beyond the age of five years
c countries with low levels of technological or economic success
d countries whose economic activity is growing quickly
e a strong desire to achieve something
f a difference

AUTHENTIC LISTENING SKILLS Focused listening

When you have some advance information about what a speaker is going to talk about, you can form ideas about what you think you will hear. This can help you to focus on the content of the talk when you listen and check if your ideas are included or not. The main aim of this skill is **not** to correctly predict what the speaker says, but to help you to focus your listening on the main ideas.

3a 🎧 **14** Work in pairs. Look at the Authentic listening skills box. Based on the information in Exercises 1 and 2, decide what aspect of world population Hans Rosling is going to talk about. Then listen to the extracts from the TED Talk. What does he say about this issue?

3b 🎧 **14** Listen again. Complete the extracts.

1 I still remember the day in school when our teacher told us that the world population had become _____ billion people, and that was in 1960.
2 And I'm going to talk now about how world population has _____ from that year and into the future.
3 The world population has _____ since I went to school.

31

3.1 Global population growth, box by box

TEDTALKS

1 ▶ **3.1** Watch the edited version of the TED Talk. Are the sentences true (T) or false (F)?

1 Each of Hans Rosling's boxes represents one billion people.
2 In 1960, there were three billion people in the industrialized world.
3 Hans Rosling uses the space between the green boxes and the blue box to represent the gap between rich and poor countries.
4 Hans Rosling states that that by 2010, the difference between very rich and very poor countries is much bigger than it was in 1960.
5 According to Hans Rosling, one of the most significant changes since 1960 was better child survival rates.
6 Hans Rosling believes that the 'old West' has no role in the modern world.

2 ▶ **3.1** Watch the first part of the talk (0.00–4.25) again. Choose the correct option to complete the sentences.

1 Hans Rosling uses the toys to represent the growing *aspirations / family sizes* of people in the different economies.
2 Hans Rosling thinks that the terms 'the West' and 'the developing world' are *still / no longer* relevant.
3 Since 1960, the most *populated / successful* 'developing countries' have become 'emerging economies'.
4 The poorest two billion people are *not as poor / just as poor* as they were in 1960.

▶ analogue BR ENG
▶ analog N AM ENG
▶ industrialized, industrialised BR ENG
▶ industrialized N AM ENG

3 ▶ 3.1 Watch the second part of the talk (4.25–6.18) again. Complete the sentences.

1 On the graph, each bubble represents a _____.
2 The graph shows the relationship between family size and _____ survival.
3 The graph shows how when more children survive, women start to have fewer _____.
4 Even with a child survival rate of 70 to 80 per cent, the population will _____ in one generation.

4 ▶ 3.1 Complete the summary of Hans Rosling's message with the sentence endings (a–c). Then watch the third part of the talk again (6.18 to the end) and check your answers.

Hans Rosling's data show that the richest countries in the world have excellent child survival and therefore [1] _____. He believes that the way to slow down population growth is [2] _____. He also thinks that green technology and other investments [3] _____.

a can achieve this
b low population growth
c to reduce poverty in the poorest parts of the world

5 Work in pairs. Have the average family size and standard of living changed in the last 50 years in your country?

VOCABULARY IN CONTEXT

6 ▶ 3.2 Watch the clips from the TED Talk. Choose the correct meaning of the words.

7 Work in pairs. Discuss the questions.

1 Do you know anyone who is an optimist? What are they like?
2 Do you know anyone who is a pessimist? What are they like?
3 What's the most remote place you've ever been to?

CRITICAL THINKING Supporting the main argument

8 Hans Rosling used a graph to support his argument that improving child survival to 90 per cent will slow down population growth. Which of the items in the list did the graph show? How successful do you think this graph was in supporting Hans Rosling's argument?

- observable facts
- personal experience
- published research
- statistical data

9 Work in pairs. Read these comments* about the TED Talk. Underline the argument in each comment. Circle the part of the comment that supports the argument. Which comment(s) do you find more convincing? Why?

Viewers' comments

A Austin – I think that saving children's lives just means more mouths to feed, more poverty, more children in the next generation – I've travelled a lot and seen the situation for myself.

A AndyT – That's very harsh! There have been plenty of studies showing exactly the opposite is true. Do a web search on UNICEF and you'll see for yourself.

B Barbara – Of course the population can double in a generation if couples have six children and four survive – that's basic maths. Rosling's point is that 90 per cent child survival is the critical figure and he's based that on what's been happening in emerging economies.

*The comments were created for this activity.

PRESENTATION SKILLS Using props

> **TIPS**
> Props are objects which can make a presentation more memorable and illustrate your ideas. Your props should be appropriate to the content of your talk as well as being:
> - easy for the audience to understand
> - interesting enough to hold the audience's attention
> - unusual enough to help your audience to remember your talk

10 ▶ 3.3 Look at the Presentation tips box. Then watch the clip from the TED Talk and say which criteria Hans Rosling's props meet.

11 Work in pairs. Discuss recent trends involving one of these areas. What props could you use to show the trends? Write a few sentences to explain the trend and practise presenting your ideas.

communication   food   games   money

12 Work with a new partner. Take turns to present your ideas. How effective are your partner's props?

▶ colours **BR ENG**
▶ colors **N AM ENG**

▶ organization, organisation **BR ENG**
▶ organization **N AM ENG**

3.2 The next economic giant

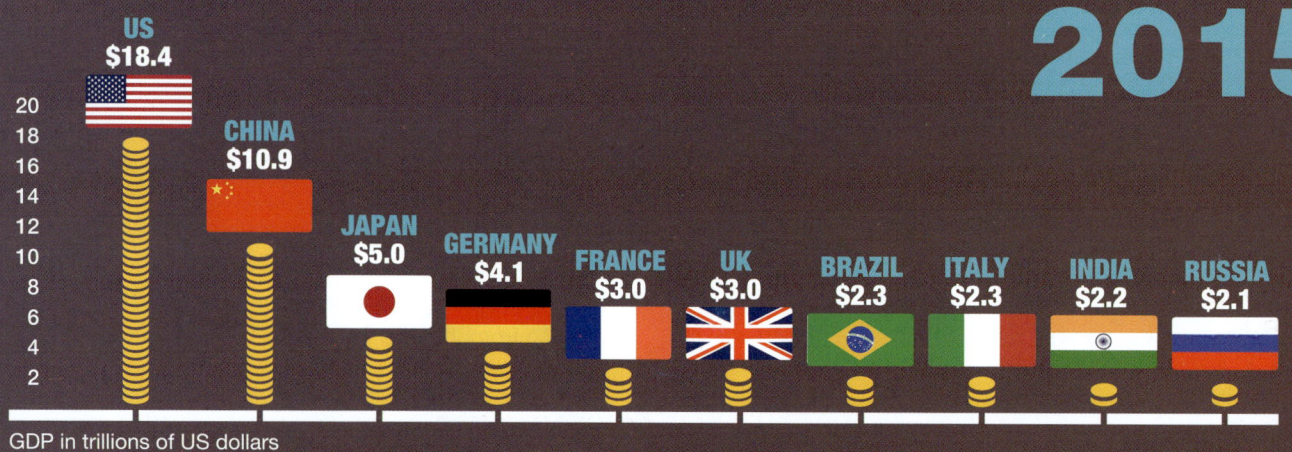

GRAMMAR Present perfect simple and continuous

1 Match the acronyms BRIC and MINT with these two groups of emerging economies.

| Brazil | China | India | Russia |
| Indonesia | Mexico | Nigeria | Turkey |

2 Look at the infographic published in 2015. Can you find any BRIC or MINT countries? Then decide if the sentences are true (T) or false (F) according to the information shown.

1 The US has maintained its position as the world's largest economy.
2 Over the last thirteen years, the UK economy has been shrinking.
3 France's economy hasn't changed since 2002.
4 The Chinese economy has increased from $1.5 trillion to $10.9 trillion in just over a decade.
5 Brazil's economy has been growing rapidly and the country is now one of the ten biggest economies in the world.
6 India's economy has overtaken Canada's since 2002.

3 Read the sentences in the Grammar box. Answer the questions (1–3).

PRESENT PERFECT SIMPLE AND CONTINUOUS

Present perfect simple

The world's top ten biggest economies **have changed** since 2002.
The world population **has jumped** to seven billion people.

Present perfect continuous

The economy of China **has been growing** for a number of years.
Some of the traditionally strong economies **have been shrinking** recently.

1 Which tense is formed with the verb *have* + *been* + *-ing* form of the main verb?
2 Which tense emphasizes the process – how the time has been spent?
3 Which tense emphasizes the results of an activity?

Check your answers on page 144 and do Exercises 1–6.

4 Read the conversations in an office. Complete the replies with the present perfect continuous form of the verbs. Underline the time expressions used with the present perfect continuous.

1 A: Have you looked at my report yet?
   B: Sorry, I _____ (reply) to emails all morning.
2 A: Are those two visitors still in Reception?
   B: Yes, but they _____ (not wait) long.
3 A: Have you seen Rashida recently?
   B: No – _____ she _____ (work) from home for the last few days?
4 A: Have you heard about the contract with India?
   B: Oh, yes. We _____ (talk) about it for weeks now.
5 A: Have you mentioned the new office plans to Jamila?
   B: Not yet. I _____ (travel) a lot recently.
6 A: Is the printer working now?
   B: No. The technician _____ (try) all day to fix it.
7 A: Have you seen that headline about credit cards?
   B: No. I _____ (not read) the finance section.
8 A: Your office has been busy this week.
   B: I know. We _____ (redesign) the website.

5 Work in pairs. Tell your partner about some of the things you've been doing recently. Use the time expressions from Exercise 4.

I've been getting ready for my trip to South Korea for the last few days.

6 🎧 **15** Look at the table from the magazine *Economic Trends*. Complete the text with the present perfect simple and continuous form of the verbs. Then listen and check your answers.

	Ten years ago	Today
clothes	8%	8%
education	5%	4%
entertainment	8%	8%
fast food	1%	3%
groceries	15%	12%
health and health products	3%	4%
household goods	6%	6%
housing and utilities	22%	26%
transport	14%	18%
miscellaneous	18%	12%

Trends in household expenditure [1] _____ (not / show) great changes over the past ten years. The biggest chunk of household spending still goes on housing and utilities, and this [2] _____ (jump) from 22 per cent to 26 per cent. Equally, transport costs [3] _____ (increase) by four per cent. These numbers are not surprising, as fuel costs [4] _____ (rise) steadily over the ten-year period. As fast foods [5] _____ (become) more and more popular, our spending on them [6] _____ (triple). We [7] _____ (also / buy) more health products – are we compensating for our poor eating habits? Unusually, given that clothes prices [8] _____ (fall) year-on-year, we still spend the same amount on clothes.

7 Work in pairs. Discuss the table in Exercise 6. How do these changes compare to your own situations?

SPEAKING Popular brands

8 **21st CENTURY OUTCOMES**

Write two brand names for these items of household expenditure. Can you add more items and brands to the list?

| clothes | entertainment | fast food |
| groceries | health products | household goods |

9 Work in pairs. Compare your lists from Exercise 8. Discuss the questions.

1 Are the most popular brands local or international?
2 What percentage of income goes on each type of expenditure?
3 Has your spending on these items changed recently?
4 How have spending habits in general in your country changed over the last few years?

21st CENTURY OUTCOMES FINANCIAL AND ECONOMIC LITERACY Make appropriate personal economic choices

3.3 Personal development

READING What do you need?

1 Look at the three diagrams. They show the three most important things that three people need in their life to make them feel happy (1 = the most important). What are the three most important things that you need to make you feel happy? Are they in the diagrams? Draw your own diagram. Then work in pairs and compare your diagrams.

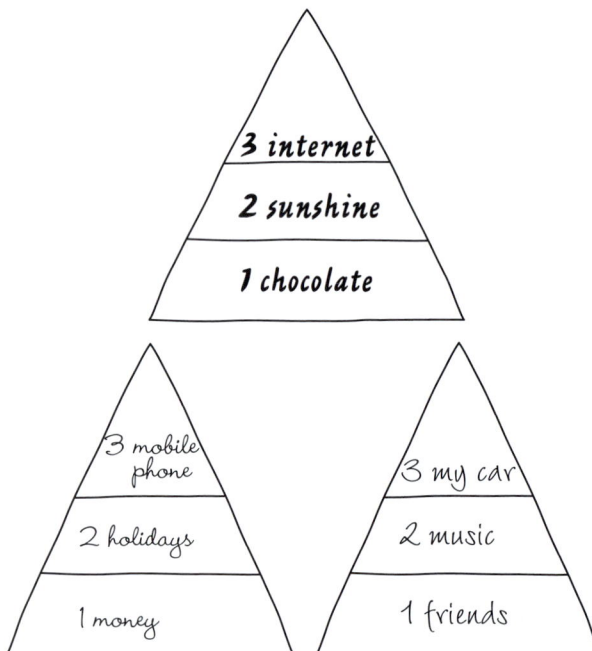

2 Work in pairs. Match the groups of words (A–D) with the headings (1–4). Are any of the things you discussed in Exercise 1 in these groups?

1 social needs	3 safety needs
2 physiological needs	4 esteem needs

A	B	C	D
drink	family	independence	health
food	friendship	prestige	job security
shelter	love	self-respect	personal
sleep	romance	status	safety
			property

3 Read the article. In what order does the article mention the needs described in Exercise 2? What is the fifth 'need'?

4 Read the article again. Are the sentences true (T) or false (F)?

1 There have been no new developments in the area of Maslow's theory.
2 Maslow thought the theory was shown most clearly as a pyramid.
3 The theory can be useful in managing how we motivate people at work.
4 It hasn't been possible to prove the theory scientifically.

5 Complete the questions with words from the text. Then answer the questions.

1 Have you ever read a book that has had an _____ on you? (line 3)
2 Do you think you have a strong instinct for _____? Would you do well alone on a desert island? (line 11)
3 Who were the people you most _____ when you were growing up? (line 17)
4 What do you think you need to reach your _____ in life? (line 28)
5 Is _____ to a group of people with similar interests or a shared background important to you? (line 37)
6 What kinds of things would you take into _____ when looking for a new job or new course of study? (line 42)

6 Work in pairs. Compare your answers and ask follow-up questions with *what*, *why*, *how*, etc.

7 Work in pairs. Discuss the questions.

1 Why are the levels described as a progression in the article?
2 According to the theory, when can a person achieve self-actualization?
3 How does the theory influence advertising?
4 How relevant is Maslow's theory today?

VOCABULARY Personal growth: abstract nouns

8 Complete the table with words from the article.

Adjective	Noun
motivated	1
2	influence
safe	3
4	success
growing	5
6	perfection
secure	7
8	quality
9	quantity

9 Work in pairs. Complete the sentences with words from Exercise 8. Then discuss whether the sentences are true for you.

1 At work, my salary is my main _____ . Without it, I'd lose interest.
2 My job is measured by the quantity of what I produce rather than the _____ of my work.
3 Personal _____ is very important to me – I want to feel fulfilled in my life.
4 In the city where I live, we don't really feel _____ on the streets at night.
5 I don't believe that advertising has any _____ on how I spend my money.
6 I'd rather be happy in my personal life than _____ in my career.

SPEAKING Are you satisfied?

10 21st CENTURY OUTCOMES

Work in groups. Discuss the questions.

1 To what extent do you think that your various needs are met?
2 What fulfils your needs more: work, family and friends, hobbies, or other things?
3 Which of your needs do you think would seem unusual to a previous generation?

What do you need?

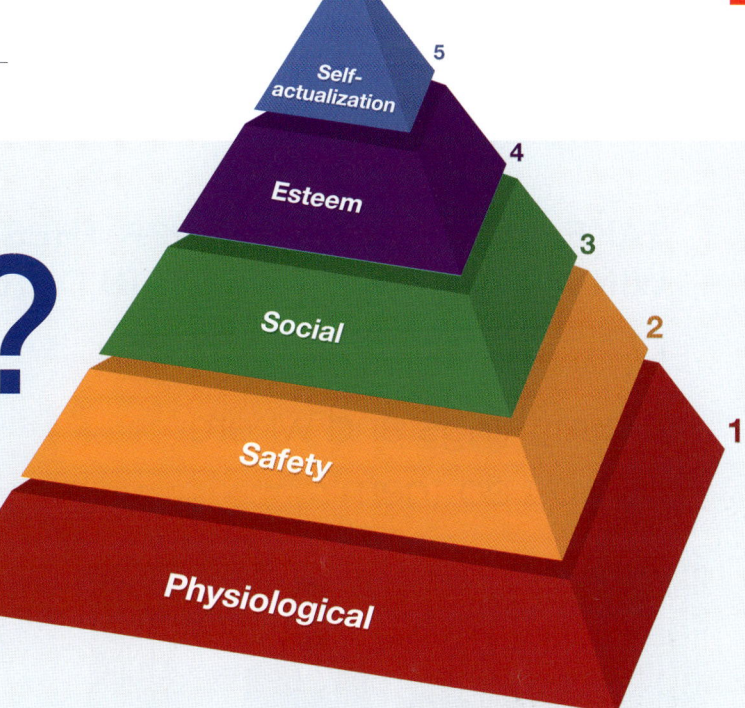

In 1954, a book called *Motivation and Personality* was published by the American psychologist Abraham Maslow. The book had an impact far beyond the academic world and the psychological theories it describes are still influential in management training today. This is despite the fact that newer theories of human developmental psychology have largely replaced Maslow's original idea, known as Maslow's hierarchy of needs.

Maslow's hierarchy suggests that people are motivated according to a progression through five different stages of 'need'. First come the most basic needs for survival such as food and water, then the need for physical and economic safety. After this is the level of social needs which refers to our relationships with others – friendship, family, and so on. The fourth level concerns respect and esteem. To be 'successful', we need to be assured of our own self-esteem, social status, to feel respected or admired in our work, etc.

The hierarchy is often shown as a pyramid even though Maslow himself didn't use this idea. The key idea in the theory is that we can't be successful in a given level unless we have fulfilled the needs in the previous level – or the ones lower down in the pyramid.

The ultimate stage in this model of personal growth is self-actualization. That is, the ability of an individual to achieve their full potential. This could be a creative talent, an achievement in sport, being successful in business or becoming the perfect parent. For each individual, the desire or goal will be different.

One of the ways in which the theory is applied in business and management is in understanding how to manage motivation. For example, it could be difficult to motivate members of a team to work together (level three) if they feel that their jobs are not secure (level two). Maslow's hierarchy of needs has also been influential in marketing, brands and advertising. For example, a pensions company may sell its products by appealing to our need for financial security or a social media service will target our 'level three' needs of social belonging.

Nevertheless, in the decades since the publication of *Motivation and Personality* there have been other studies which have questioned and criticized Maslow's theory. Some have suggested that his original study group of college students was not broad enough to take into account the differences in cultural and geo-political situations which exist in the world. Others point out that Maslow's methodology was a subjective one – a qualitative rather than a quantitative approach – and that it's difficult to test the theory in a scientific way.

Whatever current opinion, Maslow's influence can still be found in all areas of modern life.

21st CENTURY OUTCOMES   CRITICAL THINKING Analyse and evaluate claims and beliefs

3.4 Could you call me back?

LISTENING Market research

1 Work in pairs. Have you ever taken part in a market research survey? What were the questions about?

2 Answer the questions in a market research survey from a small hotel which is trying to grow its business. Which areas of business do you think the hotel is trying to develop?

3 🎧 16 Listen to four voicemails for Elaine, the manager of the hotel. Make notes on each message. What action does Elaine need to take in each case?

4 🎧 16 Listen again. Complete the expressions in the Useful language box.

LEAVING VOICEMAILS

1 This is Louisa Redhill getting _____ to you about …
2 Could you call me _____ before Friday?
3 This is a message _____ Elaine.
4 I'm calling _____ using your venue.
5 Could you email _____ your prices at Aziz at ATZ.com?
6 I'm returning your _____ .
7 You can get in _____ with me on 645 698 421.

TAKE A MINUTE TO ANSWER THESE QUESTIONS AND YOU COULD WIN A WEEKEND FOR TWO IN OUR PREMIUM COUNTRY HOTEL.

How often do you do these things and where do you do them?

Rate on a scale of 1 (not often at all) to 5 (very often).

spend the night away from home on business?
1 ○   2 ○   3 ○   4 ○   5 ○

spend time on a mini-break with your family?
1 ○   2 ○   3 ○   4 ○   5 ○

have lunch out on business?
1 ○   2 ○   3 ○   4 ○   5 ○

go out for a family meal?
1 ○   2 ○   3 ○   4 ○   5 ○

get invited to a special occasion, such as a wedding?
1 ○   2 ○   3 ○   4 ○   5 ○

go to a work conference or convention?
1 ○   2 ○   3 ○   4 ○   5 ○

go to a live music venue?
1 ○   2 ○   3 ○   4 ○   5 ○

5 Put the words in order to complete the voicemails.

1. Jane, could _____ before tonight? It's quite important.
   (back / call / me / you)
2. Could _____ as soon as you can?
   (details / email / me / you / the)
3. Can you _____ mobile? It's 619 587 135.
   (back / get / me / on / my / to)
4. Do you have an email where I can _____ ? Thanks.
   (touch / you / in / get / with)

Pronunciation Intonation in requests

6a 🎧 **17** Listen to the requests and notice the intonation. Practise saying the sentences.

1. Could you call me back before tonight?
2. Could you email me the details?
3. Can you get back to me on my mobile?
4. Do you have an email where I can get in touch with you?

6b 🎧 **18** Practise saying these requests. Then listen and check your intonation.

1. Could you get back to me?
2. Can you let me know?
3. Can you give me a ring?
4. Could you text me the prices?

SPEAKING Leaving voicemails

7 **21st CENTURY OUTCOMES**

You are going to work in pairs and leave a voicemail asking your partner something or asking them to do something. Make notes on what you need to say. Include a day, date or time.

8 Work in pairs. Take turns to read your voicemail. Make notes. Then return the call with an appropriate response.

WRITING Making notes from voicemails

9 Read these notes (1–4) made while listening to voicemails. What do you think the original voicemails said?

1. Anya can't do Mon. Will send Jul/Aug budget.
2. Confirm I can meet accountant, Fri 2nd, 10.30 am.
3. Text Nicole available days for Sept.
4. Return Jeff's call by 2 pm Thurs.

Writing skill Abbreviations

10a Look at the abbreviations we use in notes and informal writing. Which are days and which are months?

Apr	Aug	Dec	Feb	Fri	Jan
Jul	Jun	Mar	May	Mon	Nov
Oct	Sat	Sept	Sun	Thurs	Tues
Wed					

10b Complete the spoken forms of these times and dates.

1. 06.00 — six o'clock in the _____
2. 14.10 — ten past _____
3. 5.45 pm — five _____ pm
4. 7.30 am — _____ _____ seven in the morning
5. 19.50 — _____ to eight in the _____
6. 3 am — _____ am
7. 12/2 — February the _____
8. 1/10/2009 — the _____ of October two _____ and nine
9. 11/11 — the _____ of November
10. 22/5/2016 — the _____ of May twenty sixteen
11. 3/8/2000 — August the _____ two thousand
12. 30/4 — the _____ of _____

11 Make notes from these voicemails. Use abbreviations.

1. Hi, it's Janine. I've sent you some sales projections by email. Can you take a look and get back to me before Thursday next week, that's the tenth?
2. Hi, it's Scott. Can we talk about ideas for special promotions in July and August? I'm free all day on Tuesday.
3. Hi, it's Luigi. Would you be able to call me some time before the beginning of December?
4. Hi, it's Angela. I've set up a meeting with the market research people for half two on Friday afternoon. Let me know if that's OK with you.

COMMUNICATION AND COLLABORATION Speak and listen effectively to transmit information

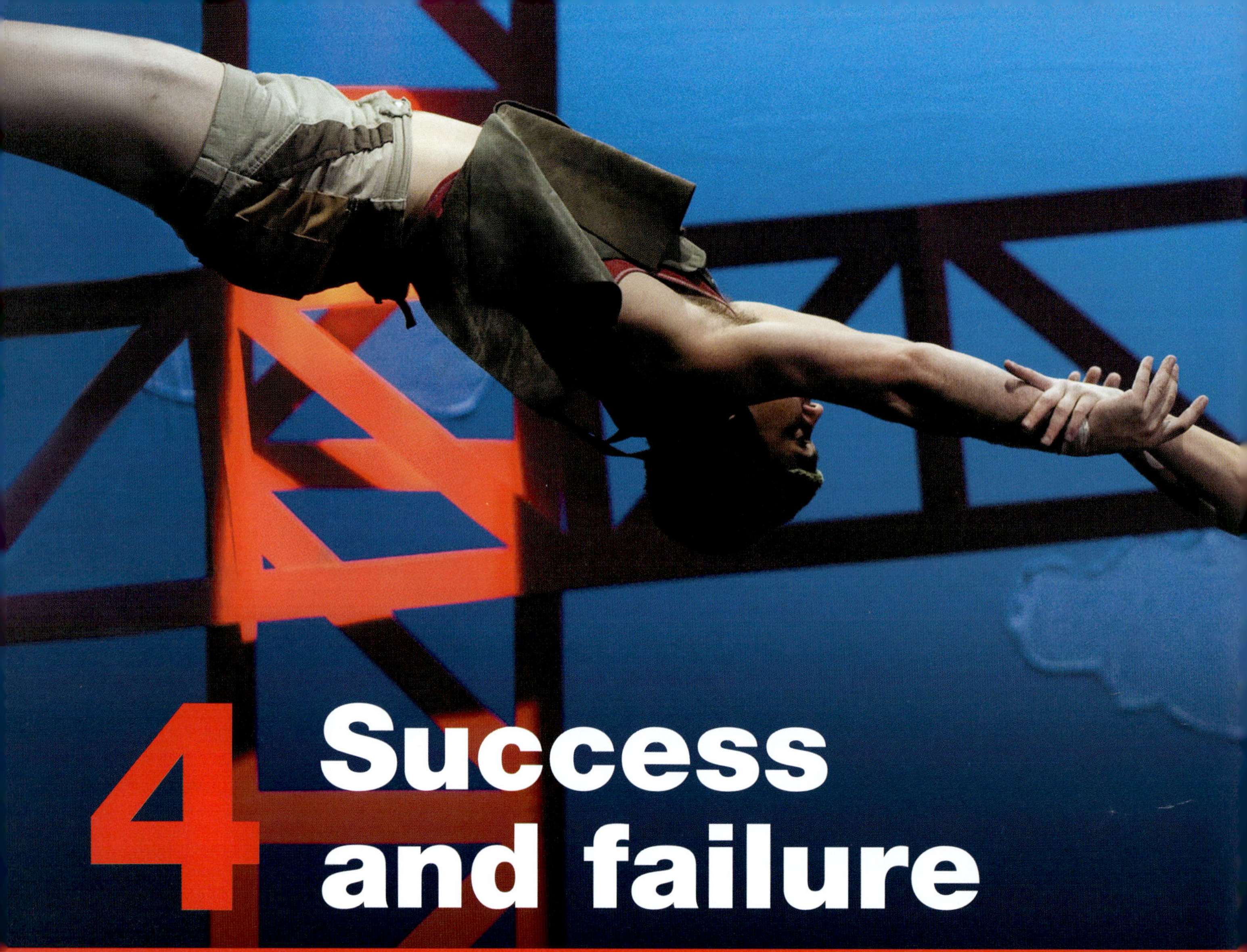

4 Success and failure

BACKGROUND

1 You are going to watch a TED Talk by Richard St. John called *Success is a continuous journey*. Read the text about the speaker and the talk. Then work in pairs and discuss the questions.

1 What words do you think might be on Richard St. John's list of eight words to summarize success?
2 Which things could make businesses succeed or fail? Make a list.
3 Are the things on your list outside factors, or are they part of the business itself?

TED TALKS

RICHARD ST. JOHN describes himself as 'an average guy' who found success doing what he loved. He spent more than a decade researching the lessons of success and says he can summarize them in eight words.

Richard St. John's idea worth spreading is that success should be thought of as a life-long journey rather than a one-way street, because the moment we think we've reached success, we may stop trying altogether and may fail.

Two trapeze artists from Circus Oz perform, New York, USA

KEY WORDS

2 Read the sentences (1–6). The words in bold are used in the TED Talk. First guess the meaning of the words. Then match the words with their definitions (a–f).

1 You always have to **push ahead** to make progress and that requires effort.
2 An artist who can't think of new ideas is suffering from **creative block**.
3 Don't be distracted by things that aren't important. You need to **focus** on the key things.
4 It's not enough just to like what you do, you need to feel **passion** for it.
5 All businesses should **serve** the needs of their customers.
6 When something doesn't work at first, you have to **persist**.

a a powerful feeling of love
b to attend to the needs of someone
c to concentrate
d to show drive and determination
e to keep trying, to not give up
f the inability to make or invent something new

AUTHENTIC LISTENING SKILLS
Collaborative listening

> Listening is not like reading – we don't get a chance to go back to parts that aren't clear. This means that you shouldn't expect to understand 100 per cent of what you hear. Also, different people understand different parts of a message and so working with others can increase your understanding.

3a 🎧 **19** Look at the Authentic listening skills box. Then listen to the beginning of the TED Talk. Write down the words you can remember.

3b 🎧 **19** Work in pairs. Compare your words with your partner. Did you write the same words? Then listen again. Did you hear more words than the first time?

4.1 Success is a continuous journey

TEDTALKS

1 ▶ 4.1 Watch the TED Talk. What does Richard St. John talk about? Choose the correct option (a–c).

   a the things he did right
   b the things he did wrong
   c both the things he did right and the things he did wrong

2 ▶ 4.1 Watch the first part (0.00–1.39) of the talk again. Match the things Richard St. John stopped doing (1–5) with the reasons (a–e).

   He stopped …
   1 pushing himself
   2 trying to improve
   3 doing things that lead to ideas
   4 focusing on clients and projects
   5 doing what he loved

   because he thought …
   a he should do things a company president should do
   b he was good enough
   c he'd made it and he could relax
   d ideas should just come to him easily
   e spending his money was more interesting

3 ▶ 4.1 Watch the second part (1.39–3.08) of the talk again. Put the events (a–e) in order.

   a He focused on spending his wealth.
   b He lost all of his employees.
   c He started working on things he enjoyed.
   d He became depressed.
   e His customers went to other businesses.

4 ▶ 4.1 Watch the third part (3.08 to the end) of the talk again. What's the difference between the two slides Richard St. John shows with his eight principles of success?

5 Work in pairs. Discuss the questions.

   1 Do you agree with Richard St. John that 'money can't buy happiness'? Why? / Why not?
   2 What are your personal criteria for 'success'?

▶ figured **N AM ENG**   ▶ real estate agent **N AM ENG**   ▶ Doc **N AM ENG**
▶ thought **BR ENG**   ▶ estate agent **BR ENG**   ▶ Doctor **BR ENG**

VOCABULARY IN CONTEXT

6 ▶ 4.2 Watch the clips from the TED Talk. Choose the correct meaning of the words.

7 Work in pairs. Discuss the questions.

1 Have you ever sat back in your comfort zone?
2 What kind of stuff did you get into when you were younger?
3 Is there anything that worries your friends but that you couldn't care less about?

CRITICAL THINKING Challenging assumptions

8 Work in pairs. Richard St. John challenged his audience to think about success in a new way. What assumption did he say people normally have about the route to success?

9 Read these comments* about the TED Talk. Discuss the questions.

1 Which comment(s) talk(s) about Richard St. John's proposed route to success?
2 How successful do viewers feel he was in achieving his purpose?

Viewers' comments

R Roberto – Great talk! So simple, but so effective. And replacing the 'ladder' of success with a circle makes the relationship between our actions and their consequences really clear too.

J Janine – Why is success always defined in the area of work? What about family, relationships, personal growth?

Y Yun – The principles illustrated here are true for any situation in life, not only business. They all need continual effort to get a result – you can never think that you've made it.

*The comments were created for this activity.

PRESENTATION SKILLS Repeating key phrases

TIPS

Repeating key phrases at certain times during your talk is a very effective way to get your message across. It can particularly help speakers whose native language is different from yours.

- Identify the important 'take away' points you want listeners to focus on.
- Think of a similar sentence pattern you can use several times.
- Prepare sentences with two parts: the repetition and the changing information.

10 ▶ 4.3 Work in pairs. Look at the Presentation tips box. Then watch the clips from the TED Talk. Which two-word phrase does Richard St. John use to introduce each of his examples?

1 _____, I worked hard, I pushed myself. But …
2 _____, I always tried to improve and do good work. But …
3 _____, I was pretty good at coming up with good ideas. […] But …

11 ▶ 4.3 Watch the clips again. What does Richard St. John repeat each time beginning with *But* … ?

12 Read the example sentence and write three similar sentences repeating the words in bold.

*When **I** worked hard, **I found** I passed my exams easily.*

- passed my exams / had more job offers
- made friends at work / enjoyed my job more
- changed jobs / earned more money

13 Work in pairs. Write a few sentences to explain different consequences of studying English. Use repetition. Practise presenting the ideas.

14 Work with a new partner. Take turns to present the ideas. How effectively do you both get your message across?

▶ let go (of employees) **N AM ENG**
▶ make (employees) redundant **BR ENG**
▶ president of the company **N AM ENG**
▶ chairman of the company **BR ENG**

4.2 Measures of success

AGE, EXPERIENCE & SUCCESS

Do people do their best work when they are young? Pop stars and actors often seem to peak in their twenties. We looked at **SIX HIGH-FLYERS** from the business world.

HOW OLD WERE THEY WHEN THEY REALLY MADE IT?

39 — opened the first Zara store

AMANCIO ORTEGA

40 — sold Birmingham City Football club for £82 million

KARREN BRADY

43 — joined the board of Facebook

SHERYL SANDBERG

47 — set up own manufacturing company

JAMES DYSON

49 — became Chief Executive, Easyjet

CAROLYN McCALL

50 — bought Telmex, the telecommunications company

CARLOS SLIM HELU

GRAMMAR Narrative tenses

1 Do you think age is important in the workplace? Are there jobs that you need to be young or old to do?

2 Look at the infographic. Find these people.

an airline executive	a fashion entrepreneur
an inventor	a sports executive
a technology executive	a telecoms magnate

3 Read the text in the Grammar box. Answer the questions.

4 Choose the correct option to complete the sentences.

1 Amancio Ortega's clothing empire *was operating / had operated* in over 80 countries when, in 2011, he *resigned / was resigning* as chairman and *moved / had moved* into property investment.

2 Before she *joined / was joining* Google, Sheryl Sandberg *was working / had been working* for the US Treasury. She *rose / had risen* to the position of Chief of Staff by the time she left.

3 Carolyn McCall *did / was doing* her degree when she met her husband. After graduating from university, she *trained / had trained* as a teacher.

NARRATIVE TENSES REVIEW

*Brady and Slim were early starters: at the age of 23, Brady took over as Managing Director of the club. And as a teenager, Slim **bought** shares in a local bank, then **worked** for his father. Sandberg **was working** as a Vice President at Google when Mark Zuckerberg approached her. She **'d had** a job in government before Google. But not everyone found success quickly: Dyson **had been trying** to sell his revolutionary vacuum cleaner for ten years before he succeeded.*

1 Which tenses are the verbs in bold?
  a past simple   c past perfect simple
  b past continuous   d past perfect continuous

2 Which tenses are used to describe these things?
  a an activity or state in progress before the main event
  b a background activity or state
  c a sequence of events
  d an action that took place at an earlier time than the main event

Check your answers on page 146 and do Exercises 1–3.

5 Complete the biography of Oprah Winfrey with the correct form of the verb.

BIO
Oprah Winfrey
- Philanthropist
- Media Owner
- Actress

Oprah Winfrey found fame on American TV and in later life ¹ _____ (go on) to become a highly successful media owner. Before she got her own TV show, Oprah ² _____ (work) as a newsreader and a talk show host. Her show gained huge audiences with celebrity interviewees ranging from artists such as Michael Jackson to politicians such as Barack Obama. Oprah's own show won multiple media awards and it ³ _____ (run) for 25 years when she ⁴ _____ (launch) her own TV network in 2011. By that time, Winfrey's wealth and influence ⁵ _____ (lead) to her being named 'America's most powerful woman' by *Life* magazine. This accolade recognized that, since the 1990s, she ⁶ _____ (use) her wealth to fund educational projects and in fact she ⁷ _____ (become) one of America's biggest philanthropists. At one time, Oprah's TV shows were shown in 150 countries. She also made films outside the United States. In 2004, while she ⁸ _____ (film) in South Africa, Oprah ⁹ _____ (decide) to establish an academy for girls, investing $40 million in the project. Oprah herself teaches at the academy via satellite.

6 Work in pairs. Tell your partner about a time you were successful at something. What were the events leading up to your success? What happened next?

GRAMMAR *used to* and *would*

7 🎧 **20** Listen to a radio interview with the founder of the children's charity Places for Kids, Gina Desai. How does she measure her success? Choose the correct option (a–c).

   a She feels powerful.
   b Her work helps to make children's lives better.
   c She heads up a very big organization.

8 🎧 **20** Listen again. Correct the factual mistake in each sentence.

   1 Gina's family used to live in Iraq.
   2 Gina's brothers and sisters wouldn't talk to her.
   3 Alisha would put her books in strange places.
   4 Gina used to be dyslexic.
   5 Gina didn't use to need glasses.

9 Read the sentences in the Grammar box. Answer the questions (1–2).

USED TO AND WOULD

Her family **used to live** in India.
She **didn't use to need** glasses.
She **used to put** her toys in strange places.
She **would put** her toys in strange places.
The other girls **wouldn't play** with her.

1 Which form describes both past habits and past states?
2 Which form describes past habits?

Check your answers on page 146 and do Exercises 4–6.

10 Choose the correct option to complete the sentences. Sometimes, both options are possible.

   1 Sue *used to know / would know* a girl called Gina.
   2 *Did Sue use to work / Would Sue work* in a bank?
   3 Where *did Gina use to hide / would Gina hide* Sue's toys?
   4 She *used to be / would be* unhappy.
   5 She *used to cry / would cry* when she was alone.

Pronunciation Elision of consonants *t* and *d*

11a 🎧 **21** Listen to the sentences. Notice how the words in bold are pronounced. Which consonant is omitted?

   1 We **used to** live in India.
   2 The other girls **wouldn't talk** to me.
   3 She **would put** my toys in strange places.
   4 I needed glasses, but I **didn't use** to wear them.

11b Practise saying the sentences in Exercise 8. Try to use elision.

SPEAKING Old habits

12 **21st CENTURY OUTCOMES**

Write sentences with *used to* and *would* about these things. The sentences can be true or false. Then work in pairs and listen to your partner's sentences. Ask questions to find out which sentences are true.

- a job I used to do
- a place I used to live
- some people I used to know
- when I was at school
- when I was looking for a job
- when I was younger

21st CENTURY OUTCOMES   **CRITICAL THINKING** Analyse information and draw conclusions

4.3 Failure is not an option

READING Lessons for life

1 Work in pairs. Discuss the questions. Try to use examples to support your opinions.

   1 When you make a mistake, does it mean you have failed?
   2 Do you learn more from your own mistakes or from other people's mistakes? What kinds of things do you learn?

2 Complete the quotations at the beginning of the article with these words. Which quotation do you find the most interesting?

   | failure   nothing   success   truth |

3 Read the article quickly. Choose the main message(s) (a–c).

   a It's impossible to succeed when you make mistakes.
   b Knowing why things go wrong teaches you nothing new.
   c Mistakes are inevitable – it's what you do next that counts.

4 Read the article again. Find examples of three kinds of mistake.

   1 lack of planning
   2 lack of knowledge
   3 multiple causes

5 What do the underlined words refer to in these extracts from the article?

   1 You can't have one without the other. (lines 5–6)
   2 … the truth is that they are a part of every decision-making process. (lines 7–8)
   3 I didn't have time to find a new one. (line 14)
   4 This nearly destroyed the company. (lines 24–25)
   5 … stop looking back and look ahead – to the next time! (line 38)

6 Work in groups. Which of these things do you think influenced the 'New Coke' disaster? Discuss your ideas.

   | advanced trialling   consumer satisfaction |
   | advertising   market research |
   | brand loyalty   product taste |
   | company strategy |

VOCABULARY Success and failure

7 Look at how these nouns are used in the article. Are they countable (C) or uncountable (U)? Which nouns can be used in both ways (B)?

   1 failure (line 1)   8 disaster (line 27)
   2 success (line 5)   9 experience (line 28)
   3 mistake (line 6)   10 expertise (line 28)
   4 truth (line 7)   11 blame (line 31)
   5 planning (line 17)   12 catastrophe (line 32)
   6 knowledge (line 21)   13 fault (line 37)
   7 error (line 24)

8 Complete the sentences with the correct form of words from Exercise 7. Sometimes, more than one word is possible.

   1 One of Coca Cola's biggest marketing _____ is its name, which is the most recognized phrase in the world after 'OK'.
   2 A series of computer _____ led to the whole system closing down in our office.
   3 It wasn't my _____ that I was late for the meeting: we were stuck in the lift!
   4 My day has been a complete _____. Everything went wrong!
   5 My colleagues at work have lots more _____ than I do, so they often help me out.
   6 The news article was full of _____. In fact, there was hardly a word of _____ in it at all.

9 Put the words in order to make questions. Then ask and answer the questions with your partner.

   1 planning / good / how / are / at / you / ?
   2 expertise / you / areas / what / would / say / your / are / of / ?
   3 useful / your / knowledge / in / or / is / experience / more / job / ?
   4 you / when / speak / mistakes / do / making / you / mind / English / ?
   5 a / disaster / have / work-related / you / ever / had / ?
   6 your / for / ever / things / take / do / the / aren't / you / blame / that / fault / ?

SPEAKING Passing on lessons learned

10 **21st CENTURY OUTCOMES**

   Work in pairs. Tell your partner about a mistake you have made, whether trivial or serious. What advice would you give someone in a similar situation?

46

EVERY SATURDAY WITH **THOMAS DOWLING**

LESSONS for LIFE

> We just calmly laid out all the options, and ... was not one of them.
>
> *Jerry C Bostick, Mission Control Apollo 13, NASA*

> If failure is not an option, then neither is ... .
>
> *Seth Godin, entrepreneur*

> In all science, error precedes the ... , and it is better it should go first than last.
>
> *Hugh Walpole, novelist*

> So winners, Hae-Joo proposed, are the real losers because they learn ... ? What, then, are losers? Winners?
>
> *from Cloud Atlas, David Mitchell, novelist*

When Jerry Bostick said that failure was not an option on the Apollo 13 rescue mission, he knew that they were dealing with a life or death situation. But this is not a philosophy that you can generally follow in more day-to-day situations. Seth Godin probably came closer to everyday reality with his observation that, really, success and failure go hand in hand. You can't have one without the other. And what's more, mistakes and failure don't necessarily go hand in hand. While it's easy to think that you should avoid making mistakes, the truth is that they are a part of every decision-making process.

Let's look at some examples of how this works. A college professor of mine used to say about mistakes, 'Understand them, learn from them and then move on.' His words came to mind the first time I gave a presentation in my new job. I had an audience of ten, but only four handouts. This was because the printer cartridge had run out when I was printing the handouts and I didn't have time to find a new one. Fortunately, I also had a slide show prepared, so the presentation wasn't a total failure. But I felt embarrassed and annoyed with myself. And this is a perfect example of one of the most common types of mistake: not planning ahead. Everything about the presentation was, in theory, within my control, but I blew it because I left everything until the last minute.

But even the best planning in the world doesn't help if you don't have sufficient knowledge about what you're doing. Someone I know set up a new business and decided to do his own tax returns rather than pay an accountant. At the end of his first year of trading, he found he owed a large sum in taxes due to his accounting errors. This nearly destroyed the company. He learned his lesson and the following year hired an accountant.

A third kind of mistake is more complicated and it's not so easy to focus on a single cause. An example is the infamous 'New Coke' marketing disaster. Despite the experience and expertise of a company like Coca Cola, when they introduced 'New Coke' in 1985, it bombed. Nobody was interested in a 'new' flavour, everyone preferred the original taste. An in-depth analysis was needed to try and work out who should take the blame for such a catastrophe – market researchers? product developer? executive decisions? In the end, Coca Cola simply recognized they'd made a mistake and moved on to something different, returning to the familiar taste of 'Coke Classic' almost immediately.

But perhaps the most important thing about analysing your mistakes is to accept the blame. You blew it, it's your fault. Once you've worked out what went wrong and why, then stop looking back and look ahead – to the next time!

Thomas.Dowling@themagazine.au

I blew it (exp) I failed completely
it bombed (exp) it was a disaster
out of the blue (exp) unexpectedly

Unit 4 Success and failure

21st CENTURY OUTCOMES — INITIATIVE AND SELF-DIRECTION — Reflect critically on past experiences in order to inform future progress

4.4 How did it go?

LISTENING Reviewing an event

1 A small company holds an Open Day every year with fun events to promote the company and to raise funds for charity. Look at the list of things that happened at last year's Open Day. Decide if the things are successes (S) or problems (P).

> **Open Day Summary**
> 1) we didn't sell all the tickets
> 2) we ran out of T-shirts to sell
> 3) we made a profit overall
> 4) two people got food poisoning
> 5) it rained in the afternoon
> 6) we got coverage on local TV
> 7) three kids suffered minor injuries
> 8) there weren't enough volunteer helpers
> 9) we got lots of donations from other local businesses
> 10) the litter bins overflowed
> 11) there was a lot of coverage on Twitter

2 🎧 22 Work in pairs. Discuss how the company could avoid repeating the problems this year. Then listen to a meeting about the Open Day. Which points do the people talk about? Did you hear any of your ideas?

3 🎧 22 Listen again. Look at the Useful language box. Match the suggestions (1–6) with the responses (a–f).

> **MAKING AND RESPONDING TO SUGGESTIONS**
>
> **Making suggestions**
> 1 Why don't we think about setting up another covered area?
> 2 We should be careful here.
> 3 I don't think we need to have a burger stall.
> 4 How about putting something out on Twitter?
> 5 We could consider other ways of getting more followers.
> 6 We'd better get more printed.
>
> **Responding to suggestions**
> a I couldn't agree more.
> b I like the sound of that.
> c I'm not sure I'm with you on that.
> d OK … or I could look at the prices first.
> e Let's look into that.
> f That's a good idea.

Pronunciation Intonation and meaning

4a 🎧 **23** Meaning is expressed not only by your words but also by your intonation. Listen to the responses in the Useful language box. For each one, decide if the speaker sounds enthusiastic (E) or unsure (U).

4b 🎧 **23** Listen again and repeat the sentences.

SPEAKING Making and responding to suggestions

5 **21st CENTURY OUTCOMES**
Work in small groups. Make suggestions for the other problems in the list in Exercise 1. Then suggest and agree on two more ideas for activities for the Open Day. Make notes on your discussion. You will use the notes in Exercise 11.

6 Choose a spokesperson from your group. Present your ideas to the class. As a class, choose the two ideas you think will raise the most money.

WRITING Minutes (1)

7 Read the email that was sent out before the meeting in Exercise 2. Which point deals with the Open Day?

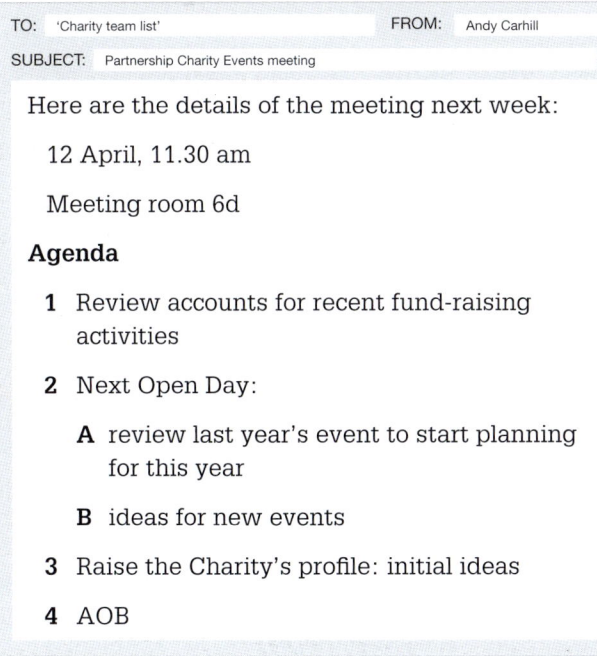

TO: 'Charity team list'   FROM: Andy Carhill
SUBJECT: Partnership Charity Events meeting

Here are the details of the meeting next week:

12 April, 11.30 am

Meeting room 6d

Agenda

1 Review accounts for recent fund-raising activities

2 Next Open Day:
   A review last year's event to start planning for this year
   B ideas for new events

3 Raise the Charity's profile: initial ideas

4 AOB

8 Read the extracts from the minutes of the meeting. Which of the points in Exercise 7 do they refer to?

> **Partnership Charity Events meeting 12 April**
> **Present:** Andy Carhill, Tamara Watson, Jason Lee
> **Apologies for absence:** Ken Sawalha, Olivia Gray

> Last year's Open Day was discussed to see what changes are needed for this year. The following points were agreed:
> • look into setting up an additional covered area (TW)
> • check caterers' certificates (AC)
> • find different burger stall to hire (AC)
> • use Twitter to get more volunteers (TW)
> • check T-shirt prices (AC)

9 Look at the email and the minutes again. What do you think these terms mean?

1 Agenda   3 Present
2 AOB   4 Apologies for absence

Writing skill Bullet points

10a Notice how the points for action are written using bullet points for clarity. Answer the questions.

1 What is the form of the verb in each sentence?
2 What do the initials after each bullet point mean?

10b How would the action points be written as complete sentences?

10c Write these sentences as bullet points.

1 We decided that we'd try to find a new venue for our next open day.
2 Andy's offered to get a quote for a children's entertainer.
3 Tamara was asked to check the latest health and safety regulations.
4 Andy's going to find a new company to design the promotional material.
5 Jason said he'd send everyone a new budget outline.
6 Tamara and Jason are going to investigate collaborations with local charities.

11 Look at your notes from your discussion in Exercise 5. Use your notes to write sections 2B and 3 from the Agenda. Use bullet points for your action points.

12 Exchange minutes with another group. Evaluate their minutes using these questions.

• Do they clearly state what action needs to be taken?
• What do you think of the other group's ideas?
• Do you think their ideas would work? Why? / Why not?

21st CENTURY OUTCOMES **PRODUCTIVITY AND ACCOUNTABILITY** Prioritize, plan and manage work to achieve the intended result

Review 2 | UNITS 3 AND 4

READING

1 Read the article about Krochet Kids. Find this information.

1. the names of the three American friends
2. the African country one of the three friends visited
3. what the hats were made of
4. the number of women working in the African project
5. the name of the second country Krochet Kids works in

2 Read the article again. Answer the questions.

1. What was unusual about Kohl's new skill?
2. Why did Kohl and his friends want to crochet?
3. How did the name Krochet Kids originate?
4. What was Stewart doing in Uganda?
5. How has Krochet Kids developed since it first began in Uganda?
6. What are some of the changes in the women's lives since they started working with Krochet Kids?

GRAMMAR

3 Complete the sentences about Krochet Kids with the present perfect simple and present perfect continuous form of the verbs.

1. Since Krochet Kids began, it _____ (increase) the number of women it helps in Uganda to 150.
2. In Northern Uganda, rebel forces _____ (fight) for more than 20 years.
3. As well as providing work, Krochet Kids _____ (give) training in money management and business skills.
4. The founders of the company _____ (develop) a system to track each woman's development.
5. The company _____ (look) for new staff to expand the Peru operation recently.
6. The women in Krochet Kids Peru _____ (make) hats since 2011.

Krochet Kids

Make your own hat   When American teenager Kohl Crecelius's older brother taught him how to crochet, neither of them knew what that simple skill would lead to. Kohl and his two friends Travis and Stewart didn't care that crochet wasn't a typical 'boy' skill – they just wanted to make their own unique and personalized hats to wear when snowboarding and skiing at the weekend. Soon they had a steady supply of customers among their school friends and they featured in a local newspaper under the headline of 'Krochet Kids'.

mentor (n) a person who gives a younger or less experienced person help and advice over a period of time, especially at work or school

Pass your skills on   Fast forward several years, and the three friends had moved to different colleges, but they kept in touch. Stewart spent a summer working in Uganda with people who had been living in government camps for more than twenty years. These people were looking for ways of earning money and becoming independent. By the following year, the three young men had set up Krochet Kids as a non-profit company and had recruited a group of women in Uganda to make the colourful woollen hats that had been so popular with their American school friends several years earlier.

Make a difference   Since 2008, Krochet Kids has expanded its operation to employ 150 women in Uganda and more in Peru. The company is committed to a business model which provides a job, an education and a mentor scheme for the women and their families. The statistics are clear. For the average woman making goods for Krochet Kids, her personal income has increased as much as ten times. She is able to save up to 25 times more money than before. Her children are 25 times more likely to have increased their school attendance. Increased earnings lead to better access to health care, and so families are five times healthier than they used to be. Some of the effects of having an income are unexpected: the incidence of domestic abuse has fallen by 40 per cent for these women and they have become more involved in decision-making in the home.

Meanwhile the product range has expanded to include scarves, bags and clothing, ensuring the long-term future of the company and the families it supports.

4 Choose the correct options to complete the text about the experience of Leonor, a woman who works with Krochet Kids Peru (KKP).

Leonor ¹ *was moving / had moved* from a mountain region to Lima at the age of fourteen, but soon she ² *found / had found* that she ³ *didn't have / hadn't had* enough money to pay her school fees. Before KKP, Leonor ⁴ *would struggle / had been struggling* to find secure employment. She ⁵ *was taking / used to take* any job that was available, and she ⁶ *was working / had worked* twelve-hour shifts in a factory when she ⁷ *heard / was hearing* about KKP. By this time, she ⁸ *had / used to have* a daughter and ⁹ *needed / was needing* work where she ¹⁰ *didn't have to / hadn't had to* leave her daughter for long periods. KKP ¹¹ *provided / had provided* Leonor with work and with a place at the KKP childcare centre.

VOCABULARY

5 Complete the sentences about Krochet Kids with the correct form of the words.

1 KKP has been influen_____ in improving access to education for the children of its workers.
2 Measuring the qualit_____ changes to women's lives is a key part of Krochet Kids' philosophy.
3 Projects like Krochet Kids offer financial secur_____ to its workers.
4 The grow_____ number of non-profit organizations shows that there is a need for this type of company.
5 The measures of succe_____ in a non-profit company are different from that of a traditional company.
6 The women Stewart met in Uganda were motivat_____ to become financially independent.
7 Working with Krochet Kids has led to greater personal saf_____ for many women.
8 The families working with Krochet Kids don't have perfec_____ lives, but they are much better than they used to be.

6 Complete the text with eight nouns from the list.

blame	catastrophe	disaster	error
experience	expertise	failure	fault
knowledge	mistake	planning	success
truth			

Non-profit companies may have different aims to commercial companies, but their ¹ _____ or ² _____ depends on business ³ _____ and good ⁴ _____ for the future just as much as any other company. Sometimes, people with good intentions make the ⁵ _____ of focusing only on the social benefits they want to achieve. But the ⁶ _____ is, as with any business, a good business model is essential. People with ⁷ _____ of their subject and extensive ⁸ _____ in the field are essential for the business to work well.

DISCUSSION

7 Work in pairs. Discuss the questions.

1 How do commercial companies usually measure success? Do you think it's the same for Krochet Kids?
2 Do you know of any small businesses that have started? What were the keys to their success or failure?
3 How do individuals measure success in their own lives? Does this vary according to the cultures they live in?

SPEAKING

8 Complete the conversations using the prompts.

A: I'd like to buy my friends some different presents this year.
B: ¹ *How about / look / Krochet Kids website?* The profits they make go to support the people who make their stuff.
A: Really? ² *like / sound / that.* I'll have a look.

C: It's Mum's birthday soon. ³ *better / book / restaurant / meal.*
D: A meal? ⁴ *Or / do / something different / this year.*

E: I think we need to make it easier for people to buy our products.
F: I agree. ⁵ *Why / not / think about / change* the payment methods on our website?
E: OK. We could add a PayPal option as well.
F: ⁶ *Yes, / good idea.*

G: I think we should redesign our website soon.
H: ⁷ *not sure / with you / that.* The current design is only a couple of years old and we're getting a lot of hits.
G: ⁸ *not think / need / completely change,* but it's important to stay up-to-date.

WRITING

9 Read the voicemails. Then complete the notes using abbreviations where possible.

1 Hi, it's Joana. Can you upload the content for the new website on Monday morning, please? I need to check it that afternoon. Thanks.
2 Hi, it's Frank. Fairtrade called. Can you get back to them this morning before midday? And Thursday or Friday are the only days I can do a meeting with them.
3 Hi, it's Adam. Are those sales figures for October to December correct? Can you confirm them and then get them to Marta, preferably by Thursday at the latest.
4 It's Mike. We can't use the town hall for the children's festival, so can you look into a new venue? I'll be in the office on Wednesday, give me a call at half three.

1 _____ website content _____ morn.
2 Return Fairtrade _____ before _____. Set up meeting _____ / _____.
3 Confirm _____ _____ _____ – _____. Forward to Marta _____ latest.
4 _____ _____ new venue children's festival. Call Mike _____ _____.

5 Exercise

BACKGROUND

1 You are going to watch a TED Talk by Nilofer Merchant called *Got a meeting? Take a walk.* Read the text about the speaker and the talk. Then work in pairs and discuss the questions.

1 Approximately how much time do you spend walking each day?
2 How do you think your level of fitness compares to previous generations?
3 What are the benefits of having 'walking meetings' according to Nilofer Merchant?

TEDTALKS

NILOFER MERCHANT was born in India and moved to the United States as a child. She founded her own company which works on business strategies with global corporations. As an author, she has written about creating better business solutions through collaboration and humanistic approaches. Nilofer Merchant's idea worth spreading is that we can all be healthier, more productive and more creative if we have meetings while we are on a walk.

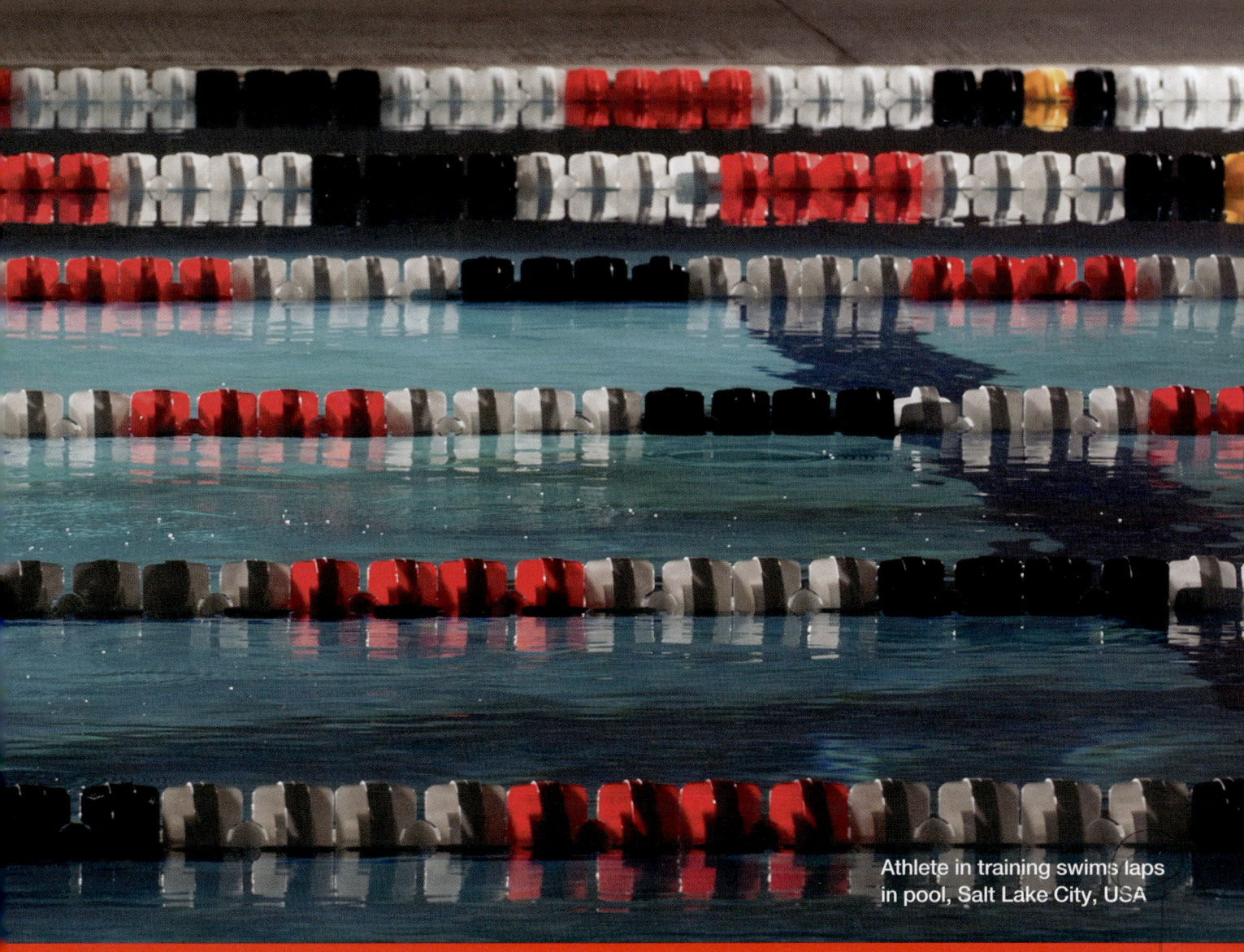

Athlete in training swims laps in pool, Salt Lake City, USA

KEY WORDS

2 Read the sentences (1–6). The words in bold are used in the TED Talk. First guess the meaning of the words. Then match the words with their definitions (a–f).

1 Certain 'lifestyle' illnesses are more **prevalent** than ever in the 21st century. c
2 It might feel as if we are healthier, but the **stats** don't agree. a
3 I'm not at all fit: I **huff and puff** if I have to run anywhere! e
4 My colleague has such inventive solutions to problems. It's real **out-of-the-box** thinking. b
5 We aren't making any progress with the problem. It's time to **reframe** our plans. f
6 Experts warn us that working as hard as many people do is not **sustainable** in the long term. d

a commonly used abbreviation for *statistics*
b unusual and original
c common, current and widespread
d able to be continued at a steady level
e to get out of breath
f to look at things in a new way

AUTHENTIC LISTENING SKILLS
Rising intonation

lengths

A rising intonation at the end of a sentence usually means the speaker is asking a question, but this is not always the case. In some accents, the rising inflection is also used with statements. Recognizing these intonation patterns will improve your understanding of the speaker's message. You can also use clues such as the grammatical structure of the sentence to help to decide if the speaker is asking a question or making a statement. / *inviting a response*

3a 🎧 **24** Look at the Authentic listening skills box. Then listen to the extracts from the TED Talk. Do they sound like questions (Q) or statements (S)?

1 _____ 2 _____ 3 _____ 4 _____

3b 🎧 **25** Read the phrases and decide if you expect them to have a rising or falling intonation. Then listen to the extracts and check your answers.

5 Now, any of those stats should convince each of us to get off our duff more …
6 I've learned a few things …
7 First, there's this amazing thing about actually getting out of the box …

5.1 Got a meeting? Take a walk

TEDTALKS

1. ▶ 5.1 Complete the summary of the TED Talk with five of these words. Then watch the talk and check your answers.

   box   ideas   life   office   physical   smoking   walking

   According to Nilofer Merchant, in health terms, sitting is the equivalent of [1] _smoking_. There are serious illnesses which are tied to our lack of [2] _physical_ activity. When she started to have meetings while walking, it changed her [3] _life_. She found that getting out of the [4] _office_ resulted in out-of-the-box thinking. Walking while talking is a way of coming up with a new set of [5] _ideas_.

2. ▶ 5.1 Watch the first part (0.00–1.22) of the talk again. Complete the notes.

   1. Hours per day people today spend sitting down: _9.3_
   2. Hours per day people today spend sleeping: _7.7_
   3. Two cancers linked to inactivity: _breast_, _colon_ 10%
   4. Percentage of heart disease linked to inactivity: _six_
   5. Percentage of type 2 diabetes linked to inactivity: _seven_

3. ▶ 5.1 Watch the second part (1.22–2.19) of the talk again. Read the extracts from the talk and answer the questions. _alone._

   1. 'What did get me moving was a social interaction.' What was that interaction? _nitga dog-walker_
   2. 'I've taken that idea and made it my own.' What does Nilofer Merchant mean? _invites others on mtg-walk_
   3. 'I used to think about it as, you could take care of your health, or you could take care of _____.' What is the second thing she mentions? _wk_

4. ▶ 5.1 Watch the third part (2.19 to the end) of the talk again. Are the sentences true (T) or false (F)?

   1. Nilofer Merchant isn't sure whether out-of-the-box thinking comes from being outside in a natural environment or actually doing exercise. _T_
   2. According to Nilofer Merchant, we often think that two ideas are incompatible with each other when in fact that isn't true. _T_ → _think of another?_

5. Work in pairs. What does Nilofer Merchant mean by _fresh air drives fresh thinking_? Can you think of a time when this was true for you? _being in nature makes you think differently._

▶ tush, duff N AM ENG
▶ bottom BR ENG
▶ directly /dəˈrektli/ N AM ENG
▶ directly /daɪˈrektli/ BR ENG
▶ regular /ˈregjələr/ N AM ENG
▶ regular /ˈregjələ/ BR ENG

VOCABULARY IN CONTEXT

6 ▶ 5.2 Watch the clips from the TED Talk. Choose the correct meaning of the words.

7 Work in pairs. Do you agree with the statements? Why? / Why not?

1 Many things that seem impossible at first turn out to be doable in the end.
2 Conditions like stress and anxiety are tied to 21st century lifestyles.
3 It's kind of odd that more companies aren't encouraging their employees to leave the office building during the work day.

CRITICAL THINKING Reflecting on experiences = implications

8 Our experiences can teach us things if we are able to reflect on them critically. Nilofer Merchant learned from walking meetings that looking after our health and working don't need to be mutually exclusive. What did this point also make clear to her? Choose the correct option (a–c).

a If you understand this point, you can extend this kind of thinking to other ideas you thought were also mutually exclusive.
b If you understand this point, the number of deaths from heart disease and illnesses from inactivity will decrease.
c If you understand this point, you can change the way you interact with people in your life.

9 Work in pairs. Read these comments* about the TED Talk. What have these people learned from their experiences and from listening to the talk?

Viewers' comments
B **Bruce** – I get up and walk around the office at least once an hour. It's just like she says – when I sit down again, my brain feels fresher.
J **Julia** – As a graphic designer, I already know that going for a walk helps me to solve design problems, but I hadn't realized there was such a health risk to sitting down. I'm doubly glad I'm active at work!

*The comments were created for this activity.

PRESENTATION SKILLS Beginning with a strong statement

TIPS
The start of the talk is your opportunity to get the audience's attention and hold it for the rest of the presentation. You can do this in a variety of ways.
- Be surprising – do or say something that your audience won't expect.
- Be controversial – say something that some members of the audience might disagree with.
- Be challenging – say something to make your listeners question themselves.

10 ▶ 5.3 Watch the clip from the TED Talk. Complete the opening sentence of the talk. Then look at the Presentation tips box. Which technique is Nilofer Merchant using?

'What you're doing, right now, at this very moment, _____ _____ _____.'

11 Prepare strong opening statements for these statistics. Use the techniques in the Presentation tips box. Then prepare the next few sentences of your presentation, explaining or commenting on the statistics.

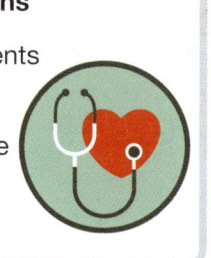

USA annual deaths
from traffic accidents over **30,000**
from heart disease **600,000**
(2012 data)

EU countries overweight adults
52%
(2012 data)

EU recommended physical activity for adults:
150 minutes per week (minimum)

12 Work in pairs. Give one of your presentations. How does your partner get your attention?

▶ walk /wɔk/ **N AM ENG**
▶ walk /wɔːk/ **BR ENG**
▶ learned **N AM ENG**
▶ learned, learnt **BR ENG**
▶ box /bæks/ **N AM ENG**
▶ box /bɒks/ **BR ENG**

5.2 Overcoming challenges

GRAMMAR Modals and related verbs: past forms (1)

1 Work in pairs. Think of at least five sports. Then order them according to how dangerous they are. (1 = the most dangerous, 5 = the least dangerous)

2 Is tennis one of the sports on your list? How dangerous do you think it is? Look at the infographic about tennis players to see if your opinion is correct.

3 🎧 26 Listen to a discussion of sports injuries on a radio programme. Choose the correct option to complete the sentences.

  1 Compared to the past, there are _____ tennis tournaments now.
   a fewer
   b more
   c the same number of

  2 Juan Martin del Potro and Novak Djokovic said they _____ as a result of what people said.
   a became injured
   b gave up
   c kept going

  3 After beating Rafael Nadal, Steve Darcis _____.
   a was beaten in the next round
   b withdrew from the tournament
   c won the tournament

  4 The presenters _____ that Andy Murray's injury has had an impact on his playing.
   a agree
   b don't agree
   c don't believe

4 🎧 26 Listen again. Read the sentences in the Grammar box. Which player does each sentence beginning *He* refer to?

5 Read the sentences again. Answer the questions (1–3).

MODALS AND RELATED VERBS: PAST FORMS (1)

can (not) + infinitive without to   ability + permission

He **couldn't defend** his Wimbledon title in 2009.
In the past, players **could rest** between big matches.

to (not) be able to + infinitive   = couldn't

He **wasn't able to recover** until the 2011 season ended.

manage to + infinitive

He **managed to keep** going with his teammates' support, despite the pain.

succeed in + -ing

He **succeeded in beating** Nadal in a first-round match.

must + infinitive without to / have to + infinitive

He **had to have** surgery on his back.

1 Which past forms are used to refer to these things?
   a the possibility of doing something
   b the ability to do something
   c the necessity to do something
2 Which past forms refer to specific times in the past?
3 Which sentences can you rephrase with other past forms from the Grammar box?

Check your answers on page 148 and do Exercises 1–4.

6 Read the text about triathletes Jenny Manners and Alison Patrick. Choose the correct options to complete the text.

Jenny Manners is a top triathlete. She also used to compete in Paralympic events with a partner who was blind. However, when her partner retired in 2014, Jenny ¹ *couldn't / had to* give this up. Then she met a new partner, Alison Patrick. Alison had been a successful runner until an injury meant she ² *couldn't / didn't manage to* continue running. She had taken up swimming instead. Jenny and Alison ³ *were able to / could* start training together. Because Jenny was her partner, Alison ⁴ *was able to / had to* take up running again. A few months later, they ⁵ *managed to / could* win a gold medal at the World Championships.

7 Read and complete people's comments about sports and fitness challenges. Use verbs from the Grammar box. Can you relate to any of these comments?

1 I've never been sporty, but I was putting on weight. Eventually, my sister _____ getting me to go with her to the gym. I quite enjoy it!
2 My friend took up jogging, but he made the mistake of not warming up first. He pulled a muscle and he _____ walk for a week.
3 Right through my childhood, I _____ swim. Then I went to Hawaii on holiday and wanted to surf, so I _____ learn. To my amazement, I _____ do it!
4 Everyone in my family decided to do half an hour's exercise every day for a month, as an experiment. We all _____ change our daily routines and in the end my brother _____ do the whole month, but everyone else _____ make it!

SPEAKING Getting motivated

8 **21st CENTURY OUTCOMES**
Work in groups. Read the list of common excuses people make for not taking exercise. Have you ever used any of them? Brainstorm different activities that people can do to get fit.

- I haven't got time to take exercise.
- I'm not sporty.
- Gyms are too expensive for me.
- I'm always too tired.
- I've got a young family / elderly parents to look after.

5.3 The bottom line

READING What's in a name?

1 Read the news headlines. Identify the sport and the sponsor in each one.

> Manchester United announce £750 million sponsorship deal with Adidas
>
> Red Bull Racing and Casio extend sponsor deal for another two years
>
> Sky continues to sponsor British Cycling following Tour success

2 What other sport sponsorship partnerships do you know? What company might sponsor these sports? Why?

> athletics   golf   sailing   skateboarding

3 Work in pairs. Discuss the questions.
1 What do sports teams or individuals get out of sponsorship?
2 What do sponsors get out of sponsorship?
3 Is there a difference between sponsorship and advertising?
4 What kind of partnerships are most typical in sports sponsorship?

4 Read the article quickly. Check your ideas from Exercise 3.

5 Read the article again. Answer the questions.
1 Why did the football club owner want to change the stadium name?
2 How did people react to this?
3 Why didn't the owner succeed in changing the name?
4 How much money is involved in sports sponsorship?
5 Why is 'live event' television so important financially?

6 Find these expressions in the article. Write the preposition that completes each expression.
1 reacted _____ anger (line 2)
2 the row _____ the proposal (line 7)
3 the reason _____ the change (lines 8–9)
4 the extent _____ which (line 19)
5 _____ a global scale (line 20)
6 raising brand awareness _____ a wide market (lines 28–29)
7 the company _____ the first electronic exercise bike (lines 31–32)
8 _____ the years to come (line 49)

7 Work in pairs. Do you think minority-interest sports find it easy to attract sponsorship? How do you think this affects them?

VOCABULARY Finance

8 Complete the expressions with these nouns. Then check your answers in the questions in Exercise 9.

| books | budget | deal | debt | event |
| fee | finances | money | offer | partnership |

1 balance the _____
2 charge a _____
3 control your _____
4 form a _____
5 get into _____
6 invest _____
7 make an _____
8 make a _____
9 sponsor an _____
10 work out a _____

9 Work in pairs. Discuss the questions.
1 What's the job title of a person who balances the books?
2 What kinds of professions charge a fee for their services?
3 Do you control your finances well, or could you improve?
4 Can you name any companies that have formed a partnership?
5 What happens when people get into debt in your country?
6 What kind of company would you invest money in, if you could?
7 Do you know anyone who's made an offer to buy a house?
8 Have you ever made a deal that saved you money?
9 Can you name a company that has sponsored an event recently?
10 Why is it a good idea to work out a budget for your personal finances?

SPEAKING A sponsored event

10 **21st CENTURY OUTCOMES**

Work in groups. You are going to organize a sponsored event to do as a class. Decide the following:
- what kind of event
- who will benefit
- where you can get sponsorship
- what kinds of sponsors to look for
- how much you want to raise
- who will be responsible for different aspects of the event

11 Present your plans to the class. Vote for the event you would all most like to do.

What's in a name?

ALICIA GRAYLING

A few years ago, the supporters of Newcastle United, an English Premiership football team, reacted with anger when the owner of the club tried to rename their stadium. Fans couldn't believe the plan to get rid of the name of St. James' Park: it had been the home of the club since 1892 and was due to host early-round matches in the Olympic Games. The row over the proposal was so great that it was even discussed in the British Parliament. And the reason for the change? Money. Specifically, the club's owner was looking for a new sponsorship deal and estimated that a new name for the stadium would bring in up to £10 million a year. Despite the controversy, the name was changed and within a few months the club managed to find a sponsor. However, the sponsor promptly restored the original stadium name, and was happy to have their company name on the players' shirts instead. This was a wise business decision as it is hard to successfully promote your company when there's controversy involved.

The story highlights the extent to which sponsorship is big business in sport. On a global scale, sports sponsorship is estimated to be worth tens of billions of dollars a year. Fees can be huge: Manchester United succeeded in reaching an agreement to the tune of £750 million over ten years with Adidas, after their previous sponsors Nike weren't able to accept the club's financial demands. Unlike advertising, sponsorship doesn't actually focus on the features or aspects of specific products. It's all about getting the company's name known and raising brand awareness across a wide market. Hence the logic of partnerships between sports products (clothing, equipment, etc.) and sports teams. For example, Life Fitness, the company behind the first electronic exercise bike seen in gyms everywhere, is an official sponsor of the Ladies Professional Golf Association.

But there's a new phenomenon in sports business which gives the big-name sports even greater financial power than before: television and broadcast rights. With the massive national and international audiences that some sports are able to achieve, media companies are eager to sign up the rights to show the events. The media companies are willing to pay such large sums since in their turn they can attract income from advertising. Recently we've seen bidding wars for the TV rights to many sports events including the Olympic Games. For broadcasters, media content today is divided into two types: live events (which clearly includes sport) and 'everything else'. The future for these companies lies in the first type, and the sports industry is very aware of this – we'll see more sky-high deals in the years to come.

---

bidding war (n) when competing companies offer money to get something from another company
broadcaster (n) a company that transmits radio or TV programmes
rights (n) legal permission to reproduce something

5.4 Who funded you?

LISTENING Young entrepreneurs

1 Where do new businesses get the money to start up? Match the terms with the definitions and complete the sentences.

| angel investors | banks | crowd funding |
| personal savings | private loan | shareholders |

1 _banks_ are commercial businesses which charge interest on loans.
2 Money you borrow from friends, family or others is a _pr. loan_.
3 Money you have accumulated is your _p. sav._
4 _Shareholders_ are private investors who want to see a return on their money.
5 Rich entrepreneurs who want to help start-ups are known as _angel inv._
6 _Crowd f._ brings you small amounts of money from a large number of people, usually via the Internet.

2 🎧 27 Listen to part of a radio programme about young inventors with new business ideas. Answer the questions.

1 What does Ryan's invention do?
2 When did he get the idea?
3 How much did he raise?
4 Where did he get this investment from?
5 What stage is the product at?

3 🎧 27 Listen again. Complete the extracts from the conversation.

1 You _____ about your amazing 'smart' cushion, aren't you?
2 Where did the idea _____?
3 _____ to a bank?
4 My partner suggested _____ for a loan, but …
5 … we worried that it would be hard to _____, but …
6 So, _____ this wonderful cushion in the shops?
7 We _____ it as much thought as …

4 Look at the Useful language box. Match the answers with the questions in Exercise 3. Then match the statements with the remaining extracts. Which words does the speaker omit in each case?

ELLIPSIS: OMITTING INFORMATION WHEN THE MEANING IS CLEAR

Answering questions

a From my final-year project at college.
b No, we didn't.
c Not yet.
d Yes, I am.

Making statements

e I didn't want to
f it wasn't
g we can

Pronunciation Word stress in ellipsis

5a 🎧 28 Listen and notice which words in the Useful language box are stressed in ellipsis.

5b Work in pairs. Ask and answer the questions using ellipsis. Pay attention to which words you stress.

1 Do you enjoy learning English?
2 Are you very sporty?
3 Where are your parents from?
4 Was the weather good yesterday?

online Q&A with Maya Penn
@MayaPenn, May 7th

Maya Penn is thirteen years old. She runs an eco-friendly fashion company, which she started at the age of eight, and an environmental non-profit organization. She also makes animated cartoons.

SPEAKING Asking questions

6 Read about Maya Penn. Then write three questions that you'd send to the online Q&A session.

7 Work in small groups. Discuss and choose the three most interesting questions to ask Maya.

WRITING An email (1)

8 Read the email from Jake to Andy. Look at the sections in *italics*. Where do these sections come from?

TO: AndyP FROM: Jake Carver
SUBJECT: Business ideas

Hi Andy

Thanks for your email. I like the sound of the business in theory – I've got a few questions, so I've added them below your ideas.

The basic idea is to offer a range of extra sports activities to schools and youth organizations across the region.

Can you explain exactly what activities you're thinking about? And wouldn't it be better to start with just one or two activities?

We'd need to set up a website to show what we offer and for people to get in touch and make bookings.

OK, but could be costly. I wonder if you could start off just using Twitter? You can upload a lot of content there for free.

We'd aim to start at the beginning of the next school term.

That's a bit soon, isn't it? I think it might be better not to rush things.

As I say, I *am* interested. We need to discuss what kind of investment you're looking for to get started – let's keep talking!

Regards
Jake

---

9 What do you think Andy's original email was about? Choose one of the options (a–c).

a offering to lend money for a new business
b asking for investment in his new business
c looking for a job in a new business

Writing skill Questions

10a Look at the questions (1–3). Find four questions in the email. Why did Jake use these question types?

1 **Negative questions**
   Don't you think that's a bit expensive?

2 **Indirect questions**
   I wonder if you can tell me what you have in mind?

3 **Tag questions**
   You're going to employ staff, aren't you?

See page 148 for more information about questions, and do Exercises 5–7.

10b Rewrite the questions from the email.

1 What activities _____?
2 Would it _____?
3 Could you _____?
4 Is that _____?

10c Rewrite these questions. Use the words and question types in brackets.

1 What time is it? (Could you tell me …)
2 Are you busy today? (tag question)
3 Do you think we should wait? (negative question)
4 Did Sue remember to phone the bank? (tag question)
5 Do they know the price of the tickets? (I wonder …)
6 Is this a bad idea? (Don't you think …)

21st CENTURY OUTCOMES   COMMUNICATION AND COLLA

6 Values

BACKGROUND

1 You are going to watch an edited version of a TED Talk by Jill Shargaa called *Please, please, people. Let's put the 'awe' back in 'awesome'*. Read the text about the speaker and the talk. Then work in pairs and discuss the questions.

1 How easy is it to understand humour in a foreign language? What things can make it easy or difficult?
2 A similar sense of humour can make people feel part of the same group. What other things make people feel connected to each other?
3 Jill Shargaa's talk focuses on a word that has recently become very popular. What words or expressions are fashionable at the moment in your country? Do you use them?

TEDTALKS

JILL SHARGAA is an American who is both a designer and a comedian. She started her career in comedy in 1979 and has appeared in several TV shows. As the founder of her own design company, she's worked with Universal Studios and Walt Disney Imagineering.

Jill Shargaa's idea worth spreading is that the word *awesome* is used too much, and we should find more appropriate ways of describing enjoyable things – including her TED Talk.

Danny MacAskill reaches the top of the Inaccessible Pinnacle, Isle of Skye, Scotland

KEY WORDS

2 Read the sentences (1–6). The words in bold are used in the TED Talk. First guess the meaning of the words. Then match the words with their definitions (a–f).

1 I'm full of **admiration** for the way Sue has passed her exams in such difficult conditions.
2 The new concert hall is absolutely **majestic**. It's a fantastic building.
3 It was so disappointing when the goalkeeper let the ball **roll** past him and into the net.
4 Napoleon still amazes historians today with his skill in planning a military **invasion**.
5 I was astonished when the horse crossed the river in one **leap**.
6 It's astonishing the way the same **conveyor belt** moves the TVs through the whole production process.

a magnificent and very special
b entering a country by force
c a jump over a large distance
d great liking and respect
e a continuous line of products in a factory
f to move by turning over repeatedly

AUTHENTIC LISTENING SKILLS Listening for gist

> When you listen to a native speaker, there are things you can do to understand the gist – the overall idea of the talk. Relax and focus on what you do understand, not what you don't understand. Don't worry if you don't understand all the details, such as specialist terms or jokes, but focus on the general sense of the message. Try to work out the connections between the main ideas you hear.

3a 🎧 29 Look at the Authentic listening skills box. Then listen to the opening sentences from the TED Talk. Focus on the general sense. In which order (1–3) does Jill Shargaa do these things (a–c)?

a She says what she's going to talk about.
b She asks a question about the word *awesome*.
c She makes a comment about the audience.

3b 🎧 30 Listen to the next few sentences from the talk. Try to get the general sense. Which of these things (a–c) does Jill Shargaa do?

a She argues a point of view.
b She explains some specialist terms.
c She tells a quick story.

6.1 Please, please, people. Let's put the 'awe' back in 'awesome'

TEDTALKS

1 ▶ 6.1 Watch the edited version of the TED Talk. Jill Shargaa mentions all of these things. Tick (✓) the things she says are *awesome*.

visiting a restaurant	the Allied invasion of Normandy ✓
PDFs	bees ✓
sandwiches	the Wright Brothers
the wheel ✓	Rolling Stone Magazine
the Great Pyramids ✓	sharks ✓
the Grand Canyon ✓	her PowerPoint
photography ✓	

2 ▶ 6.1 Watch the first part (0.00–2.35) of the talk again. Are the sentences true (T) or false (F)?

1 Jill Shargaa says she had a fantastic experience dining in an outdoor café. F *Merely good*
2 She thinks her co-worker's comment on saving files was too strong. T
3 She thinks that the word *awesome* is frequently overused. T
4 According to a dictionary, *awesome* means producing feelings of fear and admiration. T
5 Jill Shargaa says the way we use *awesome* gives it more power. F
6 She suggests that if we say everything is *awesome*, we don't value high points and low points in our experiences. T

▶ dining **N AM ENG**
▶ having dinner **BR ENG**
▶ server **N AM ENG**
▶ waiter/waitress **BR ENG**
▶ co-workers **N AM ENG**
▶ colleagues **BR ENG**

3 ▶ 6.1 Watch the second part (2.35 to the end) of the talk again. Here are six of the things Jill Shargaa describes as *awesome*. Choose the reason (a–b) she gives.

1 the wheel
   a helps you to move things
   b rolls everything to your home
2 the Great Pyramids
   a are incredibly old
   b were the tallest structures for thousands of years
3 the Grand Canyon
   a is millions of years old
   b gets 80 million visitors a year
4 bees
   a pollinate crops
   b make honey
5 the moon landing
   a was 66 years after the first airplane flight
   b is 240,000 miles away
6 sharks
   a have teeth that move forward
   b have 30,000 teeth in their jaw

4 Work in pairs. Discuss the questions.
   1 One dictionary definition of *awesome* says it's a feeling caused by majestic things. What things would you add to Jill Shargaa's list of awesome things?
   2 She suggests that, depending on context, more appropriate words for *awesome* include *good*, *great*, *thank you*, *delicious* and even *nearby*. In what situations could you use these words?

VOCABULARY IN CONTEXT

5 ▶ 6.2 Watch the clips from the TED Talk. Choose the correct meaning of the words.

6 Work in pairs. Discuss the questions.
   1 Has anything ever given you a feeling of fear mingled with admiration?
   2 What kinds of things do people whip out of their pockets or bags?
   3 What kinds of situations do you take shots in? Do you use a phone or a camera?

CRITICAL THINKING Reading between the lines

7 Work in pairs. Jill Shargaa stated: *So in other words, if you have everything, you value nothing. […] There's no dynamic, there's no highs or lows, if everything is awesome.* Discuss which of these statements (a–c) could also be part of Jill Shargaa's message.
   a It's better not to have ups and downs in life.
   b We can't appreciate the variety of our experiences when we say it's all wonderful.
   c We should be more conscious of the value of what we have.

8 Read these comments* about the TED Talk. To what extent have the viewers understood Jill Shargaa's message?

Viewers' comments
J **Jaycee** – Very funny talk, but with a serious point, I feel. We're so lazy with the way we use language these days.
K **Kristen** – Awesome talk! The world is full of brilliant things and we should celebrate them every day!
A **Andreas** – Oh dear, I'm one of those people who use 'awesome' without really thinking about it. Everyone I know does it!

* The comments were created for this activity.

PRESENTATION SKILLS Being authentic

TIPS

The way you deliver your presentation should reflect your own personality. Don't copy a style that is not your own. Whether you are naturally funny, serious, shy or self-confident, you should be yourself.

- Relax your body so that you move and gesture naturally. Try relaxation techniques before your talk to help with this. When your body is relaxed, your voice becomes clearer and easier to understand too.
- Wear clothes you feel comfortable in, but don't choose anything that will distract your audience too much.
- Use words and expressions that you normally use. They are part of your personal style.
- Don't worry about being perfect. It's natural to feel a bit nervous. Audiences respond to speakers who are natural and 'human'. They want your talk to be successful for you and for them.

9 ▶ 6.3 Look at the Presentation tips box. Then watch the clip from the TED Talk. Do you think Jill Shargaa's presentation reflected her personality? Which of these adjectives do you think describe her?

| comfortable | confident | engaging |
| enthusiastic | funny | relaxed |

10 You are going to give a short presentation about something you're interested in. A hobby? A book? An issue? Think of what you could say about your interest. Have you any photos on your phone you can share? You can think about:
- describing your interest
- saying why it's important to you
- suggesting why others might find it interesting

11 Work in pairs. Give your presentation. Try to speak naturally. Then discuss whether your presentation styles are different or not.

▶ blowout **N AM ENG**
▶ whitewash **BR ENG**

▶ pants **N AM ENG**
▶ trousers **BR ENG**

▶ jackass **N AM ENG**
▶ idiot **BR ENG**

6.2 Getting value for money

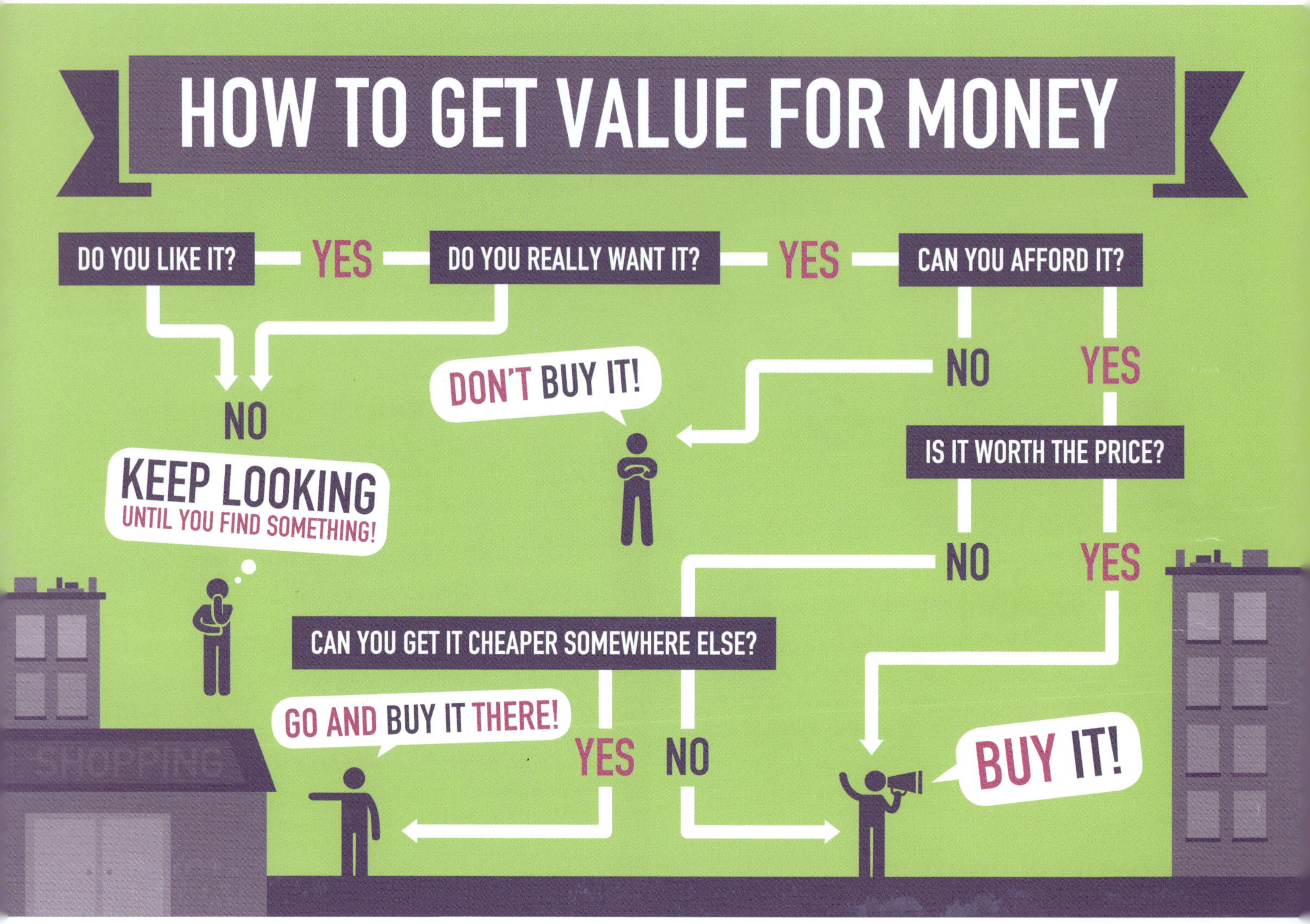

HOW TO GET VALUE FOR MONEY

- DO YOU LIKE IT? — YES → DO YOU REALLY WANT IT? — YES → CAN YOU AFFORD IT?
- NO → KEEP LOOKING UNTIL YOU FIND SOMETHING!
- DON'T BUY IT!
- IS IT WORTH THE PRICE?
- CAN YOU GET IT CHEAPER SOMEWHERE ELSE?
- YES → GO AND BUY IT THERE!
- NO → BUY IT!

GRAMMAR Zero, first and second conditionals

1 Work in pairs. Find out if any of these statements are true for your partner.
   1 I never buy things if I think they aren't value for money.
   2 I've occasionally bought stuff I've never used.
   3 I can't control myself when I buy online.
   4 I love bargains! I always buy things in the sales.

2 Look at the infographic. Answer the questions.
   1 What does the flowchart help with?
   2 Do you usually follow these steps when shopping? Tell your partner.

   If I really want something, I don't think about whether I can afford it!

3 ∩ 31 Listen to two conversations in a shop. Look at the photos. What are the shoppers interested in buying?

drill

laptop

tablet

toolbox

4 🎧 **31** Listen again. Answer the questions.

1. What problem does the first shopper have with his existing item?
2. What does the assistant say about last year's laptops?
3. What two problems does the first shopper mention?
4. What does the second shopper say about the brand?
5. What does the second shopper decide to pay with?

5 Read the sentences in the Grammar box. Answer the questions (1–2).

ZERO, FIRST AND SECOND CONDITIONALS

1 Zero conditional

If/When laptops **slow down** like that, **there's** not much you can do to fix them.

2 First conditional

If you **decide** to buy before the end of the month, we**'ll extend** the guarantee for two years.
If you **don't make up** your mind soon, **I'm going to get** a coffee.
If **I've gone** over my limit already, it **won't make** any difference.

3 Second conditional

If it **wasn't** so pricey, **I'd be** really tempted.
If you **got** that drill, how often **would** you **use** it?

1. Which tenses are used in each type of sentence?
2. Look at the conditional clauses (with *if*). Which type of conditional do we use to talk about these things?
   a something that is generally true
   b something that the speaker thinks is likely to happen in the future
   c something that is the opposite of the real situation or that the speaker thinks is unlikely to happen in the future

Check your answers on page 150 and do Exercises 1–4.

6 Match the two parts of the sentences. Then say which kind of conditional sentence they are and why.

1. If I see some clothes I can't afford,
2. If I wanted you to come shopping with me,
3. If you buy this today,
4. If this television wasn't so expensive,
5. If you've spent all your money,

a would you buy it?
b you should go home.
c I would ask you.
d you won't regret it.
e I look for something cheaper.

7 Work in pairs. You are looking for an unusual gift for a friend and have found some suitable things online. However, you have to bid for them in an online auction. Complete the first conditional sentences with your own ideas.

1. We're only going to bid if …
2. If the bid has gone too high, …
3. If we're going to limit our spending, …
4. If we can't find exactly what we want, …
5. We won't buy anything unless …
6. If someone's already bought it, …
7. You'll have to let me use your card if …
8. If we haven't found anything in an hour, …

8 Read the sentences (1–6). Write conditional sentences using the words in brackets.

I want to buy the tablet, but it's not worth that much money. (better value for money)

I'd buy the tablet if it was better value for money.

1. My car's breaking down a lot these days. I might need to look for a new one. (keep on)
2. Some things are advertised on TV. This doesn't influence me. (a product)
3. I have so much stuff because I can't help buying things. (have more self-control)
4. I spend too much on takeaways. I'm thinking about making food at home. (save money)
5. There's too much packaging on everything, so our recycling bin is always full. (less packaging)
6. The shops have special offers, so I'm always tempted. (so / so many)

9 Work in pairs. Discuss the conditional sentences in Exercise 8. Can you imagine saying any of these things?

SPEAKING Consumerism and the economy

10 **21st CENTURY OUTCOMES**

Work in groups. Discuss the consequences of each situation.

What would happen if …
- electrical goods and gadgets didn't stop working after a few years?
- nobody bought any more new clothes?
- there was no TV advertising?

21st CENTURY OUTCOMES   ECONOMIC LITERACY Show understanding of the role of the economy in society

6.3 Is it worth it?

READING Ethical consumption

1 Work in pairs. Make a list of three things you each bought this week. Can you answer these questions?

1 How much did they cost you?
2 Where were they produced?
3 Who produced them?
4 Are they eco-friendly?

2 Read the questions in the article about ethical consumption. What would you reply? Tell your partner.

3 Read the whole article and see if your answers from Exercise 2 are mentioned.

4 Read the questions. Choose the correct option (a–c) according to the information in the article.

1 Are disposable cups incredibly wasteful?
   a Yes, compared to ceramic cups, they use up more resources.
   b Yes, but no more so than reusable cups when everything is taken into account.
   c No, the actual coffee inside the cup is more eco-unfriendly than the cup itself.

2 Is it really unethical to buy fake products?
   a No, everyone does it and it does no harm to anyone.
   b No, designer items are not worth the price anyway.
   c Yes, there are legal and humanitarian issues with such goods.

3 Does buying out-of-season produce contribute to climate change?
   a Yes, but not as much as you might think.
   b No, because most of it comes from parts of the world where it grows all year round.
   c Yes, flying food around the world has a major impact on CO_2 emissions.

5 Would you change your buying habits after reading the article? Why? / Why not?

6 Work in pairs. Look at how these words are used in the article. Are they nouns, verbs or adjectives? Can you work out their meaning?

1 single-use (line 3)   4 deprive (line 30)
2 reusable (line 17)   5 produce (line 43)
3 upgrading (line 27)   6 seasonal (line 51)

VOCABULARY Consumerism: phrasal verbs

7 Find forms of these phrasal verbs in the text. What do the verbs mean?

1 take away (line 3)   4 break down (line 33)
2 throw away (line 14) 5 blow up (line 34)
3 turn out (line 14)   6 cut back (line 47)

8 Complete ... from Exe...

1 We're ... We'll h...
2 I was p...
3 The mi... morni...
4 'Two te... or to ___
5 'Where ... ___ it ___.'
6 Check that your car hire insurance covers you in case you ___.

SPEAKING Ethical awareness

9 **21st CENTURY OUTCOMES**

Work in pairs. Read the statements (1–5) in the quiz. Match the statements with the areas (a–e). Then do the quiz and find out how aware you are about ethical issues in consumerism.

a Animal welfare
b Company ethics
c Environmental impact
d Product sustainability
e Workers rights

ARE YOU AN ETHICAL CONSUMER?

Choose **YES** for the statements that describe you and **NO** for the ones that don't. Check what your scores mean below.

1	There is no tropical hardwood furniture in your home.	○ YES ○ NO
2	You always take your own shopping bags with you to the shops.	○ YES ○ NO
3	You don't buy cheap fashion items made in sweatshop conditions.	○ YES ○ NO
4	You know where your bank invests its money.	○ YES ○ NO
5	You only eat free-range organic chicken.	○ YES ○ NO

Mostly YES You are aware of the impact of your actions on the natural world and the people in it. Well done!

Mostly NO Perhaps you need to think a bit more about the impact you have on the environment and those who live in it – it's yours to protect.

Ethical consumption

You ask, we answer …

Are disposable cups evil?

Q Every time I get a coffee these days it comes in a single-use cup, whether it's to take away or drink in the café. Isn't this incredibly wasteful? Why can't cafeterias wash cups?

A This is an interesting question. According to the WWF, it takes 200 litres of water just to make one takeaway coffee. That includes the materials and process of making the throwaway cup, which then ends up in a landfill rubbish site rather than being recycled. But if we compare ceramic cups, we also have to factor in the resources used in manufacture, the energy used in washing them and the high number that get broken and thrown away. It turns out that each cup is as eco-friendly (or indeed unfriendly) as the other. So if you don't want to give up drinking takeaway coffee, you'll need an innovative solution such as the reusable portable cup – yes, it exists. There are already several brands available, and most importantly, you can take your own cup into most of the big coffee chains.

What's wrong with fake fashion?

Q Designer goods are unaffordable for normal people like me. I can't be the only person who buys fakes instead. Is this really unethical?

A Counterfeit products are an ethical minefield. But as more and more of us simply can't resist upgrading to the latest model of our favourite gadget or choosing a shirt just because of its logo, buying fakes has become normal behaviour. However, fake versions are often associated with organized crime and they deprive companies of income, thus affecting costs and ultimately the price of goods. As a consumer, you have no guarantee if your purchase falls apart, breaks down or even blows up. So is it really value for money? And you have no idea who makes your 'designer' item, how much they get paid and what conditions they work under. Perhaps a better question to ask is 'Would I be really unhappy if I just stopped worrying about designer stuff?'

Food miles and saving the planet

Q I want to eat a healthy varied diet all year round, but I feel I have to buy fruit and vegetables that have been imported. My partner says that flying in produce from around the world contributes to CO_2 emissions and climate change. Who's right?

A It depends on who you talk to. Some experts claim that if the UK didn't air-freight fresh food from producers in Africa, it would only cut back carbon emissions by 0.1 per cent. The UK spends £1 million on such imports every day, so you can imagine the knock-on effect on those producers if we all ate only seasonal and locally-produced food. More important considerations, perhaps, are what are known as the water footprint and pesticide footprint. According to Waterfootprint.org, every kilo of ripe mangoes needs 1,800 litres of water. As for pesticides and fertilizers, the overuse of these chemicals is truly disastrous for the environment. So rather than arguing with your partner about where your 'five-a-day' are from, you should probably be looking at how they are grown.

---

air-freight (v) to transport products and produce by plane
knock-on effect (n) a secondary or unintended consequence of an action

21st CENTURY OUTCOMES   **ENVIRONMENTAL LITERACY** Show understanding of your impact on the natural world

6.4 Shopping around

LISTENING Sales talk

1 Work in pairs. Discuss the questions.

1 Do you have any of these services on contract?
  a mobile phone
  b landline phone
  c Internet
  d satellite/cable TV
2 Do you know how much you pay for each one?
3 How do you pay the bill?
4 How often do you check that you're getting the best deal?

2 🎧 32 Listen to the conversation about mobile phone contracts. Answer the questions.

1 What's the customer's enquiry about?
2 What are the two tariffs mentioned?
3 What does the customer decide to do?

3 🎧 32 Listen to the conversation again. Look at the Useful language box. Tick (✓) the expressions for requesting and giving clarification that the speakers use.

REQUESTING AND GIVING CLARIFICATION

Requesting clarification

What's the difference between … and … ?
So can I just check that … ?
So if I … , would … ?
What would happen if … ?
Did you say … ?
What was … again?
Can you tell me about … again?
Does that mean … ?

Giving clarification

Let me put it another way.
Not exactly, no.
Yes, that's correct.
As I said, …
What that means is …

Pronunciation Words beginning with *u*

4a 🎧 **33** Listen and repeat the pronunciation of these words from the conversation in Exercise 2. What are the two different sounds for *u*?

unit   unlimited   upgrade   usually

4b 🎧 **34** How is the *u* pronounced in these words? Listen and check.

umbrella   unfriendly   unique   utilities

SPEAKING Consumer to consumer

5 **21st CENTURY OUTCOMES**

Work in groups. Share your knowledge as consumers in these areas. Ask for and give clarification as necessary.

1 You want to upgrade your smartphone. What do your classmates advise? Which providers offer a good service? Does it matter what make of phone you get?
2 You want to find out about internet deals in the area you live in. What's the broadband speed? Is there fibre optics? Does it include internet on your TV?
3 You are thinking of replacing your PC with a tablet. What kinds of things do you need to know about tablets? What other options are there?

WRITING A consumer review

6 Read the feedback comments about a product which was bought from an online store. Look at the photos. What is the product?

★ **CONSUMER REVIEWS** ★

Fred Q
★★★★
We bought these to take away on holiday with us to listen to music in our hotel room. They were amazingly cheap, so we didn't expect much. But the sound quality was incredibly good!

B Ferry
★☆☆☆
Very disappointing. You can't get the volume up at all. Totally useless. What a waste of money.

Dinah
★★★★
I use these to plug in my phone in the kitchen when I'm cooking – I find earphones really annoying. I'm completely satisfied with this product – it's absolutely brilliant value for money.

Writing skill Intensifiers

7a Look at these sentences. Which adjective is stronger, *poor* or *appalling*? What type of adjective do we use the intensifier *very* with? Underline seven intensifier + adjective combinations in the comments.

> The quality of the speakers was very poor.
> The quality of the speakers was absolutely appalling.
>
> See page 150 for more information about intensifiers, and do Exercises 5–7.

7b Cross out any words which are not possible in these sentences.

1 I was *incredibly / totally / really* disappointed with the sound quality.
2 This is a very *interesting / excellent* app.
3 The DVD player was *really / very / totally* expensive and not good value for money.
4 The picture on this player was *really / very / particularly* awful.
5 I am very *disgusted / unhappy* with the after-sales service and won't shop there again.
6 I found this function to be *completely / really / very* useless.

8 Write a short online review for a product you bought recently. Use at least two intensifier + adjective combinations.

9 Work in pairs with someone who reviewed a similar product. Exchange reviews and ask a follow-up question.

emergency battery charger for mobile phone

portable DVD player

speakers for an MP3 player

CRITICAL THINKING Interpret information and draw conclusions based on analysis

Review 3 | UNITS 5 AND 6

LISTENING

1 Read about FooARage Skateboard Company. Answer the questions.

1. What does the academy teach?
2. What is its aim?
3. Who are its students?

2 🎧 35 Listen to a radio interview with Jamila, a youth worker. Are the sentences true (T) or false (F)?

1. Jamila works with young people in schools.
2. Workshop participants design and decorate ready-made skateboards.
3. The workshops combine academic and personal skills.
4. Everyone who works at FooARage Skateboard Company is a volunteer.
5. According to Jamila, skateboarding is open to anyone.

3 🎧 35 Listen again. Complete each sentence with one word from the interview.

1. According to Jamila, _____ often gets kids interested in learning.
2. Making a commitment over a period of time was a _____ forward for many kids.
3. The company gets funding from _____, donations and partnerships.
4. According to Jamila, skateboarding keeps you _____.

GRAMMAR

4 Complete the sentences with six of these modals and related verbs.

| could | couldn't | didn't have to | didn't succeed in |
| had to | managed to | succeeded in | weren't able to |

1. The founders of FooARage _____ find a skateboard maker in the UK at first.
2. After months of looking in the UK, FooARage _____ go to Canada to buy the wood they needed.
3. When the company realized they _____ build the skateboards without power tools, it meant the activity was safe for kids.
4. FooARage Skateboard Company _____ getting support from a number of new sponsors last year.
5. Jamila's organization was created to help teenagers who _____ cope with traditional schools.
6. Despite having no previous experience, the kids who attended the first workshop _____ make their own skateboards.

5 Complete the conditional sentences.

1. Many educational projects wouldn't be successful if they _____ (not / have) sponsorship.
2. Projects like FooARage will make a difference if they _____ (reach) the kids who need help.
3. If children _____ (not / be) interested in an activity, they won't learn very much.
4. Teenagers won't get involved at school if they _____ (have) significant personal problems.
5. _____ so many kids _____ (have) problems at school if they got more support?
6. If a teenager has rejected school, it _____ (not / be) easy to involve them in education again.
7. If the new FooARage project is a success, they _____ (go / offer) it to more schools.
8. When a boy _____ (enjoy) making skateboards, he _____ (bring) his friends to the project.

FooARage
Skateboard Company

The FooARage Skateboard Company is a part of the FAR Academy. Their message is *Changing Lives Through Education and Skateboarding*. This UK charity is the first organization to teach young people how to design and build professional skateboards. It aims to teach life and employment skills to young people. It hopes to reach young people who do less well in traditional academic situations.

VOCABULARY

6 Read the text about business-activity projects for teenagers. Complete the finance expressions. The first letter is given.

Many teenagers have great ideas for money-making projects and this is a great way to teach them about economics and finance. Several charities that work with young people ¹ sponsor an e_____ _____ to get teenagers involved with their projects. A typical project shows participants how to ² control their f_____ and to ³ work out a b_____ for the money they have. These are skills needed in personal finance as well as in business. Teenagers who want to put their ideas into practice can learn how to find people who will ⁴ invest m_____ in their ideas. If their business idea involves offering a service, they also need to understand how to ⁵ charge a f_____ that is realistic. One of the key skills for business finance is ⁶ balancing the b_____ and, of course, how not to ⁷ get into d_____. One of the valuable things that teenagers can learn is what they are really good at: having ideas or having a good business mind. Often it's a good idea to form a ⁸ p_____ that brings both sets of skills together.

7 Use the correct form of five of the phrasal verbs to complete the paragraphs.

| blow up | break down | cut back |
| take away | throw away | turn out |

The FooARage Skateboard Company doesn't ¹ _____ any wood that is not used in building the skateboards. They also recycle second-hand boards so that they ² _____ on the need to use new materials.

The opening of our new skateboard park last weekend ³ _____ really well with loads of visitors. We'd publicized it by ⁴ _____ a huge inflatable skateboard that floated in the air. We gave everyone a skateboard key ring to ⁵ _____ so that they'd remember us!

DISCUSSION

8 Work in small groups. Discuss the questions.

1 Do you know how these people have combined their sports careers with successful businesses?
- David Beckham (UK, footballer)
- George Foreman (US, boxer)
- Tony Hawk (US, skateboarder)
- Michael Jordan (US, basketball player)
- Cristiano Ronaldo (Portugal, footballer)
- Venus Williams (US, tennis player)

2 Can you think of any more people who have moved from success in one field to be successful in business? Why do you think there aren't more people who do this?

SPEAKING

9 Complete the conversation between a sports instructor (I) and a teacher (T) about archery classes. Use the prompts.

I: We offer classes for all ages and in several locations.
T: ¹ *Did / say / run / kids' courses?*
I: Yes, from age eight up to twelve. For beginners, there's the Silver course. Then we have Gold and Platinum courses at a more advanced level.
T: ² *difference / Gold / Platinum?*
I: Platinum is for people with more than 30 hours' experience, basically.
T: And all for kids?
I: ³ *Yes, / correct.* As I said, up to twelve years old.
T: ⁴ *Can / tell / the beginners' course / again?*
I: Yes, the Silver course. It's for people – kids – who are doing archery for the first time.
T: ⁵ *What / happen / if / have / mixture of kids / different experiences?* Could they be in the same session?
I: It would depend on how many participants there were. We can definitely look into that.
T: ⁶ *So / I / check / the kids* have to be at least eight years old?
I: Yes. Eight is the youngest we can cater for.
T: OK. Well, let me talk to the head teacher and I'll get back to you as soon as I can.

WRITING

10 Read the email from Rob to Matt. You are Matt. Write a reply. Include questions about the underlined parts of the email. Use these question forms or similar ones.

Can you explain … ?	I wonder if … ?
Wouldn't it be … ?	Don't you think … ?
… , isn't it?	… , aren't they?

TO: Matt Moxley
SUBJECT: Archery classes

Hi Matt

As I mentioned the other day, I've arranged for <u>some archery classes</u> for <u>year 4 pupils</u>. They'll all be <u>in the school lunch hour</u>. I <u>don't know the exact cost yet</u>, but it won't be too much.

I think we could start <u>next month</u>, probably. We'd need to <u>send an email</u> to parents. Let me know what you think.

Rob

11 Work in pairs. Exchange emails with your partner. Did you include the same questions?

73

7 Innovation and technology

American rock climber, engineer and biophysicist, Hugh Herr at Quincy Quarries near Boston, USA

TEDTALKS

DAVID SENGEH grew up in Sierra Leone, where many people became amputees in the civil war there. When he noticed that people weren't wearing their prosthetic limbs, he investigated the reasons for this and then, as part of his PhD at MIT (Massachusetts Institute of Technology), he tried to work out a solution to the problem.

David Sengeh's idea worth spreading is that those who have a disability should have the opportunity to live active, enjoyable lives – beginning with more comfortable prosthetics.

BACKGROUND

1 You are going to watch an edited version of a TED Talk by David Sengeh called *The sore problem of prosthetic limbs*. Read the text about the speaker and the talk. Then work in pairs and discuss the questions.

1 What problems do you think amputees might face in everyday life?
2 David Sengeh was able to solve a problem for amputees using technology. How could these areas also help with the problems you discussed in question 1?

| housing | access to information | legal changes |
| financial aid | transport | |

3 What kinds of skills do you think define the kind of person who finds solutions to problems?

KEY WORDS

2 Read the sentences (1–6). The words in bold are used in the TED Talk. First guess the meaning of the words. Then match the words with their definitions (a–f).

1 A **prosthesis** takes the place of a missing limb for amputees.
2 A patient who can't change the position of their body easily can get **pressure sores**.
3 The **magnetic resonance imaging (MRI)** scan showed where my leg was broken.
4 When a person's arm comes out of their shoulder **socket**, it's quite easy to put it back into place.
5 Patients who have to spend a lot of time in bed find that **pillows** can make them more comfortable.
6 Paralympic athletes compete in sports classified by their **disability**, such as sight problems or being an amputee.

a an artificial part of the body
b a type of medical technology that takes pictures of the body
c soft cushions
d painful damage to the skin
e a cup-shaped part of a device that another part fits into
f a physical or mental condition that can affect the way a person functions

AUTHENTIC LISTENING SKILLS
Dealing with accents

You will hear many different accents from both native and non-native English speakers. There are ways that you can prepare yourself so that you find it easier to understand different accents: for example, by listening to speakers on the Internet, on the radio and in films. Non-native speakers often find it easier to understand other non-native speakers than native speakers do.

3a 🎧 36 Work in pairs. Look at the Authentic listening skills box. Then listen to the beginning of the TED Talk. Did you find any aspect of David Sengeh's English different from the spoken English you're used to? Tell your partner.

- the pronunciation of some of the words?
- the stress and rhythm of his speech?
- something else?

3b 🎧 36 Listen to the beginning of the talk again. Underline the parts that sound different from what you expected.

'I was born and raised in Sierra Leone, a small and very beautiful country in West Africa, a country rich both in physical resources and creative talent. However, Sierra Leone is infamous for a decade-long rebel war in the '90s when entire villages were burnt down. An estimated 8,000 men, women and children had their arms and legs amputated during this time.'

3c Work in pairs. Read the beginning of the talk to your partner. What differences do you notice in your stress, rhythm or intonation?

7.1 The sore problem of prosthetic limbs

TEDTALKS

1. ▶ **7.1** Watch the edited version of the TED Talk. Choose the correct option to complete the sentences.

   1. David Sengeh was a *young man / boy* during the war.
   2. Many people who had suffered amputation *didn't wear / couldn't afford* prosthetic limbs.
   3. The prosthetic limbs available in Sierra Leone were *comfortable / painful* to wear.
   4. While he was *still at school / doing his PhD*, David Sengeh developed a solution to the prosthetic problem.
   5. The sockets David Sengeh makes are *cheap / expensive* to produce.
   6. David Sengeh wants to make functional prostheses for use *in Sierra Leone / anywhere*.

▶ burned **N AM ENG**
▶ burned, burnt **BR ENG**
▶ molding **N AM ENG**
▶ moulding **BR ENG**
▶ figure it out **N AM ENG**
▶ work it out **BR ENG**
▶ custom **N AM ENG**
▶ custom-made **BR ENG**

2 ▶ 7.1 Complete the sentences with five of these words or expressions. Then watch the first part (0.00–2.20) of the talk again and check your answers.

acceptable	as a result of	before
easy to find	find	fit
make	promised himself	

1 About 8,000 men, women and children were amputees ___as a result___ the war.
2 David Sengeh ___promised hims___ that he would contribute to a better future for his country.
3 The main problem with prosthetic limbs was that they didn't ___fit___ properly.
4 It can take years for an amputee to ___find___ a prosthesis that is comfortable.
5 David Sengeh thought that conventional, uncomfortable prosthetics were not ___acceptable___ in today's world.

3 ▶ 7.1 Watch the second part (2.20–3.45) of the talk again. Put the events (a–e) in order.

a He got very positive feedback from a recent trial. 5
b They discussed solving the problem of painful sockets. 2
c He produced the sockets with a 3D printer. 4
d He met Professor Hugh Herr. 1
e He used medical technology to look at individual patients. 3

4 ▶ 7.1 Watch the third part (3.45 to the end) of the talk again. Do you think these sentences represent David Sengeh's views?

1 His work should do more than simply help people to live a normal life. ✓
2 Comfortable prostheses heal people psychologically as well as physically. ✓
3 Good prosthetic limbs can transform people's lives. ✓

5 Work in pairs. Discuss the questions.

1 In your country, do any of these technological innovations help people with disabilities in daily life?

   wheelchair ramps
   adapted public transport
   audio as well as visual signals on street crossings
   braille in lifts and on cash machines

2 What additional technologies or changes would make life better for disabled people in your community?

VOCABULARY IN CONTEXT

6 ▶ 7.2 Watch the clips from the TED Talk. Choose the correct meaning of the words.

7 Work in pairs. Complete the sentences in your own words.

1 One thing that troubles me is that …
2 … is simply unacceptable in our age.
3 I don't know how … , but I'd love to figure it out.

CRITICAL THINKING Asking significant questions

8 When presenting a solution to a problem, it's important that your audience identifies the problem as a real one. Read this comment* about the TED Talk. What was 'the right question' (a–c) that David Sengeh asked?

a Who can provide amputees with prosthetic limbs?
b What can amputees do to improve their lives?
c Why do amputees choose not to wear their prostheses?

then do Gemini task.

Viewers' comments

K Kurt – What I admire in David is that not only did he solve the problem, he asked the right question in the first place.

*The comment was created for this activity.

9 Work in pairs. Why was David Sengeh's question 'the right question'? What did it lead to?

PRESENTATION SKILLS Taking the audience on a journey

TIPS

In a talk, you take your audience on a journey.
- Know where you want to take them: make sure your talk has a beginning, a middle and an end.
- Check that your talk structure is clear. Think of the sub-title you could give each section. If this is hard for you, you're not ready to give your talk.

10 Look at the Presentation tips box. Then identify these parts of David Sengeh's talk as the beginning (B), middle (M) and end (E).

- explaining the problem
- implementing a solution
- describing the situation

11 ▶ 7.3 Watch the clips (1–3) from the TED Talk. Match the clips with the three parts (B, M, E).

12 Work in pairs. You are going to give a presentation to explain how a problem was solved. Choose one of the innovations you discussed in Exercise 5. Structure your presentation to talk about the situation, the problem and the solution.

13 Work with a new partner. Give your presentation. Are the three parts of your presentation clear?

▶ modeling **N AM ENG**
▶ modelling **BR ENG**
▶ manufacture /ˌmænjəˈfæktʃə/ **N AM ENG**
▶ manufacture /ˌmænjuˈfæktʃə/ **BR ENG**
▶ wrapped up **N AM ENG**
▶ concluded **BR ENG**

7.2 Developing new technology

RESEARCH AND DEVELOPMENT

- IDENTIFY existing needs
- DEVELOP solutions
- REVIEW results
- IMPROVE design and efficiency
- APPROVE the new product

GRAMMAR Passives

1 Work in pairs. Match the inventions with the dates of their development.

3D printer	1880s
computer mouse	1950s
driverless car	1960s
electric car	1970s
fibre optics	1980s
smartphone	1980s
solar cells	1990s
stem cell therapy	2000s

2 Look at the infographic showing the process of research and development. Do you think any of the inventions in Exercise 1 followed this process? Which ones?

3 Read the text in the Grammar box. Answer the questions (1–2).

PASSIVES

Fibre optics is a technology which allows information to be transmitted along a flexible, transparent fibre. The technology was initially researched in the mid-20th century. The term was made popular in 1960 following an article in Scientific American by Narinder Singh. By the 1970s, the first commercially successful optical fibre had been developed. Since then, many uses for fibre optics in telecommunications and medicine have been identified. New applications are being tested all the time and it's clear that fibre optics will be used in a wide range of contexts in the future.

1 Underline the passive forms of the verbs. Which verb is used with the past participle to form the passive?
2 Which information (a–d) does a passive sentence <u>always</u> give?
   a who does the action
   b when it happens
   c why it happens
   d what happens

Check your answers on page 152 and do Exercises 1–6.

4 Complete the paragraph about nanotechnology with these passive verbs.

can't be seen	has been used
needs to be regulated	should be handled
will be disposed of	~~was inspired~~

Nanotechnology (*nano* means extremely small) is a relatively new technology which ¹ *was inspired* by ideas that the physicist Richard Feynman had 50 years ago. The actual materials – nanomaterials – are so tiny that they ² _____ with a standard microscope. They include materials such as carbon or silver. Recently nanotechnology ³ _____ to improve products as diverse as sunscreen, solar cells and bandages. There are some worries about the long-term effects of nanomaterials and some scientists warn that they ⁴ _____ very carefully or that their use ⁵ _____ by governments. One problem is how products containing nanomaterials ⁶ _____ or recycled in the future.

5 Read about a new way of giving medicines to people. Choose the correct form of the verbs, active or passive, to complete the article.

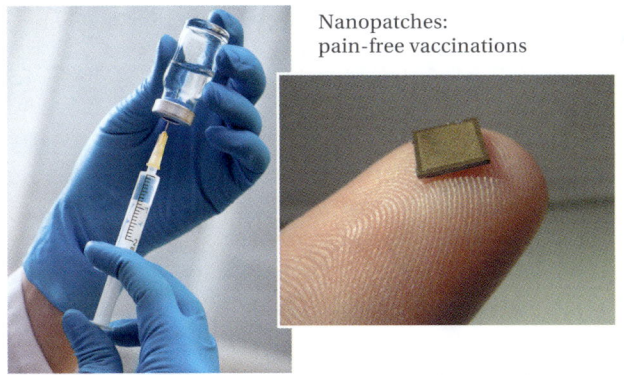

Nanopatches: pain-free vaccinations

In medicine, many technological solutions ¹ *have developed / have been developed* for specific problems. A good example of this is giving medicine to prevent diseases, such as flu, which ² *cause / are caused* by infection. Most of these medicines ³ *deliver / are delivered* by needle. But approximately twenty per cent of people are afraid of needles. This ⁴ *can stop / can be stopped* them going to the doctor's. According to the WHO, half of the vaccines which ⁵ *give / are given* in tropical areas don't work because they ⁶ *haven't kept / haven't been kept* cold enough. Now a new way of giving these medicines to people – the nanopatch – ⁷ *is testing / is being tested*. The nanopatch is a small patch that sticks to your skin. Mark Kendall and his team at the University of Queensland in Australia ⁸ *have been working / have been worked* on the nanopatch for several years. He hopes that the nanopatch ⁹ *will make / will be made* a big difference to the number of deaths (currently 17 million a year) from infectious diseases.

6 Read the article in Exercise 5 again and choose the preposition used to say:

1 why many technological applications have been developed   *by / for*
2 how a lot of medicines are delivered   *by / for*

7 Complete the sentences with *by* and *for*.

1 Calculations that would take humans years can be done _____ computers in minutes.
2 The authorities say that the disease can't be spread _____ animals.
3 The medicine should be taken _____ mouth.
4 Samples have been taken _____ analysis and the results will be available tomorrow.
5 Following complaints, all the products are being checked _____ faults.
6 Better results would be achieved _____ repeating the trial with more people.

SPEAKING Technology in everyday life

8 **21st CENTURY OUTCOMES**

Work in small groups. Look at the list of inventions and discuss what you know about each one. Then decide what problem each one solves or what purpose it has. Choose the two inventions you think are the most important.

- electric cars
- driverless cars
- 3D printers
- bionic limbs
- waterproof coatings
- biodegradable plastic
- solar panels
- smart materials (that react to changes in their environment)

21st CENTURY OUTCOMES   **TECHNOLOGICAL LITERACY**   Understand how technology can be used to achieve a specific goal

7.3 Innovative approaches

READING The real value of digital tools

1 What experiences have you had of digital technology as a student? Think about when you were at school or at college, or any other learning experience.

- online learning ✓
- tablets ✓
- school or student websites ✗
- video chat ✗

2 Read the article about technology in education. Which digital technologies in Exercise 1 are mentioned in the text?

3 Read the article again. Are the sentences true (T) or false (F)?

F 1 According to the European Commission, young people have the knowledge and ability to work in digital technology.
F 2 According to the article, European schools are slow to use new technology with their students.
?F 3 Currently, computer programming is taught too traditionally.
T 4 Using new technology in the classroom doesn't always change the way subjects are taught.
T 5 Students can study a topic before going to a class if digital media are available to them.
T 6 Studying later in the day can lead to better results for some students.

4 Find these words in the article. Choose the correct meaning (a–c).

1 **recreation** (line 6)
   a education
   b) leisure
   c work
2 **hardware** (line 18)
   a) computer equipment
   b computer experts
   c computer programmes
3 **shortage** (line 19)
   a excess
   b) lack
   c number
4 **passive** (line 33)
   a enthusiastic
   b) inactive
   c uninterested
5 **access** (line 37)
   a produce
   b) find
   c understand
6 **device** (line 44)
   a) machine
   b page
   c system
7 **flexibility** (line 52)
   a difficulty
   b time
   c) variation
8 **key** (line 65)
   a frequent
   b) important
   c rare

5 Work in pairs. Discuss whether or not you agree with these suggestions made in the article.

1 Being able to use digital media is not the same thing as understanding how it works.
2 It's a good idea to teach schoolchildren how to write computer code.
3 Digital technology allows schools to try out innovative ways of teaching.

VOCABULARY Innovation: verbs

6 Match the words in bold in the sentences with these verbs.

enable 5	exploit 3	get round 7
improve 4	inspire 6	introduce 2
put into practice 8	replace by	

1 All the old computers have been **changed for** tablets that are much easier to use.
2 Our school has **started** a new assessment system. Now we only have one exam each term.
3 The college could do better if it **used** its resources in a better way.
4 The headteacher wants all the students to **do better** this year.
5 The new school website **allows** parents to contact us more easily.
6 The visit to the science museum **encouraged** us to change how we teach science to our students.
7 Using video chat with students in Spain **solved** the problem of our students not having experience of native Spanish speakers.
8 Student satisfaction has gone up since we **implemented** our personalized online feedback.

7 Work in pairs. Tell your partner about three of these things.

- a way of exploiting your time to study English more effectively
- a place, person or event that inspired you to do something
- a change that has been introduced or you'd like to introduce in your work or studies
- something you learned that enabled you to do more in your life
- something you've replaced recently or would like to replace
- something you feel you have improved in

SPEAKING New ideas for unexpected problems

8 **21st CENTURY OUTCOMES**

Read the beginning of the news item. What answer do you think the teacher expected?

> Teachers at Coal Hill Primary School decided to set up a school garden after a pupil answered the question 'Where do we get milk from?' with 'The supermarket.'

9 Work in small groups. Discuss how you would help schoolchildren to understand more about where their food comes from, how it is produced and how it gets to their plates. Think about what you want to achieve, how to do it and what results you would like to see.

THE REAL VALUE OF DIGITAL TOOLS

A recent European Commission event (European e-Skills Week) focused on the lack of skills in digital technology among young people. While most young people use digital media for recreation – games and social networking – they are not necessarily competent in the skills needed to work in the digital economy, according to the European Commission.

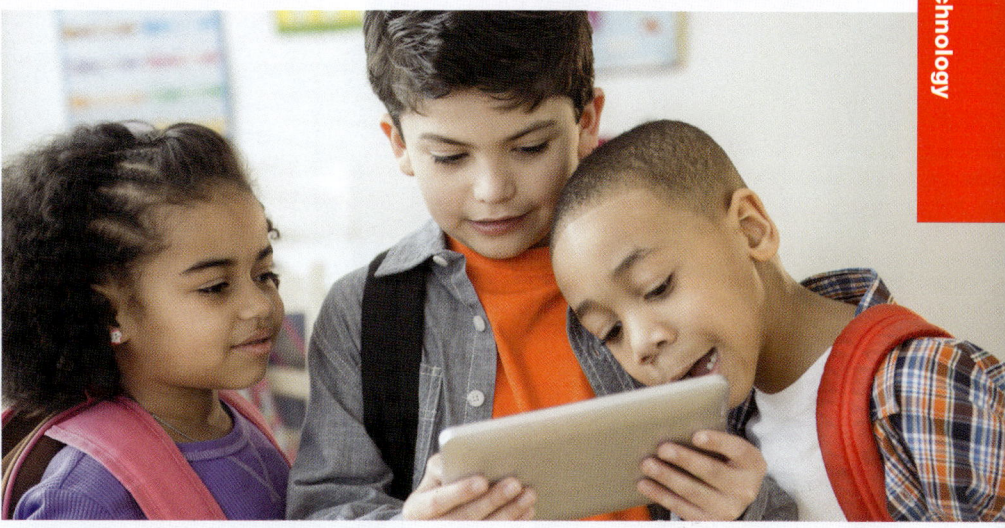

Digital technology is an increasingly familiar part of the school environment. Tablets have been introduced into many schools as the prices have dropped and versions for schools become available. Traditional chalkboards have been replaced by digital whiteboards in classrooms across Europe. In short, there's been a massive investment in both hardware and software in education. Nevertheless, there is still a shortage of people who are skilled and qualified in information and communication technologies (ICT). So where does the problem lie?

For some education experts, the issue is that pupils are not taught about how digital resources work. These experts are in favour of teaching computer coding and programming in the same way as other traditional school subjects. Others point out that the potential of the digital classroom has not been fully exploited yet: in effect, the argument is more about how the new technological tools can be used to revolutionize learning rather than the actual tools themselves. One expert, Gareth Mills, points out that an interactive whiteboard might still be used with a traditional teaching style where the teacher talks to a passive group of students. This is to ignore the possibilities that putting the tools into the hands of the pupils can lead to. In Wales, a recent report recommended that, despite fears that students would be distracted if they had access to social networking sites, such sites should not be blocked in schools – they can in fact be used as a platform for sharing learning materials.

The reality is that digital media can truly inspire and enable new approaches to teaching and learning. For example, when students can view the content of a lesson before and after the class via a computer or mobile device, this frees timetabled class time for interactive and more focused work with the teacher. Gareth Mills explains the benefits of working together on practical tasks and inter-school or even inter-country projects where students can develop problem-solving skills. This is precisely the type of skill that is needed to understand how ICT works, as the European Commission points out.

In addition, sharing learning materials can give schools more flexibility in the traditional organization of school timetables. For teenagers in particular, changing the school day so that lessons start later can have an important impact on how well they learn. One UK school ran a trial where lessons began at 10 am instead of 9 am. The exam results at the end of the year showed improvement across all subjects, with pass rates going up by 20 per cent in English and by 34 per cent in ICT.

The real value of digital tools, therefore, lies not only in the way they can deliver content to students but in the way they can change the whole landscape of classroom interaction. Events like the European e-Skills Week are key opportunities to show that where digital skills are concerned, schools need to look not only at what but also how they teach.

---

computer coding (n) writing in language of computer programmes
e-skills (n) the skills needed to work in digital technology
neuroscientist (n) an expert in how the human brain works
platform (n) a computer system or programme

7.4 It can all be done online

VOCABULARY Online operations

1 Work in pairs. Which of these operations do you do online? Do you feel safe when you do online operations?

- buying insurance
- buying a travel ticket
- online banking
- paying a bill
- using a credit card

2 Choose the correct option to complete the sentences.

1 Your *PIN number / email address* is private to you and not known by other people.
2 Only you know the answer to your *username / security question*.
3 The first step with most online systems is to *log in with / save* your details.
4 With *e-tickets / touchscreens* you don't get a paper copy of the document.
5 You should never write down your *bank account number / password*.

LISTENING New ways of doing things

3 🎧 37 Listen to three conversations. Match each situation with one of the operations in Exercise 1.

4 🎧 37 Listen again. Look at the expressions in the Useful language box and answer the questions. Then work in pairs and compare your answers.

ASKING HOW SOMETHING WORKS

1 How does that work?
   Will I have to download an app to use them?
   How would I do that?

2 And what do I need to do now?
   How will I know if it's been paid correctly?

3 When would the money be taken from my account?
   How often are the statements sent out?
   Where do they go?

Pronunciation Linking with /w/

5a 🎧 38 Listen to the way the underlined words are linked with the /w/ sound.

1 How will I know if it's been paid correctly?
2 Could I just ask a couple of questions about how it works?
3 How often are the statements sent out?

5b 🎧 39 Listen to how the same /w/ sound links these words.

1 There's no extra charge for paying by card.
2 How do I pay my electricity bill?
3 Let me show you how to do it.
4 the one from the bill
5 So I'm interested in getting your store credit card.
6 It's easy to arrange today.

5c Practise saying the sentences.

SPEAKING Asking and talking about how something works

6 **21st CENTURY OUTCOMES**

Work in pairs. Take turns to tell your partner about something you do online either in your personal life, or in your studies or job. Ask questions about how the process works.

WRITING A formal online message

7 Read the online message from a bank to its customers. What's the purpose (a–c) of the letter?

a to apologize for problems with the online banking service
b to announce a new range of online banking services
c to explain what is going to happen to a part of the online banking service

---

**Important changes
to our online banking service**

Dear Customer

From November of this year, the system for logging in to your bank account online will change.

The existing security questions will be replaced by a secure number system. You will receive instructions on how to generate your personal secure number by letter to your home address.

These changes will ensure that our online banking service is safer than ever and will enable you to access your account more easily when you are mobile.

You do not need to do anything at this time.

Yours sincerely

Pauline Harris

Online Services Director

---

8 Look at the features of a formal communication (a–e). Underline and label the parts of the message that match the features.

a a subject line
b the job title of the sender
c no personal name of the recipient
d the way the sender has written their name
e no verbal contractions

Writing skill Being clear and precise

9a Underline the parts of the letter that give this information:
1 What is the change?
2 When will it take place?
3 How will it happen?
4 Why is it happening?
5 What action is needed?

9b Read the comments. Then complete the sentences so that they give the same information clearly and precisely. Use the words in brackets.

1 I'm going to put the form in the post for you, probably this week if I have time. (send)
I will _____

2 You know that they're stopping check-in at the airport next month, don't you? (not available)
From next month, _____

3 You don't pay by the hour anymore in this car park – they've changed it. (apply)
New charges _____

4 Apparently, you can't take your bike on trains anymore because there's no room. (allow)
Due to lack of space, _____

5 You'll have to phone the insurance company with your new address. (change)
You have to contact _____

6 We're changing our opening hours so that customers can call in to the bank before going to work. (improve our service to customers)
Our new _____

10 **21st CENTURY OUTCOMES**

You've tried several times to get into your online bank account, but your screen freezes when you type in your details. Complete your bank's 'Send us a message' online form explaining the problem clearly, giving as many details as you can and asking for help.

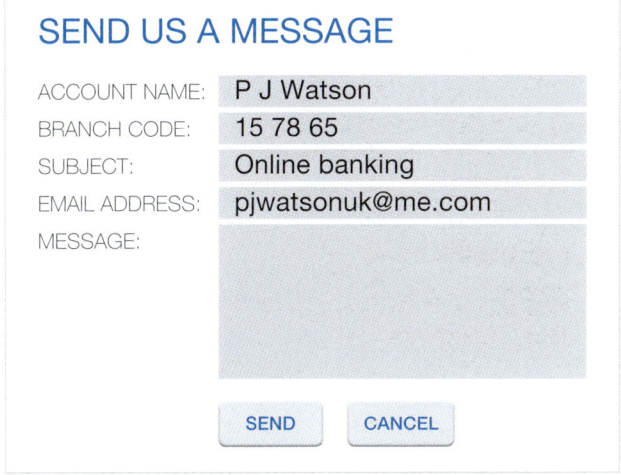

11 Work in pairs. Exchange messages with your partner. Check that the message explains when and how the problem happens.

21st CENTURY OUTCOMES **EFFECTIVE COMMUNICATION** Articulate ideas and information effectively using oral and written skills

8 Balance

A group slackline over the Andaman Sea at sunset, Krabi, Thailand

TED TALKS

NIGEL MARSH is an Australian author and marketer. As well as working in marketing, he writes and gives presentations about business and personal life, and how these two things interact.

Nigel Marsh's idea worth spreading is that achieving a work–life balance doesn't have to require a dramatic change in your lifestyle. If we take the time to take care of relationships, it can vastly improve our quality of life.

BACKGROUND

1 You are going to watch an edited version of a TED Talk by Nigel Marsh called *How to make work–life balance work*. Read the text about the speaker and the talk. Then work in pairs and discuss the questions.

1 What do you know about the term 'work–life balance'? Give an example that shows what it means.
2 You will hear Nigel Marsh talk about relationships. Which relationships do you think could be affected by a person's work?
3 In what ways do you think relationships can have an impact on someone's quality of life?

KEY WORDS

2 Read the sentences (1–6). The words in bold are used in the TED Talk. First guess the meaning of the words. Then match the words with their definitions (a–f).

1 The great thing about **flexitime** is you don't need to worry about being late for work.
2 Some companies don't do **dress-down Fridays** because people there dress casually anyway.
3 **Paternity leave** makes sense in today's world where dads are so much more involved with their kids.
4 Being unemployed for a long period can lead to a sense of **desperation**.
5 The author's main **contention** is that too many people work for too many hours.
6 In parts of the country there are no **childcare facilities**, so it's hard to work when you have very young children.

a a nursery or similar place which looks after young children during the day
b a period of time off work for men after their child is born
c a policy which lets employees wear informal clothes one day a week
d an idea or an opinion that someone expresses in a discussion
e a system which lets employees choose which hours they work each day
f the feeling of being in a very bad situation which you'll try anything to change

AUTHENTIC LISTENING SKILLS

Elision: dropped vowels

Sometimes you may not recognize a word you hear because its spoken form is different from its written form. An example of this is words with compressed syllables: for example, *comfortable* is pronounced with three syllables: / comf / or / ta / ble /. When you know how words are pronounced, you will understand what you hear more easily.

3a 🎧 40 Look at the Authentic listening skills box. Then listen to the phrases from the TED Talk. Underline the syllable that is not pronounced in the word in bold.

1 your **miserable** existence
2 classic **corporate** warrior
3 neglecting the **family**

3b 🎧 41 Work in pairs. Look at the words in bold from the talk. How many syllables are pronounced? Then listen to the phrases and check.

4 **especially** when the money runs out
5 enforcing the **boundaries**
6 I've got no mates or **interests** left

3c 🎧 42 Listen to the six words again. Practise saying the words.

8.1 How to make work–life balance work

TEDTALKS

1 ▶ 8.1 Nigel Marsh once gave up work for a year to spend time with his family. In this TED Talk, he shares four observations about the work–life balance with the audience. Watch the edited version of the talk and tick (✓) the four observations he shares.

- **a** An honest debate about the work–life balance is essential.
- **b** He's never met anyone who has found a happy balance between life and work.
- **c** Finding balance depends on individuals taking control of their lives.
- **d** We need to be realistic about the time frame we use to achieve balance.
- **e** Employers play a key role in this debate.
- **f** We need to look at work–life balance in a balanced way.

2 ▶ 8.1 Watch the first part (0.00–3.06) of the talk again. Complete the sentences with the words and expressions Nigel Marsh uses.

1. When Nigel Marsh turned 40, he decided to try and turn his _____ around.
2. He learned that it was quite _____ to balance work and life when he didn't have any work.
3. He says so many people talk so much _____ about work–life balance.
4. He thinks that going to work on Friday in _____ doesn't get to the root of the problem.

▶ rubbish **BR ENG**
▶ garbage **N AM ENG**
▶ flexitime **BR ENG**
▶ flextime **N AM ENG**
▶ stop **BR ENG**
▶ quit **N AM ENG**

3 ▶ 8.1 Watch the second part (3.06–5.51) of the talk again. Are the sentences true (T) or false (F)?

1 Nigel Marsh thinks childcare facilities in the workplace are both a good and a bad thing.
2 He says the time frame we give ourselves to achieve balance should be neither too short nor too long.
3 He advised a friend whose life was out of balance to join a gym and get fit.
4 He believes that the intellectual, emotional and spiritual sides of life are part of the balance.

4 ▶ 8.1 Work in pairs. Watch the third part (5.51 to the end) of the talk again. Listen to the story Nigel Marsh tells about the afternoon he spent with his son Harry. Then work with your partner and try to retell the events of the afternoon. What did they do? What was Harry's reaction?

5 Work in small groups. Read the extract from Nigel Marsh's concluding comments. Do you agree with him? Can you think of some examples of the 'small things' you can do?

'Now my point is the small things matter. Being more balanced doesn't mean dramatic upheaval in your life. With the smallest investment in the right places, you can radically transform the quality of your relationships and the quality of your life.'

VOCABULARY IN CONTEXT

6 ▶ 8.2 Watch the clips from the TED Talk. Choose the correct meaning of the words.

7 Work in pairs. Complete the sentences in your own words.

1 It's better to face the truth than …
2 Sometimes people with money problems fall into the trap of …
3 It's nice to mess around … at the weekend.

CRITICAL THINKING Convincing the listener

8 Nigel Marsh aimed to convince his audience that small changes can lead to a better work–life balance. Two of the techniques he used were general observations and first-hand experience. Read these comments* about the TED Talk and say which technique convinced each viewer.

Viewers' comments

Jamila — I could really identify with what he said about spending time with his little boy. I've spent lots of afternoons just like that.

Frank — The story about the woman who joined the gym made me laugh so much! But it's true that we get so involved in things we lose all perspective.

*The comments were created for this activity.

9 Work in pairs. Discuss the questions.

1 Did you relate to what Nigel Marsh said about small changes making a difference?
2 Do you think that he explained his idea convincingly?
3 What did he say or do that was particularly effective, in your opinion?

PRESENTATION SKILLS Pace and emphasis

TIPS

The way you speak to the audience is an important part of getting your message across successfully. Two key things to consider are pace – the speed at which you talk and how often you pause – and emphasis.

- Don't speak too quickly to be clearly understood.
- Vary the speed to keep the audience engaged and interested.
- Pause for emphasis at the most essential points in your talk.

10 ▶ 8.3 Look at the Presentation tips box. Then watch the clip from the TED Talk and say which techniques Nigel Marsh uses.

11 Prepare a short anecdote about one of these topics or an idea of your own. Then work in pairs and practise telling the story. Use the techniques in the Presentation tips box.

- something you did with a member of your family
- something funny that happened to you or someone you know
- something you learned from a mistake

12 Work with a new partner. Give your presentation. Do you use the same techniques? How do your presentations differ?

▶ mate **BR ENG**
▶ pal **N AM ENG**
▶ realize, realise **BR ENG**
▶ realize **N AM ENG**
▶ pyjamas **BR ENG**
▶ pajamas **N AM ENG**

8.2 Can we 'have it all'?

GRAMMAR Verb patterns with -ing and infinitive

1 Work in pairs. Discuss the questions.

1 What does 'having it all' mean? Is this a common expectation in your country?
2 What does a 'typical' day consist of for a working adult in your country?
3 Do people in your country feel that stress is an issue in their lives?

2 Look at the infographic and read what the people are saying. Have you ever done any of these things?

3 Read the sentences in the Grammar box. Find sentences in the infographic that have the same patterns. Then answer the questions (a–b) in the box.

VERB PATTERNS WITH -ING AND INFINITIVE

1 *10% of people had **considered changing** their jobs.*
2 *10% of employees **plan to take** early retirement.*
3 *15% of managers **expect their teams to work** overtime.*
4 *20% of companies **let male employees take** paternity leave.*
5 *85% of workers **like spending / to spend** time with their colleagues.*
6 *90% of people **remember starting** their first job.*
7 *30% of people **don't remember to switch off** their work computers.*

a What are the sentence patterns used in sentences 1–4?
b Look at sentences 5–7. Which verb changes its meaning with different sentence patterns?

Check your answers on page 154 and do Exercises 1–6.

4 Complete the sentences with the -ing form and the infinitive.

1. My friends and I often arrange _____ (meet) after work.
2. I've persuaded a friend _____ (come) travelling with me.
3. I dislike _____ (have) too many things to do at once.
4. I can't imagine _____ (work) until I'm 68!
5. Last year I managed _____ (do) a full-time job and study for a professional exam.
6. I promise _____ (not / take) work home with me this weekend.
7. Have you finished _____ (read) the report yet?
8. I hope _____ (see) you at the party on Saturday.
9. Our boss keeps _____ (bring) us cakes for our break.
10. Most people want _____ (feel) fulfilled in their lives.

5 Write a new sentence or question with each verb in Exercise 4. Make them relevant to you and your partner.

My sister and I usually arrange to go on holiday together once a year.
When do you arrange to meet your friends?

6 Work in pairs. Compare your sentences and ask your questions from Exercise 5.

7 Complete the conversation between two friends with the correct verb forms. In some cases, both forms are possible.

A: I'm sure my boss is a workaholic.
B: What makes you say that?
A: Because he loves ¹_____ (get) to the office first and ²_____ (leave) last.
B: Well, being the boss means ³_____ (keep) an eye on things, doesn't it?
A: Yes, but last week he stayed late and forgot ⁴_____ (pick up) his kids from school!
B: So he's forgetful …
A: Yes and he goes on ⁵_____ (find) things to do in the office even when everything's done.
B: Hmm. Do you think he loses track of time, then?
A: Oh definitely. He doesn't stop ⁶_____ (have) lunch until mid-afternoon.
B: Perhaps you should try ⁷_____ (say) something to him.
A: I'm not sure. Maybe he likes ⁸_____ (be) that way.

LISTENING Adjusting the balance

8 🎧 43 You are going to hear part of a radio programme about a decision taken by an American Chief Executive Officer (CEO), Max Schireson. Complete the sentences with the verbs. Then listen and check.

being	following	helping	limiting	slowing
travelling	to do	to find	to give up	

1. He decided _____ his job as the CEO of a big database company.
2. Doesn't he risk _____ his career opportunities in the future?
3. He doesn't miss _____ from New York to San Francisco.
4. He doesn't regret _____ down his career.
5. His colleagues encouraged him _____ what he felt was right for him.
6. He now enjoys _____ involved in day-to-day childcare.
7. He loves _____ his kids with their homework.
8. Does he recommend _____ in his footsteps?
9. Everyone needs _____ the right balance for themselves.

SPEAKING Making the most of your time

9 **21st CENTURY OUTCOMES**

Look at the diagram. Draw a similar diagram for yourself with the hours you spend on each activity every day. Add any additional activities you do.

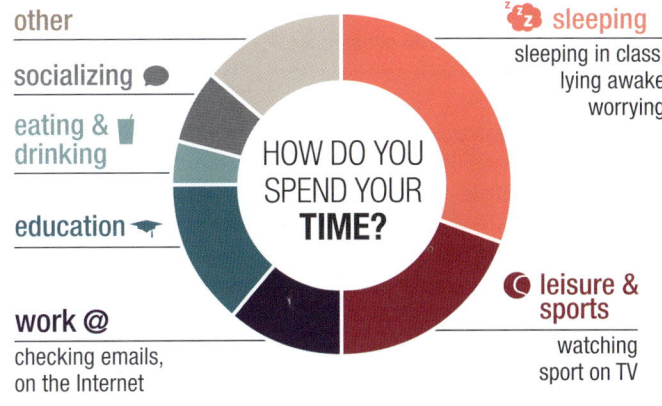

10 Work in small groups. Compare your diagrams, and find the main similarities and differences in the way you spend your day. Is there anything you'd like to change about how you spend your time? What?

21st CENTURY OUTCOMES   **HEALTH LITERACY** Understand ways of reducing physical and mental stress

8.3 Taking it easy

READING Leisure time around the world

1 Work in pairs. Discuss the questions.

  1 Are activities involving these things popular in your country?
  2 When do people do the activities?
  3 What other activities are common?

  - cinema
  - entertaining friends and family
  - museums and heritage centres
  - religious events
  - theatres and other performing arts
  - watching / taking part in sports

2 Read the newspaper article. How many leisure activities can you find? Compare with your partner.

3 Read the sentences. According to the article, are they true (T) or false (F), or is the information not given (NG)?

  1 Going shopping is a popular weekend activity among UK residents.
  2 Fulfilment and work are closely connected in Asian cultures.
  3 The OECD carried out extensive research into leisure activities in 2009.
  4 The leisure industry needs statistics on how people around the world spend their free time.
  5 Theme parks have been shown to be successful all over the world.
  6 One current idea is that gender is one of the main factors affecting leisure activities.

4 Find these expressions in the article. Then complete the sentences with the expressions. Are any of the sentences true for you?

the key question is (line 8)	The idea is that (line 21)
In other words (lines 12–13)	On the contrary (line 35)
Things like (line 19)	What's interesting is (line 40)

  1 I kept a diary of all my activities for a week. _____, I go online much less than I thought.
  2 I'm not keen on outdoor activities. _____ hiking and cycling just don't appeal to me.
  3 I want to go from full-time to part-time, but _____ can I afford to?
  4 I thought learning English would be difficult, but _____, it's quite easy!
  5 I'm organizing a charity karaoke night. _____ everyone pays to sing.
  6 I've got too much to do. _____, I haven't got time to study any more.

5 Work in pairs. Discuss the questions.

  1 Did you learn anything from the article? What?
  2 How far do you agree with the writer's comment about age and leisure activities?

VOCABULARY Relaxation

6 Match the expressions (1–8) with their definitions (a–h).

  1 take annual leave / have a day off
  2 catch up with friends / go out
  3 get away from it all / have a change of scene
  4 put your feet up / take it easy
  5 spend quality time
  6 recharge your batteries / feel refreshed
  7 switch off / clear your head
  8 unwind / chill out

  a to have time doing things you enjoy with family
  b to have a paid period of holiday from work
  c to socialize
  d to get your energy back
  e to have a change from your normal routine
  f to stop thinking about work or study
  g to rest physically
  h to relax

7 Complete the sentences with your own words. Compare with your partner and ask a follow-up question.

  1 The people I like to spend quality time with are …
  2 I try to catch up with friends …
  3 For me, switching off from my work/studies is …
  4 My ideal place for a change of scene would be …
  5 If I have a day off, I …
  6 My idea of chilling out is …

SPEAKING Giving advice

8 **21st CENTURY OUTCOMES**

  Work in small groups. Discuss what advice you would give to the following people.

  Andy, 24, call centre worker: 'I work long hours because I'm trying to save up for a car. I deal with lots of dissatisfied customers and when I get home, it's hard to put them out of my mind.'

  Diane, 29, sales manager: 'I spend a lot of time travelling to the various shops I'm responsible for and at the weekend I feel too exhausted to do anything.'

  Sunetra, 22, administrative assistant: 'The work I do is boring and I'm stuck in front of the computer all day. I can't believe I've got backache at my age.'

weekend business blog

LEISURE TIME
around the world

September 24 | Janet Barker

It's the weekend, you're not at work. So what are you doing? If you're in Switzerland, you might be hiking through the countryside, or if you're in the UK, you might be hiding from the rain in your local shopping centre. If you're in Japan, you're possibly travelling to see family, or if you're in South Korea, entertaining friends. Where you live and the culture you live in affects what you choose to do with any leisure time you have.

But if we're looking at leisure, the key question is whether 'leisure' is essentially a Western concept. Or are there different meanings for the idea of leisure in different cultures? Some writers have highlighted the contrasting views of leisure as a route to fulfilment in Western and Eastern cultures. In other words, traditional Asian cultures see fulfilment as something which comes from work. In the West, on the other hand, there is a clear distinction between work and leisure, and Westerners are more likely to associate fulfilment with leisure.

However, as well as these cultural influences on the concept of leisure, there are many factors that affect the actual leisure activities that people engage in. Things like climate, infrastructure and gender come into play in different cultures. The idea is that people who live in places with cold or wet weather might be more likely to spend their free time indoors, for example. According to a study by the Organization for Economic Co-operation and Development (OECD) in 2009, people in France spend twice as much time eating and drinking, at home and in restaurants, as people in Mexico. Other studies show that live music and dancing events are more popular in African countries, where many populations have limited electricity supplies, compared to North America, where TV and the Internet are among the top leisure interests.

For companies in the leisure and recreation industry, this kind of information is not simply interesting but key to their growth. An American theme park developer, for example, can't assume that the Western leisure model will be automatically successful in another culture. On the contrary, the assumption should be that activities with such strong cultural influences will be much harder to get right without extensive research into the market. The picture is complicated even further by the fact that trends in leisure activities are changing all the time.

What's interesting is, age and social background also influence the kinds of activities people choose to do: visiting historic sites is popular in Europe but not, perhaps, among the young so much as the older generations. Perhaps now more than ever, the real division in cultures from all around the world is that of age. The generation that has grown up with the Internet is more likely to be spending free time in online activities such as gaming, chatting or watching videos, no matter what their cultural background is. Take a look around you – can you predict what your friends and family are up to this weekend just by their age? I have a feeling you can!

8.4 I need a break!

LISTENING Taking a break

1 What do people in your country like to do on a national holiday or a long weekend?

2 🎧 44 Listen to the conversation between two colleagues. Write down the options they discuss for the long weekend.

3 🎧 44 Listen again. Look at the Useful language box and write C (Carla) and S (Steve) next to the expressions.

DISCUSSING OPTIONS

1 That's a possibility.
2 I'd prefer (not) to …
3 What are the alternatives?
4 On the other hand, …
5 I'd rather … than …
6 You have to think about …
7 You'd be better off …ing …
8 Not only that, …
9 I can see your point.
10 The only problem would be …ing.
11 I'd better make my mind up.

Pronunciation Stress in expressions

4a 🎧 45 Listen to three sentences from the Useful language box. Underline the word that is stressed.

1 That's a possibility.
2 What are the alternatives?
3 I can see your point.

4b 🎧 46 The words that are stressed in a sentence are usually the nouns or the verbs, but sometimes other words are stressed. Listen to four sentences from the Useful language box and underline the bold word that is stressed.

1 **I'd prefer not to** deal with airports on a long weekend.
2 **On the other hand,** I've been to London so many times.
3 **I'd rather do something new** than visit the same old places.
4 **You have to think about** the expense – London's not cheap.

4c 🎧 46 Listen to the sentences in Exercise 4b again and repeat. Then complete the expressions in bold with your own endings. Work in pairs and give the sentences to your partner to read out.

SPEAKING A day off

5 Work in small groups. Imagine you have a day off next week. Discuss some of the things you could do, either together or on your own, on that day. Use the expressions in the Useful language box.

WRITING An email (2)

6 Read the email which was sent out after a meeting. Answer the questions.

1 Who's the email from?
2 Who's it to?
3 What was the meeting about?
4 What are the three options that were discussed?
5 Which option was chosen?
6 What action should the reader take?

FROM: Sports and Social Committee
TO: All staff
SUBJECT: End-of-year social event

Dear colleagues

We haven't been able to have an end-of-year social event for the past two years due to our limited funds in the Sports and Social Club. This year, however, the company is going to support an event. We discussed various options, such as an office party, a meal out and a day trip.

Firstly, we considered an office party held on the premises. The main advantage of this would be that it avoids any need for people to make special travel arrangements. On the other hand, the building doesn't really have a space that is suitable.

We therefore looked at a meal out. There are a number of suitable restaurants and hotels close to the office. One argument against this was that sitting at tables is not a very good way for us to mix and get to know people from other departments.

Finally, we discussed a day trip, for example to a local tourist spot. The main drawback of this is the cost. In addition, it's difficult to find somewhere that caters for all of our needs and interests.

Taking all of the points into consideration, we propose an office party for all staff, to be held in the main reception area. Date and time to be confirmed.

Please let us know your opinion, preferably before the end of next week.

Thank you.

SaSC

Writing skill Linking expressions

7a Look at the groups of linking expressions (1–7). Underline twelve linking expressions in the email. Add the linking expressions to these groups.

1 Listing and adding points
In the first place,
Secondly,
Furthermore,
_____
_____

2 Introducing examples
For instance,
like
_____

3 Introducing advantages
The most important benefit of
Many people argue that
_____

4 Showing contrast
However,
Nevertheless,
Despite (this),
_____

5 Giving reasons
For this reason,
As
_____

6 Introducing disadvantages
The main disadvantage of
_____
_____

7 Concluding
To conclude,
To sum up,
All in all,
_____

7b Choose the correct option to complete the sentences.

1 The economy is still slow. *For instance, / Despite this,* our sales figures are good.
2 *To conclude, / The most important advantage of* we found no reason why we should not go ahead with the bonus scheme.
3 *Secondly, / All in all,* despite some initial problems, we had a productive meeting.
4 No agreement was reached. *However, / For this reason,* we arranged to have a second meeting.
5 *As / Many people argue that* more breaks help people to concentrate.
6 The team reported on issues *like / as* frequent absence from work.
7 *In the first place, / The main disadvantage of* flexitime is the effect on planning.

8 21st CENTURY OUTCOMES

Imagine you prefer one of the other two options in the email. You are going to write to the Sports and Social Committee giving your opinion, with reasons. Work in pairs, and discuss the advantages and disadvantages of each option. Then work on your own and write an email following the structure of the email in Exercise 6.

9 Exchange emails with a new partner. Check that the ideas in your partner's email flow well. Does their choice follow logically from the reasons they give?

21st CENTURY OUTCOMES PRODUCTIVITY AND ACCOUNTABILITY Participate actively

Review 4 | UNITS 7 AND 8

READING

1 Read the article about Enova. Match the headings (1–3) with the paragraphs (A–C).

1 An innovative approach
2 Award-winning social enterprise
3 Making sure it works

2 Read the article again. Find this information:

1 the organization that gave the Tech Award
2 the country Enova works in
3 the founders of Enova
4 Jorge Camil Starr's area of study
5 the first thing Enova did
6 two things Enova decided to do
7 an unexpected consequence of teaching the children
8 three ways Enova measures its success rates

GRAMMAR

3 Complete the paragraph about Enova video games with passive forms of the verbs.

The educational games that the students use ¹_____ (design) by Enova. The games ²_____ (can / find) on a free internet portal. The portal ³_____ (visit) more than 31,000 times since it ⁴_____ (set up). The 26 games ⁵_____ (play) in 46 countries so far. At any given moment, the portal ⁶_____ (access) by some of the 1,540 registered users. As Enova continues to grow in the future, more games ⁷_____ (develop). While the games follow the Mexican Public Education criteria, they ⁸_____ (can / use) as part of the education programmes of other countries.

4 Read the comments about a computer learning system. Complete the sentences with the -ing and infinitive forms of the verbs.

1 Educational software allows teachers _____ (monitor) students' progress more easily.
2 The system lets teachers _____ (choose) which learning activities to use.
3 Most teachers recommend _____ (check) the system at least once a week.
4 The teachers plan _____ (use) the technology with more classes.
5 We regret not _____ (start) this method before now.
6 The students enjoyed _____ (show) their parents how the games worked.
7 More adults continue _____ (come) to class when these systems are used.
8 The education authority intends _____ (fund) new systems in the future.

ENOVA

A In 2013, the Mexican learning and innovation network, Enova, was recognized with a Tech Award. The awards are given annually by The Tech Museum of Innovation in the USA. Enova delivers education to people in Mexico who don't have any other access to computers. The non-profit network was founded by Jorge Camil Starr along with two of his oldest friends. When they were growing up, they travelled around Mexico to go surfing and saw the potential that was being wasted in small towns with no infrastructure. Jorge later explained how doing his degree in economics around the time that the Internet was developing led to the idea of taking quality education to these low-income towns via technology.

B Enova's first task was to look at the failure of the existing systems. Computers had been used in community development for twenty years in Mexico, but the success rate of these projects was poor. Jorge realised that the systems had to be simplified. Enova took two important decisions. The first was that each educational centre would be run by only one person with full responsibility. The second was in the way they would deliver educational content – using video games. Almost all of Enova's academic material has been designed as games. The children were motivated to learn because the games were fun to play. But to the surprise of Enova, they found that the children's mothers also wanted to play the games as well. Enova had discovered a way to bring education to adults too.

C Jorge is keen to emphasize that Enova doesn't assume it's successful just because people go to their centres – the impact of the educational programmes is carefully measured. Enova follows the students who graduate and those who drop out. Students who abandon their studies are asked why, and the information is used to try and improve the programmes. Enova also measures students' success on the external government exams, which gives an independent assessment of its impact. Although there are still about 80 million people in Mexico without computer access, there are now 70 Enova centres reaching over 350,000 people.

94

VOCABULARY

5 Complete the sentences with the correct form of six of these verbs.

enable	exploit	get round
improve	inspire	introduce
put into practice	replace	

1 A visit to the Tech Fair last month _____ us to use tablets with all our students.
2 After a lot of discussion, we finally _____ our ideas to improve our systems.
3 Changing our email system _____ us to speed up our office communications.
4 Our intranet worked better when the old PCs _____ by Mac computers.
5 We need a new approach to _____ the problem of the intranet crashing.
6 When we have internet access, we can _____ the learning resources much more.

6 Complete the sentences about relaxation. The first letters of the expressions are given.

1 The weekends are when I spend q_____ t_____ with my family.
2 I've got a d_____ o_____ tomorrow, so I'm going shopping.
3 We're all going out for pizza tonight. It will be great to c_____ u_____ with my friends.
4 When I go on holiday, I can't s_____ o_____ until the second or third day.
5 Jan's been working so much recently. She really needs to t_____ it e_____ for a while.
6 What's the best way to r_____ b_____ when you're tired? Personally, I like a day on the beach.
7 If you're really tired, why don't you p_____ f_____ up for a couple of hours?
8 I'm fed up with this office. I really need a c_____ of s_____.
9 In our house, Sunday mornings are for c_____ o_____ with the Sunday papers over breakfast.
10 Once a year, we try to g_____ a f_____ it all and take a trip somewhere.

DISCUSSION

7 Work in small groups. Discuss the questions.

1 At one time, it was suggested that technological innovations would mean that people would work less and have more leisure time. What do you think of this suggestion?
2 In your experience, what are the advantages and disadvantages of computerized or online learning?

SPEAKING

8 Complete the conversation about taking an Italian class. Use the prompts.

A: Are you going to do your Italian class again this year?
B: Yes, but [1] *prefer not / go* to a class three times a week. The travelling takes ages.
A: Well, maybe [2] *better off / do* an online course.
B: That's a possibility. [3] *How / work*?
A: Usually you can join a group and it's like a virtual classroom.
B: [4] *have to / download* any special software to do the course?
A: I don't think so.
B: So it would be less time than going to a class.
A: [5] *have / think about* how much time you really have. I mean, you still have to study and hand homework in.
B: And I'd have to do a lot on my own. [6] *only problem / speak* to other people.
A: My colleague is doing a course where they speak on Skype. It sounds easy.
B: Hmm. [7] *rather speak face to face / on Skype*, but it might be OK.
A: Yes, I think it would be nicer to do it from home.
B: Well, [8] *better make / mind*. The enrolment for my usual course starts tomorrow.

WRITING

9 Read the conversation between two colleagues at Blackthorn & Sons. Write the email. Include some of these linking expressions. Begin your email *Dear colleagues* and end with the names of the organizers.

| for this reason | furthermore | in addition |
| like | such as | that's why |

Anya Waite: So, we need to write to everyone to ask them if they're interested in the idea of a social and educational association. We should mention we can offer social events, a cinema group, language classes, and things like that. And say something about organizing trips to other places people might be interested in.

Jess Lynne: I've set up a wiki page and a survey so that people can tell us what they think, and if they're interested. I'll send you the links to include in the email.

Anya Waite: OK, I'll write the email this afternoon and send it out.

10 Work in pairs. Exchange emails with your partner. Did you include the same linking expressions?

9 Creative thinking

Artist H.A. Schult transforms rubbish into 'Trashmen', Barcelona, Spain

TEDTALKS

SUNNI BROWN is an American who has been called one of the '100 most creative people in business'. Her area of expertise is visual literacy and showing how the use of art and games can help in problem-solving.

Sunni Brown's idea worth spreading is that while doodling may seem like a simple or idle pursuit, it's actually a powerful way to inspire and organize our ideas.

BACKGROUND

1 You are going to watch an edited version of a TED Talk by Sunni Brown called *Doodlers, unite!* Read the text about the speaker and the talk. Then work in pairs and discuss the questions.

1 Which of these things best help you to learn or come to a decision about something: drawing pictures, writing ideas down, going for a walk, talking about things with another person?
2 Which of the things in question 1 does Sunni Brown specialize in?
3 Which of these 'drawings of ideas' are you familiar with: mind maps, flow charts, symbols, concept maps?

KEY WORDS

2 Read the sentences (1–6). The words in bold are used in the TED Talk. First guess the meaning of the words. Then match the words with their definitions (a–f).

1 To take an **intellectual** approach, you need to consider the facts and not your feelings.
2 A sentence with incorrect grammar can seem **meaningless**.
3 Teachers often **scold** their pupils for bad behaviour.
4 Discussions in the **boardroom** can cover all aspects of a business.
5 When we are reading and listening, we focus on **verbal information**.
6 I'm a **kinaesthetic** language learner. I like to walk around and stick labels on things in my house.

a without a purpose or meaning
b where the directors of a company have meetings
c related to ideas and information
d facts or ideas expressed in words
e related to physical movement
f to speak to someone angrily when they do something wrong

AUTHENTIC LISTENING SKILLS
Understanding fast speech

In some languages, each syllable in a spoken word has the same length. In spoken English, syllables vary in length. This means that sentences with different numbers of syllables can actually take the same time to say – as in *It's a good thing to know* and *It's an important thing to understand*, for example. For the listener, varying syllable length can make it more difficult to understand speakers who talk quickly. It's useful to recognize which words in a sentence become shorter in fast speech and which parts are stressed.

3a 🎧 **47** Work in pairs. Look at the Authentic listening skills box. Then listen to the opening sentences from the TED Talk and write down the words that are stressed. Try to reconstruct the sentences.

3b Work in pairs. Read these sentences to your partner first slowly and then quickly. Which parts 'disappear' and which parts do you stress?

1 So, I discovered some very interesting things.
2 Additionally, I've heard horror stories from people whose teachers scolded them, of course, for doodling in classrooms.
3 And they have bosses who scold them for doodling in the boardroom.

3c 🎧 **48** Listen to the sentences from Exercise 3b. Did you stress the same words as Sunni Brown?

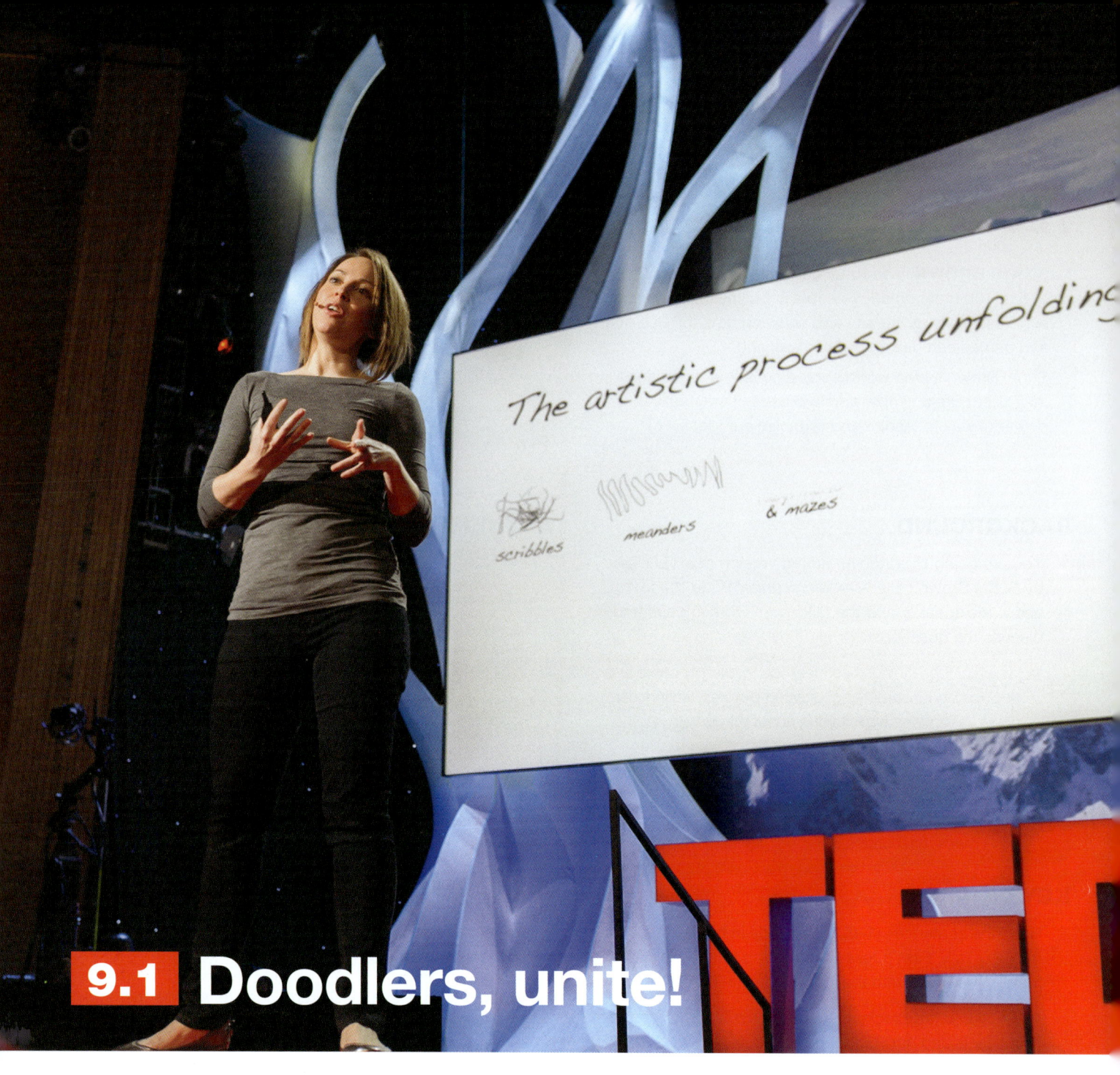

9.1 Doodlers, unite!

TED TALKS

1 ▶ 9.1 Look at this list of key points that Sunni Brown makes in her TED Talk. Then watch the edited version of the talk and tick (✓) the points that she shows in her slides.

a The meaning of the word *doodle* has changed over time.
b Doodling has traditionally been considered as something negative.
c We are so focused on verbal information that we don't realize that doodling is valuable.
d We need to relearn how to doodle.
e She proposes a new definition of doodling.
f Doodling helps you to remember more efficiently.
g There are four main ways people take in information.
h Doodling should be used when people have to process a lot of information.

2 ▶ 9.1 Watch the first part (0.00–2.02) of the talk again. Choose the correct option to answer the questions.

1 When was *doodle* used with these meanings?
 a a corrupt politician
 b a fool
 c to do nothing of value
 d to make fun of someone
2 Which groups of people sometimes do these things?
 a object to people doodling at work
 b use negative verbs to describe people who doodle
 c tell people off for doodling in class

▶ adult /ədʌlt/ N AM ENG
▶ adult /ædʌlt/ BR ENG
▶ anti-intellectual /ˌæntaɪ ɪntɪˈlektjuəl/ N AM ENG
▶ anti-intellectual /ˌænti ɪntəˈlektʃuəl/ BR ENG
▶ process /ˈprɑses/ N AM ENG
▶ process /ˈprəʊses/ BR ENG

3 ▶ **9.1** Watch the second part (2.02–3.14) of the talk again. Choose the correct option (a–c) to complete the sentences.

1 Sunni Brown believes … .
   a her culture understands doodling
   b we don't feel comfortable doodling
   c we pay too much attention to language
2 Her new definition of doodling suggests that … .
   a it helps you to think clearly
   b it's an activity that not many people really do
   c it's harmless drawing

4 ▶ **9.1** Complete the summary with these words. Then watch the third part (3.14 to the end) of the talk again and check your answers.

| all | anyone | children | decisions | thought | two |

When we make [1]_____, we need to process information in at least [2]_____ of four ways: visual, auditory, reading and writing, and kinaesthetic. Doodling actually uses [3]_____ of these ways simultaneously. Research with [4]_____ suggests that doodling is a natural thing to do. It is very easy for [5]_____ to do and it helps with intellectual [6]_____ processes.

5 Work in pairs. Discuss the questions.

1 In what situations have you doodled?
2 Why did you doodle?
3 Did you feel it was a bad thing to do?

VOCABULARY IN CONTEXT

6 ▶ **9.2** Watch the clips from the TED Talk. Choose the correct meaning of the words.

7 Work in pairs. Discuss the questions.

1 What kinds of problems might you encounter when learning a foreign language?
2 In what situations can people tend to lose focus?
3 In your opinion, what's the best setting for successful learning?

CRITICAL THINKING Supporting arguments

8 Which sentences (a–e) describe Sunni Brown's arguments?

a Doodling helps us to process information.
b Doodling can aid concentration.
c Doodling is a natural skill which we shouldn't ignore.
d Doodling should be taught in schools.
e Doodling shouldn't be thought of as a negative thing.

9 Work in pairs. Read these comments* about the TED Talk. Which of these comments support(s) Sunni Brown's arguments?

Viewers' comments
T Tim – I have to say that if I'm doodling, I don't think about what my teacher's saying. It's one or the other for me.
G Grace – Since I started doodling a few years back, I do it all the time to get my ideas clear.
L Luca – Speaking as a person who finds it hard to sit still in meetings, I find doodling a great help. But I try not to be obvious about it!

*The comments were created for this activity.

PRESENTATION SKILLS Supporting key points with slides

TIPS

Slides should support what you want to say in your talk. They can be useful when your talk contains a lot of information, explains theoretical concepts or uses specialist terms. They can be a useful support when your audience includes people whose first language is not the one you use for your talk.

- Use clear, simple visuals which your audience can understand at a glance.
- Use simple phrases so that the audience doesn't have to divide its attention between you and your slide.
- Limit each slide to two or three points.

10 ▶ **9.3** Look at the Presentation tips box. Then watch the clips from the TED Talk and say which techniques Sunni Brown uses.

11 Work in pairs. Make a slide that supports one of these ideas. Then write a few sentences to explain the idea. Practise presenting the idea with the slide.

- Visual instructions are better than text for assembling furniture.
- Pictures are a great aid in language learning.
- Using a map helps you to get to your destination.

12 Work with a new partner. Take turns to present the idea and the slide. How well does your partner's slide support their words?

▶ favorite **N AM ENG**
▶ favourite **BR ENG**
▶ horror /ˈhɔrər/ **N AM ENG**
▶ horror /ˈhɒrə/ **BR ENG**
▶ analyze **N AM ENG**
▶ analyse **BR ENG**
▶ simultaneous /ˌsaɪməlˈteɪniəs/ **N AM ENG**
▶ simultaneous /ˌsɪməlˈteɪniəs/ **BR ENG**

9.2 Looking for inspiration

THE CREATIVE PROCESS

THE BIG PICTURE
What are we doing?

THE OBJECTIVE
What does the client want to achieve?

THE SLOGAN
What's the key idea?

THE TARGET AUDIENCE
What do we want to communicate to them?

THE VISUALS
How can we show the idea with images?

THE BACKGROUND
Who are the competitors?

GRAMMAR Relative clauses

1 Work in pairs. Discuss the questions.
   1 What kinds of organizations use advertising – companies, political parties, … ?
   2 What aims do different organizations have for advertising – sell more, build an identity, publicize a message, … ?

2 🎧 49 Look at the infographic. Then listen to an interview with a creative consultant. Number the sections in the order he mentions them.

3 🎧 49 Listen again. Answer the questions.
   1 What two jobs did Chris do before being a consultant?
   2 Does he work differently for different clients?
   3 Why is it important to find out about competitors?
   4 Which is Chris's favourite part of the creative process?

100

4 Read the sentences in the Grammar box. Answer the questions (1–4).

RELATIVE CLAUSES

Defining relative clauses

*The big picture is the basic **idea that** describes what we're going to do.*
*The overall goal is **something which** tells us what the organization wants to achieve.*
*The **people** **(who)** we want to reach are the target audience.*
*That's the part of the **process** **(that)** I most enjoy.*

Non-defining relative clauses

*The **slogan, which** is a phrase or a sentence, should be short and memorable.*

Reduced relative clauses

*You need to look at the **competitors operating** in the same areas.*
*You were responsible for **adverts seen** by millions.*

1. Complete the list of relative pronouns: *where, when, whose,* _____, _____, _____.
2. Which type of relative clause gives information that is essential for the sentence to make sense: defining or non-defining?
3. Which type of relative clause gives information that can be omitted and the sentence will still make sense: defining or non-defining?
4. Which type of relative clause never includes a relative pronoun?

Check your answers on page 156 and do Exercises 1–6.

5 Match the two parts to make sentences about terms in advertising.

1. Advertising agencies who listen to their clients
2. Television, where most people will see an advert,
3. Drawing the storyboard, which is a series of simple pictures,
4. The art director, whose job is to control the whole process,
5. All the different activities which promote a product
6. The concept, which is essential to a successful advert,

a. are called the campaign.
b. get the best results.
c. has to really represent the product.
d. is the first stage in making a video.
e. is the most expensive media.
f. is the key person.

6 In which sentences in Exercise 5 can you replace the relative pronoun with *that*?

7 Rewrite the sentences using defining and non-defining clauses.

1. The CLIO Awards celebrate creative and inventive thinking. They are given annually.
2. A graphic designer won the design award. Her style is really original.
3. Some adverts are too entertaining. They don't help the audience to remember the product.
4. Outdoor adverts use large billboards. They need to have visuals with a big impact.
5. Talented people can earn a lot of money when they work for big agencies.
6. The Internet is a place with adverts. The most creative advertising ideas are found there.
7. An advert won the top prize. It was voted for by most people.
8. Viral videos can be a form of advertising. They appear on the Internet.

8 Which of the sentences in Exercise 7 can be rewritten with reduced relative clauses?

9 Read the description of an advert from which the relative pronouns and commas have been removed. Add ten relative pronouns and eight commas. Then underline the three reduced relative clauses.

'One of the most memorable adverts I've ever seen was for a bank name I can't even remember. But the advert was promoting some kind of savings product was very funny. You see two bank employees working at their desks. They're both answering phone queries. The office they are in looks grey and boring. Then one of the employees is very serious says something sounds like a line from a pop song. It's a song heard a lot on the radio. The other one sitting next to him starts to sing and dance. She's trying to make him laugh. The idea is simple is good, but it's the actors make it really funny.'

10 Work in pairs. Do you think the advert described in Exercise 9 was successful? Why? / Why not? Tell your partner about an advert that you remember.

SPEAKING Are you persuaded?

11 **21st CENTURY OUTCOMES**

Work in small groups. Brainstorm a list of five TV adverts you are all familiar with. Then give them stars (five stars = the best) according to these questions. Which advert gets the most stars overall?

1. Is it more entertaining than the TV programmes on at the same time?
2. Is the concept original?
3. Is the message about the product memorable?
4. Are the claims it makes believable?
5. Does it persuade you to buy the product?

21st CENTURY OUTCOMES **MEDIA LITERACY** Examine how media can influence beliefs and behaviour

9.3 Agreeing to differ

READING The left brain – right brain debate

1 Work in pairs. Do you know anyone who fits these descriptions? Tell your partner about the people. Do some people fit more than one description?

Someone who …

- paints and draws a lot.
- never makes decisions in a hurry.
- is great with words and can express themselves well.
- has a good head for numbers and can keep track of their finances.
- plays a musical instrument.
- is sensitive and acts according to their feelings.

2 Read the article. Decide whether the descriptions in Exercise 1 refer to a 'left brain' or a 'right brain' thinker.

3 Read the sentences. Whose views do they represent? Write CW (Cary Wilson) and KM (Kirk Monroe) next to the sentences.

1 Humans are not the only species where functions are connected to the different sides of the brain. _____
2 The fact that you can take tests to show what side of the brain you use most doesn't mean the tests are valid. _____
3 The brain works as a whole more than as separate sections. _____
4 The ideas suggested by left–right brain thinking help us to improve our skills. _____
5 It's good to know more about the way our brains work. _____

4 Look at how the words (1–8) are used in the article. Match the words with their meaning (a–h).

1 feeding (line 17)
2 predators (line 18)
3 exaggerated (line 21)
4 countless (line 22)
5 nonsense (line 29)
6 strengths (line 38)
7 weaknesses (line 38)
8 boost (line 43)

a a very large number of things
b animals that kill and eat other animals
c finding food to eat
d skills that you are not particularly good at
e skills that you are particularly good at
f something that is untrue or silly
g to improve or increase
h something which is made to seem more important than it really is

5 Work in pairs. Discuss the questions.

1 Have you ever done one of the tests mentioned in the article? What were the results?
2 Do you consider you have more 'left-brain' or 'right-brain' skills?
3 Whose views do you find more convincing? Why?

VOCABULARY Personality adjectives (1)

6 Complete the table with these adjectives.

emotional	sensible	illogical
unimaginative	sensitive	irrational
realistic	careful	analytical

Noun: concept person	Adjective	Opposite
analysis / analyst	1	–
art / artist	artistic	–
care	2	careless
dynamism	dynamic	–
emotion	3	unemotional
imagination	imaginative	4
logic	logical	5
precision	precise	imprecise
–	rational	6
realism / realist	7	unrealistic
–	8	foolish
sensitivity	9	insensitive

7 Choose the best option to complete the sentences.

1 I have a friend who makes good financial decisions. She's very *sensible / foolish* about money.
2 One of my friends is afraid of tomatoes and eggs, which seems totally *rational / irrational* to me!
3 My colleague is so *precise / careless* – her work always has to be perfect.
4 Some people are dreamers. They tend to be *realistic / unrealistic* about their plans.
5 A sad film always makes me cry. I'm so *emotional / unemotional*.
6 Thinking about other people shows that you are a *sensitive / insensitive* person.

8 Does your job or area of study attract people with any of the personality types in Exercise 7? Which ones?

The LEFT BRAIN / RIGHT BRAIN debate

Is it possible to become more of a creative person than you are? Or are you stuck as a 'left brain' thinker? There's a popular theory that our creativity and other aspects of our personalities are determined by which side of our brain is dominant. But is that a helpful theory? And is it even based on fact?

We invited a psychologist, Cary Wilson, and an educationalist, Kirk Monroe, to discuss the question *Is the left–right brain idea useful?*

KM Yes. It's been shown many times that there are some brain functions that we can clearly associate with either the right or the left side of the brain. Language is located in the left side and visualization in the right, for example. There have also been studies which show something similar in animals; that is, things like feeding or escaping from predators are types of behaviour that seem to originate in different sides of the brain.

CW No. The problem with this idea is that it has been exaggerated to describe whole personality types. If you go online, you'll find countless tests which will tell you in a matter of seconds if you are a right-brain creative, artistic, musical and intuitive person who is influenced by their emotions, or alternatively that you are a left-brain thinker who's logical, analytical and takes decisions objectively. You'll even find lists of famous 'left-brain' people: Albert Einstein or Stephen Hawking, and 'right-brain' people: Leonardo da Vinci! It's nonsense. It's not useful to put people into categories like this. In fact, I believe it is harmful. Not only is there no real evidence to support it, there are now some very convincing studies showing that both sides of the brain are active and neither side is stronger than the other.

KM I agree that we use the whole brain to process things. However, it can be very useful in education, at work and in our daily lives to have a better understanding of our strengths and weaknesses. Let's say you've done one of these tests and it tells you you're a left-brain thinker. Perhaps you recognize that in yourself, because creativity is an area you want to improve in. Having this knowledge might encourage you to look for things you can do to boost your creativity.

CW I can't disagree that understanding more about how we think and function as individuals can benefit us. But for me, the key thing is to remember that there's no scientific basis for this theory. Do the tests for fun, but don't take them seriously.

---

intuitive (adj) instinctive, not based on learning or outside evidence

visualization (n) the technique of making mental images

SPEAKING Boosting your creativity

9 **21st CENTURY OUTCOMES**

Work in groups. Discuss the questions.

1. Is being creative important to you?
2. How would you define 'being creative'?

10 Look at the list of suggestions to boost your creativity. Have you ever tried any of these things?

11 As a group, choose one of the activities and try it out. As an individual, choose one to try out before the next class. Compare your experiences in the next class.

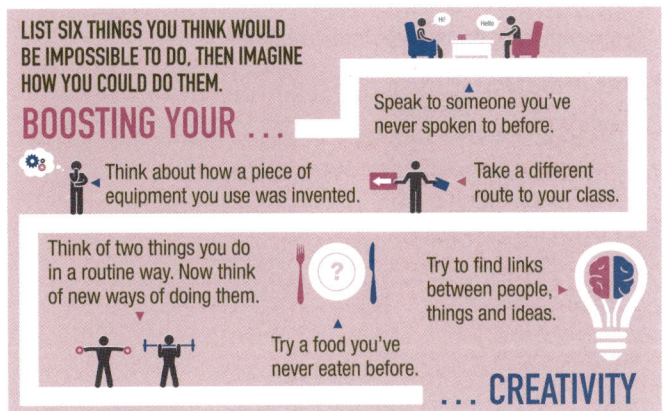

21st CENTURY OUTCOMES — **CREATIVITY AND INNOVATION** Use idea-creation techniques such as brainstorming

9.4 It's a great idea

LISTENING Launching a new product

1 Have you ever queued up to buy anything or pre-ordered anything online? Discuss your experiences.

> tickets for an event   sales goods   new gadgets   toys

2 🎧 50 Listen to a discussion about the launch of a new video game. Answer the questions.

1 What are the two aspects of the launch being discussed?
2 What are the suggestions?
3 Which idea do the speakers agree about, and which idea do they not agree about?

3 🎧 50 Listen again. Look at the Useful language box and tick (✓) the expressions you hear.

Pronunciation Stress and meaning

4a 🎧 51 Listen to two ways of asking two questions from the Useful language box. Write the word you think is stressed in each case.

1a _____   1b _____
2a _____   2b _____

CO-OPERATING IN A DISCUSSION: TURN TAKING

Inviting someone to take a turn

What do you think about … ?
What are your thoughts on … ?
How about you?
How do you feel about … ?
Would you like to say anything … ?
I'd like to know what you think about …
I'd be interested in your opinion.

Taking a turn

I just wanted to say …
If I could say/add something here.
I'd just like to make a point here.
Let me just say that …

4b Which questions in Exercise 4a show that the person's opinion is more important? Which questions show that the topic is more important?

4c Complete the questions in the Useful language box with your own ideas. Then practise the two different stress patterns.

SPEAKING Organizing a campaign

5 Work in groups. You are going to discuss ideas for an advertising campaign for your English course. Make notes on some ideas. Then discuss your ideas. Use at least four expressions from the Useful language box.

WRITING A personal account

6 Read the article from a website for people who run small businesses. Answer the questions.

1. What field does the writer work in?
2. What is the purpose of the article?
3. What happened in the two experiences she describes?

LIGHTBULB MOMENTS

Where do entrepreneurs get their ideas from?

Leanne Jones, CEO NowApp

People are always asking me how I came up with my ideas and how I made money from them. I feel some of these people might be too focused on the second part of the question! Because I've got to say that, in my case at least, there were loads of ideas that went nowhere. But thinking about it, there are a couple of tips I can pass on. One is about spotting problems. I'm the kind of person who tries to find better ways of doing things. So when I got frustrated buying something online, I asked myself if I could do it better. That's how one of my most successful apps came about. So frustration can end up being pretty productive! And then, there's a trick I use, which is to not think about things. I know, it sounds a bit weird. But I've had most of my best ideas when I was out running or driving. You're not really thinking about work, but your mind is free to make random associations. Once, I was flying off on holiday, dreaming about lying on the beach, and an idea for a flight-checking app just popped into my head. So my ideas came from being both curious and distracted, I think.

Writing skill Informal language

7a Look at the list of features (1–12). Decide which features are used in formal writing (F) and which are used in informal writing (I). Then underline examples of informal writing in the article.

1. active verb forms
2. contractions
3. conversational expressions
4. formal linking expressions
5. imprecise terms
6. no contractions
7. objective comments
8. passive forms
9. personal details
10. phrasal verbs
11. subjective opinions
12. exclamation marks

7b Rewrite the sentences in a more informal style by making the changes in brackets.

1. The development team which I lead is highly experienced. (phrasal verb, adverb)
2. The product was developed by my team. (active verb form)
3. We did not expect it to be successful. (contraction)
4. On one occasion, we discussed cancelling the project. (phrasal verb)
5. However, we had almost completed a prototype. (linking word, contraction)
6. We decided to continue with the development. (phrasal verb)
7. The product received positive reviews in the media. (imprecise verb)
8. We now have a 28 per cent market share. (contraction, exclamation mark)

8 **21st CENTURY OUTCOMES**

Work in groups. Choose a popular product that you all know about. Imagine you were involved in its development. Brainstorm ideas and vocabulary to write a paragraph about your experience. Work together to write the opening sentence.

9 Work on your own. Complete the paragraph. Then exchange your paragraph with someone in your group. Make two suggestions to improve your partner's writing.

21st CENTURY OUTCOMES CREATIVE WORKING WITH OTHERS Incorporate group input and feedback into your work

10 Connections

BACKGROUND

1 You are going to watch an edited version of a TED Talk by Julian Treasure called *5 ways to listen better.* Read the text about the speaker and the talk. Then work in pairs and discuss the questions.

   1 Think about times you have been in shops or hotels. What kinds of music, announcements or other sounds did you notice?

   2 What kind of advice do you think Julian Treasure's company gives?

   3 Think about different situations in which you listen to English: in a classroom, one-to-one conversation, films or videos, radio or podcasts, for example. Which situations do you find easier than others? Which do you find more difficult? Why?

JULIAN TREASURE is a British author and blogger. He runs a company that advises retail, hotel and other businesses on how to use sound. He defines listening as 'making meaning from sound', but says that in general, we only remember about 25 per cent of what we hear.

Julian Treasure's idea worth spreading is that in a fast-paced world where everyone is competing for attention, 'conscious listening' may be the only way we can truly understand each other and maintain meaningful relationships.

Two women sew fishing nets, Ninh Hai village, Vietnam

KEY WORDS

2 Read the sentences (1–6). The words in bold are used in the TED Talk. Match the words with their definitions (a–f). Then ask and answer the questions with a partner.

1 Does your hearing have a **filter** to cut out background noise while you're studying?
2 What do you put a **premium** on in friendship – being a good listener or giving good advice?
3 Have you ever been in a class where there was such a **cacophony** you couldn't understand the teacher?
4 What would be your favourite **soundscape**? Mine is all the sounds by the seaside.
5 Do you ever feel like you're in a **bubble** when you're listening to music through headphones?
6 Are you disturbed by **mundane** sounds from around your house when you try to study?

a great value
b lots of different sounds competing with each other
c a separate space from everything around
d something that helps to separate things into different parts
e ordinary, routine, everyday
f the overall effect of lots of sounds

AUTHENTIC LISTENING SKILLS Dealing with unknown vocabulary

Unknown words don't make it impossible to understand a speaker. For example, speakers often follow a technical term with an example or an explanation of the term.
- Learn to distinguish between the key words you need in order to understand the talk and other unknown words.
- Pay attention to what the speaker says immediately after a term you don't know.

3a 🎧 52 In his TED Talk, Julian Treasure talks about a listening technique called *pattern recognition*. Listen and complete the extract.

'We use some pretty cool techniques to do this. One of them is **pattern recognition**. So in a cocktail party like this, if I say, '_____, _____, _____,' some of you just sat up. We recognize patterns to distinguish _____ from signal, and especially our name.'

3b 🎧 53 Listen and complete these extracts.

1 **differencing** is another _____ we use
2 **filters** take us from all sound down to what we _____ _____ to

10.1 5 ways to listen better

TEDTALKS

1 ▶ 10.1 Watch the edited version of the TED Talk. Match the parts of the talk (1–3) with the things Julian Treasure talks about (a–c).

1 techniques we use to listen
2 reasons we are losing our ability to listen
3 exercises to improve conscious listening

a spend time in silence
  identify different channels of sound
  enjoy mundane sounds
  move your listening position
  use the RASA technique

b more and more audio and video recordings
  the world is noisy
  we are impatient

c recognizing patterns
  listening to differences
  paying attention to different sounds

2 ▶ 10.1 Watch the first part (0.00–2.17) of the talk again. According to Julian Treasure, are the sentences true (T) or false (F)?

1 We can hear our own names when there's lots of noise.
2 When there's a constant background noise, we can ignore it.
3 Most people don't use filters when they listen.
4 Sound gives us information about where we are.

▶ recognize, recognise BR ENG
▶ recognize N AM ENG
▶ scenario /sɪˈnɑːriəʊ/ BR ENG
▶ scenario /səˈneriou/ N AM ENG
▶ desensitized, desensitised BR ENG
▶ desensitized N AM ENG

3 ▶ 10.1 Complete the sentences with four of these words. Then watch the second part (2.17–3.57) of the talk again and check your answers.

| carefully | conversation | headlines | interesting |
| loudly | noise | tiring | understanding |

1 Recordings mean the need to listen _____ has disappeared.
2 It's very _____ to listen when there's so much noise in the world.
3 The media screams at us with _____ to get our attention.
4 Without conscious listening, there's no _____.

4 ▶ 10.1 Watch the third part (3.57 to the end) of the talk again. Answer the questions.

1 How many minutes of silence each day does Julian Treasure recommend?
2 What example of a noisy environment does he use?
3 What examples of a mundane sound does he use?
4 Julian Treasure says if you can take just one technique away from his talk, it should be what?
5 What do the letters RASA stand for?

5 Work in pairs. Review the Authentic listening skills you have worked on in Units 1–9. Are they similar to or different from Julian Treasure's techniques? How?

VOCABULARY IN CONTEXT

6 ▶ 10.2 Watch the clips from the TED Talk. Choose the correct meaning of the words.

7 Work in pairs. Complete the sentences in your own words.

1 Most of the time, all we hear is sound bites from …
2 One of the things I most appreciate about my friends is …
3 I reckon when we watch TV, we pay attention roughly …

CRITICAL THINKING Identifying problems and solutions

8 Julian Treasure structured his talk by pointing out a problem and then offering some solutions. What was the problem? Do you think the structure of the talk was effective?

9 Read the comment*. Discuss what Jerome's problem could be. Would any of the techniques from the talk help him? Which one(s)?

Viewers' comments

Jerome – I can certainly think of times when I've come away from a conversation thinking one thing, then found out later that I'd missed the point. So I guess I am doing something wrong!

*The comment was created for this activity.

PRESENTATION SKILLS Body movement and gesture

TIPS

There are two reasons why you need to think about how you use your body. First, it helps you to relax and so to give a more successful talk. Second, your body language and gestures can reinforce your listeners' understanding of your message, *or* they can distract from this comprehension.

- Pay attention to what you might be doing because you're nervous. Do you sway? Pace the floor?
- Try to keep parts of your body (arms, legs, hands) open rather than holding them tightly closed.
- Try to keep your upper body calm.
- Gesture with your palms out and open.
- Use arm and hand movements that help to illustrate your message.

10 ▶ 10.3 Look at the Presentation tips box. Then watch the clips from the TED Talk. Answer the questions.

a In the first two clips, what does Julian Treasure do with his hands when he says the words in bold?
1 Now not **you**, not **this** talk, but **that** is generally true.
2 And then there is **a whole range of filters**. […] But they actually create our reality in a way, because they tell us what **we're paying attention** to right now.

b What techniques does he use in the third clip?

11 Work in pairs. Look at the slide about different levels of noise, which is measured in decibels. Prepare a few sentences to present the information. What gestures could you use? Practise your presentation.

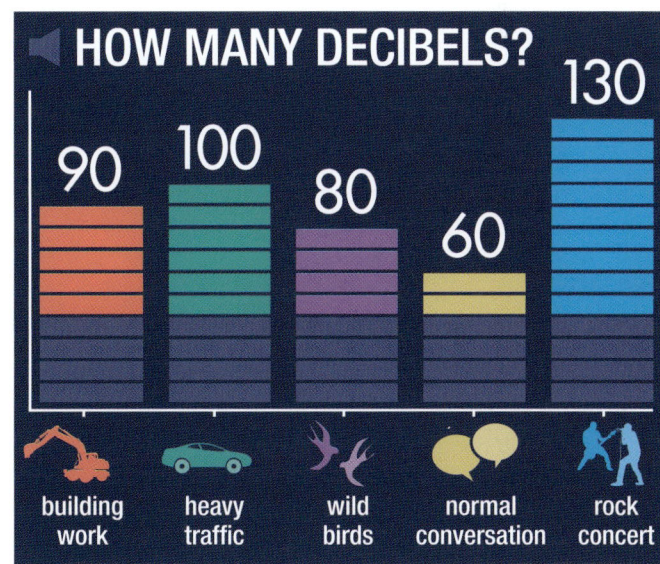

12 Work with a new partner. Give your presentation. How well do you use the techniques in the Presentation tips box?

▶ coffee bar BR ENG
▶ coffee shop N AM ENG
▶ savouring BR ENG
▶ savoring N AM ENG
▶ lever /ˈliːvə/ BR ENG
▶ lever /ˈlevər/ N AM ENG

10.2 How can I help?

CUSTOMER SERVICE: THE IMPACT ON FUTURE BUSINESS

THINK OF A CUSTOMER SERVICE EXPERIENCE YOU HAD. WAS IT GOOD OR BAD?

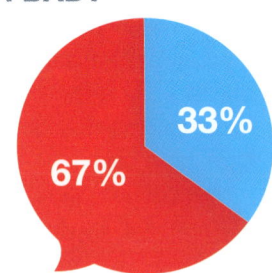

- 33% 'The experience I remember was good.'
- 67% 'The experience I remember was bad.'

HOW MANY PEOPLE DID YOU SHARE THAT CUSTOMER SERVICE EXPERIENCE WITH?

GOOD
- 'I told fewer than five people.' 52%
- 'I told more than five people.' 48%

BAD
- 'I told fewer than five people.' 46%
- 'I told more than five people.' 54%

AFTER A GOOD EXPERIENCE …
- 55% 'I will consider using the company again.'
- 25% 'I will recommend the company to others.'

AFTER A BAD EXPERIENCE …
- 45% 'I have used social media to share my views.'
- 13% 'I might consider complaining to the company.'
- 24% 'I won't use that company again.'

GRAMMAR Reported speech

1 Work in pairs. Tell your partner about an experience you had with a customer service department. How would you rate your level of satisfaction on a scale of 1 (unsatisfactory) to 5 (completely satisfied)?

2 Look at the infographic. How would you respond to the survey about customer service?

3 Compare the reported statements and questions in the Grammar box with the statements and questions in the infographic. Answer the questions (1–4) in the box.

REPORTED SPEECH

Reported statements

*67% of respondents said (that) the experience they **remembered** had been bad.*
*54% said (that) they **had told** more than five people about bad customer service.*
*45% told us (that) they **had used** social media to share bad experiences.*
*13% told us (that) they **might consider** complaining to the company.*
*24% said (that) they **wouldn't use** companies again after bad service.*

Reported questions

*We asked if respondents' customer service experiences **had been** good or bad.*
*We asked how many people the respondents **had shared** their experiences with.*

1 How do the verbs change?
2 How do the pronouns change?
3 Do we use an object pronoun with *say* or with *tell*?
4 Do we use an *if*-clause when reporting *yes/no* questions or *Wh-* questions?

Check your answers on page 158 and do Exercises 1–3.

4 Read the news item about Twitter and customer service. Complete the reported comments with these verbs.

was	was going to be	were
were using	had	didn't mean
had decided	had tweeted	had been travelling
could deal with	wouldn't bother	

These days, smart businesses are using Twitter to improve their customer service. One national power company told us that more and more customers ¹_____ Twitter to complain, and said that they ²_____ to respond to complaints the same way. The spokeswoman said that they ³_____ problems quickly, effectively and in a more personal way. Another big retailer told us that real dialogue with customers ⁴_____ the 'next big thing'. They said that people usually ⁵_____ to make complaints if the process ⁶_____ too difficult, but that ⁷_____ they ⁸_____ satisfied customers. We asked some companies if they ⁹_____ any examples of how they use Twitter in this way. One train company told us that a passenger ¹⁰_____ in a cold train and she ¹¹_____ about it. A company employee read the tweet, contacted the train driver and he turned up the heating!

5 Read the news item about a hotel review. Then rewrite the sentences with quotes as reported speech. Change the verbs, pronouns and adverbs as necessary.

1 The hotel owner said (that) they would refund the money that day.

TAKING THINGS TOO FAR?

BRUCE SHIELD | A hotel in Australia which charged customers a 'fine' of $100 for posting a bad review on a website now say they will refund the full amount. The hotel owner said, 'We will refund the money today.' We asked the owner about the controversial policy and he told us, 'We introduced the policy because some customers were abusing feedback websites.' And a bad review can have a dramatic effect on a business. 'How did your policy improve customer relations?' we asked the owner. He said that the situation was difficult since 'customers will threaten us with a bad review because they want a discount.' In this case, the hotel guests were a young couple, who were furious at the fine. They said, 'We found an extra charge of $100 on our credit card bill.' The next day the couple asked their bank 'Is this legal?' The case quickly attracted nationwide publicity, leading to the hotel's change of heart.

6 Work in pairs. Imagine you have witnessed situations like these. Tell your partner what happened, what was said and how the situation ended.

- A traveller arrived at an airline check-in with an enormous suitcase.
- A delivery man brought a damaged parcel to someone's door.
- Someone was smoking a cigarette at reception where a no-smoking sign was clearly visible.
- A waiter spilt a drink as he brought it to someone's table.
- Someone tried to jump the queue to get served before their turn.

A: *I was standing in the queue at check-in at Sydney airport when the man in front of me went up to the counter. His suitcase was enormous. He could hardly lift it. The check-in assistant weighed the suitcase and told him that it was much too heavy. She said he would have to go and buy two smaller ones.*
B: *And what did the man say?*
A: *He told her he ...*

LISTENING AND SPEAKING Two sides to every story

7 21st **CENTURY OUTCOMES**
🎧 54 Listen to a phone call between a British tourist staying in self-catering accommodation in France and the agent responsible for the house. What's the problem? What does the tourist ask for?

8 🎧 54 Listen again. Complete the sentences.

1 François asked if _____
2 James asked how _____ and what _____
3 François then asked if _____
4 James asked François if _____

9 Work in small groups. Discuss the questions.

1 How do you think François reported the conversation to the owner of the house?
2 How do you think James reported the conversation to the owner of the house?
3 How well do you think each man handled the situation?
4 Do you think any mistakes were made? What?
5 Would you give a refund? Why? / Why not?

10 Work in pairs. Have a conversation about the same situation that ends satisfactorily for both people.

10.3 The customer is always right

READING Cross-cultural awareness

1 In your country, which of these service industries are most likely to be used by foreign visitors? Have you experienced problems yourself in these areas when travelling abroad?

banking	hair & beauty	health care
restaurants	retail	tourism
transport	travel	utilities

2 Read the feedback from four students on a college website. Find this information. Would you choose to do either of these units?

1 the course the students did
2 the two units the students comment on
3 positive comments about the units
4 negative comments about the units

3 Read the feedback again. Look at the syllabus of the Cross-Cultural Awareness Module below. Complete the headings with the topics mentioned in the students' feedback.

BYWELL COLLEGE Auckland New Zealand
Hotel and Catering Level 2

Cross-Cultural Awareness Module (HC2.2)

Unit A: Cross-cultural misunderstandings

1 Awareness
 1.1 _____
 1.2 customs
 1.3 _____
 1.4 _____
 1.5 the family
2 Strategies
 2.1 Overcome personal prejudice
 2.2 Learn _____

Unit B: Cross-cultural communication

1 Verbal communication
 1.1 Appropriate speech
 1.2 _____
 1.3 _____
2 Non-verbal communication
 2.1 Appropriate _____
 2.2 International signs

BYWELL COLLEGE Auckland New Zealand
Hotel and Catering Level 2

I recently completed the Cross-Cultural Awareness module (HC2.2). The module is a compulsory part of the Hotel and Catering Level 2 course and I understand that it has been substantially changed since last year. On the whole, I think the course was excellent and that it has prepared me very well for working with both colleagues and customers from different cultural backgrounds.

BYWELL COLLEGE Auckland New Zealand
Hotel and Catering Level 2

I would like to highlight the HC2.2 unit on Cross-cultural misunderstandings (Unit A), which covered issues I had not given any consideration to before. While I knew that religion and ways of dressing can be sensitive areas, I was unaware of how important formality is, especially the idea that being too formal can be as inappropriate as being too informal. Here in the UK we do expect friendliness to be part of a service, so it's useful to learn that for some other cultures what we think of as unfriendly or impolite is simply viewed as professional. The only thing I would say is that the tutor could have given more specific information about different cultures and what they regard as unacceptable so that we can avoid giving offence. On the other hand, I now know greetings and basic terms in six languages, which is great as I've always been unable to learn a foreign language. I was amazed at how easy this was and how confident I now feel using the greetings. It was a very enjoyable class too.

BYWELL COLLEGE Auckland New Zealand
Hotel and Catering Level 2

For me the most practical HC2.2 unit was Unit B: Cross-cultural communication. The tutor, Ms Mackay, warned us that we would feel uncomfortable at times and she was right! But using video really helped us to see what our body language looks like to others. This was invaluable given that most of what we communicate is actually non-verbal. I also found the active listening workshops useful. These were ideas that were completely new to me. Following on from this, watching the videos, we were able to really understand how frequently we interrupted the other person and how we hardly ever gave them feedback during the conversation. I would have liked more time to practise the effective questioning techniques, as I am still unclear on how to use reflective questions and paraphrasing. I think that this is one aspect of the unit that could be improved.

BYWELL COLLEGE Auckland New Zealand
Hotel and Catering Level 2

I'd just like to say that the tutors on the Cross-Cultural Awareness module were among the best I've had at this college. They gave us lots of positive feedback. They were also sensitive in helping us to understand that sometimes we aren't aware of how negative our own behaviour can be.

---

paraphrasing (n) a way of stating the same idea using different words

4 Look at how these words are used in the students' feedback. Which words have negative meanings? Are the other words positive or neutral? Underline the prefixes.

1 misunderstandings (line 8)
2 unaware (line 10)
3 inappropriate (line 12)
4 informal (line 12)
5 unfriendly (line 14)
6 impolite (line 14)
7 unacceptable (line 17)
8 unable (line 20)
9 uncomfortable (line 25)
10 invaluable (line 27)
11 non-verbal (line 28)
12 unclear (line 34)

5 Complete the sentences with words (with or without the prefix) from Exercise 4.

1 The problem is quite _____ now that you've explained it.
2 I'm very sorry. We were _____ that you'd been experiencing difficulty with our service.
3 We respectfully ask guests to wear _____ dress in the hotel restaurant.
4 I regret that there have been some _____ over our refunds policy.
5 I agree that this kind of behaviour is simply _____ and I will take steps to ensure it doesn't happen again.
6 The directions were absolutely _____ – we'd never have found the hotel without them.

6 Work in pairs. Discuss the questions.

1 What experience do you have of cross-cultural misunderstandings? How did you feel in these situations? How might the cross-cultural units described in the students' feedback have helped you?
2 What do you think are the best ways to avoid difficulties arising from cross-cultural misunderstandings? How can any difficulties be resolved?

VOCABULARY Customer service

7 Complete the expressions with these verbs. Who does these things – the customer or the service provider?

| ask for | behave | give | leave | make | pay |
| provide / offer / charge for / pay for | | | | | |

1 _____ appropriately / politely / professionally / badly / offensively
2 _____ a service charge / a bill
3 _____ a tip / a refund
4 _____ a tip
5 _____ a service / extras
6 _____ a mistake / an apology
7 _____ an apology / a refund

8 Read and complete the conversation with some of the expressions from Exercise 7. Change the verb forms where necessary.

A: I always feel so uncomfortable if I have to complain about bad service.
B: Really? I don't think you should. As long as you just point out the problem and you ¹_____, what's the problem?
A: Yeah, but sometimes it's just that someone's ²_____ in the bill or whatever.
B: So? They'd probably thank you for telling them so that they don't get into trouble from their boss. Anyway, if a place is ³_____, they should get it right.
A: I guess so. Fortunately I've never had to ⁴_____ of any money. But there've been loads of times in restaurants when I haven't ⁵_____ – like when the service has been really slow or the waiter just doesn't seem to be listening and you have to ask for things repeatedly.
B: I don't like it when you have to ⁶_____ that already includes a service charge. It should be up to me!

SPEAKING Leaving tips

9 21st CENTURY OUTCOMES

Work in groups of three. Read the comment from a British student. What is normal tipping behaviour in your country?

I'm planning a trip to the States soon, and a friend has just told me that not only is it compulsory to leave a tip in restaurants, but that I should leave 15–25 per cent of the bill! Is my friend joking?

10 Work in the same groups of three. Decide who is Student A, Student B and Student C. Read your information on page 164. Then discuss what you would say to the British student.

21st CENTURY OUTCOMES   GLOBAL AWARENESS Get a better understanding of other nations and cultures

10.4 Any other business?

LISTENING Helplines

1 Work in pairs. What do you value most when you deal with a company's helpline?

- a free phone number
- friendliness as well as politeness
- knowing the person's name
- no waiting time on the phone
- a personal response
- prompt follow-ups to your enquiry

2 🎧 55 Listen to a meeting of a Customer Care team. What is the topic of the meeting? Choose the correct option (a–c).

a helplines versus websites
b response times on helplines
c charges on helplines

3 🎧 55 Listen again. Make notes about:

1 the problem
2 a suggestion
3 the reaction
4 an offer

TAKING PART IN MEETINGS: RASA

Receive – paying attention

| Yes. |
| Great. |
| You're absolutely right. |

Appreciate – showing understanding

| oh | OK | yeah |
| uhuh | hmm | |

Summarizing what you've heard

| So … |
| In other words, … |
| What you're saying is … |

Asking questions

| And is that … ? |
| Do you mean … ? |

Pronunciation Sounds and meaning

4a 🎧 **56** Listen to the responses for showing understanding in the Useful language box. You will hear each response twice. For each one, decide if the speaker's intonation shows understanding, surprise or disagreement.

	Understanding	Surprise	Disagreement
1		✓	
2			
3			
4			
5			
6			
7			
8			
9			
10			

4b 🎧 **56** Listen again and repeat the different intonations.

SPEAKING Comparing experiences

5 **21st CENTURY OUTCOMES**

Work in small groups. Discuss your experiences and opinions of the options in Exercise 2. Try to use the expressions in the Useful language box. When you finish, spend two minutes making notes about the discussion. You will need your notes in Exercise 8.

WRITING Minutes (2)

6 Read the minutes of the meeting in Exercise 2. Are they similar to your notes in Exercise 3?

> **Customer Care meeting January 7th**
> **Present:** Pat Jones, Rory Scott, Neil Anderson
> **Helpline**
>
> PJ informed the meeting that there has been considerable customer dissatisfaction with the charges for the helpline. Currently this is an 0845 number. She suggested switching to a free phone number. NA agreed that this was an issue that needs to be looked into. RS offered to work out the additional cost of a free line and report back.
>
> There was no other business. NA reminded everyone to check their email for the venue of the next meeting, as this will be different due to office redecoration.

Writing skill Reporting verbs

7a Look at the groups of reporting verbs (1–5). Underline five reporting verbs in the minutes that have the same patterns. Add the reporting verbs to these groups.

> 1 verb + *-ing*
>   recommend, propose, _____
>
> 2 verb + *(not) to* + infinitive
>   promise, refuse, _____
>
> 3 verb + object + *(not) to* + infinitive
>   invite, ask, _____
>
> 4 verb + *that*
>   explain, realize, _____
>
> 5 verb + object + *that*
>   tell, warn, _____
>
> See page 158 for more information about reporting verbs, and do Exercises 4–6.

7b Choose the correct option to complete the sentences.

1 The agent *said / told* me that my complaint was being looked into.
2 The committee *asked / proposed* waiting for the results of the survey.
3 My friend *explained / told* that there was a way to speak to an agent immediately on the phone.
4 The person I spoke to *asked / suggested* me to send proof of my identity.
5 The company *recommended / warned* clients that all deliveries would be delayed by two days.
6 The hotel owner *has invited / has refused* us to write about our experience on their website.
7 My friend *informed / promised* not to get angry when he complained about the food.
8 The company *refused / reminded* to give us our money back.

8 Use your notes from Exercise 5 to write the minutes of your discussion. Use at least three reporting verbs.

9 Exchange minutes with someone from your group. How similar are the points you remember? Have you used the same reporting verbs?

Review 5 | UNITS 9 AND 10

LISTENING

1 Read about Alpha Communication. Answer the questions.

1 What business model does Alpha Communication follow?
2 What business sector do they work in?

2 🎧 57 Listen to a radio interview about Alpha Communication. Are the sentences true (T) or false (F)?

1 In the UK, co-operatives are limited to a narrow range of business sectors.
2 As a co-op, Alpha Communication is unique among communications companies.
3 There are benefits from Alpha for both local people and the co-op owners.
4 The same creative team has worked at Alpha since it began.
5 Alpha's clients are similar organizations.

3 🎧 57 Listen again. Complete each sentence with one word from the interview.

1 Co-ops are run by people who are equal _____.
2 Co-ops provide both goods and _____.
3 Edwina Jones describes the Alpha group as _____.
4 Alpha's core values are co-operation, honesty, _____, fairness and respect.
5 Edwina Jones was shown a campaign for a Fairtrade _____.

ALPHA COMMUNICATION

Alpha Communication is a UK marketing and design company which is also a co-operative social enterprise. They produce marketing, design and communication materials for businesses mostly also in the UK. They define themselves as 'nerds' who love research, data and doing new things.

nerd (n) a person who is very interested in one subject, especially computers, and knows a lot of facts about it

GRAMMAR

4 Read about the Mondragon Corporation. Add the missing relative pronouns and commas to the text. Underline the four reduced relative clauses.

The Mondragon Corporation is a collection of worker co-operatives based in northern Spain, in the Basque Country. The name comes from the town the first co-op was founded. The co-op was started in 1956 by a group of people had studied locally. The first product made by the co-op was a heater. Now the Mondragon Corporation is the biggest business group in the region. In the first twenty years, the Corporation grew quickly with the addition of companies business models followed co-operative principles. The Mondragon Corporation now includes more than 250 companies operates in four sectors: finance, industry, retail and knowledge. The sector growing most rapidly is probably knowledge. There are fifteen technology centres together have more than 1,700 employees working in research and development.

5 Write the statements and questions as reported speech.

1 Tyne Co-op said, 'Alpha has come up with a highly original campaign that we're really pleased with.'
_____

2 Bill Rylands told us, 'I'm very happy with Alpha and I won't use any other company.'
_____

3 KidCare asked, 'How much does a typical website cost?'
_____

4 Sandra Brown asked, 'Can I change the website content myself?'
_____

5 Tyne Co-op said, 'The team were making improvements to our video until the last minute.'
_____

6 FruitStore told us, 'We haven't had a website before. It's really making a difference to our business.'
_____

7 Bill Rylands asked, 'How long does it take to make a typical video?'
_____

8 Alpha asked, 'Did we provide the quality you expected?'
_____

VOCABULARY

6 Read about teams in business. Complete the nouns and adjectives in the text.

Co-ops usually value teamwork very highly. The success of any team is about getting the balance right. A company like Alpha Communication needs to have ¹imaginat_____ and ²art_____ staff to create content for clients. At the same time, the creative team shouldn't be ³unreal_____ – it must work within given limits. Care and ⁴precis_____ are essential to deliver the message the clients want. For a healthy business, the team needs someone with an ⁵analy_____ approach. There's no room for ⁶emot_____ in business finance. As a whole, the team needs the ⁷dynam_____ required to drive the business forward.

7 Read the comment from the director of a communications agency. Complete the text with the correct form of appropriate verbs.

'We haven't had many bad experiences with our clients. Occasionally we ¹ _____ a mistake with an invoice, but we sort it out immediately. I can only remember a few problems, but in each case the client ² _____ politely and never offensively. We ³ _____ a service that is quite specialized and sometimes a client might not realize they need to ⁴ _____ for extras. In general, though, our clients ⁵ _____ their bills on time. In our business, clients usually give approval to our ideas and so if a campaign isn't successful, we don't ⁶ _____ a refund! But we do try to build a good relationship so that our clients come back to us in the future.'

DISCUSSION

8 Work in small groups. Discuss the questions.

1 What aspects of customer experience influence your decision on whether to use a company again?
   - after-sales service
   - expert knowledge
   - friendly interactions with staff
   - personal attention
   - price and availability of product/service
   - professionalism of staff
   - quality of the product

2 If you had your own small business, what would be the three most important guidelines you would give your staff regarding customer service?

SPEAKING

9 Complete the conversation between five friends, Tim, Eve, Pete, Anya and Meena, who want to start a food co-op. Use the prompts.

T: OK, so we're all here to talk about the idea of forming a co-op to sell the fruit and vegetables that we grow. ¹*What / you / think / about* letting each person speak in turn?
E: That sounds OK to me. ²*How / you,* Pete?
P: Yeah, fine. ³*I / want / say* that I'm here because Susan can't come, so I'll need to check everything with her.
T: OK, sure. Anya, ⁴*what / thoughts* on a co-op?
A: I think it could be a great idea. I'm not clear on how we can organize it, though.
P: ⁵*Let / say* that there's loads of information online.
T: Yes, I've been having a look. ⁶*like / know / think* about the 'small co-operatives' site.
A: That's the best site I've seen. Meena, ⁷*you like / say anything?*
M: My feeling is that we need to find out if there are similar co-ops already in our area.
E: ⁸*If / say / something here.* I think Meena has a good point. There's a similar group in the next village.

WRITING

10 Read these comments made by the owners of a co-operative restaurant about how they started. Complete the text using the correct patterns with the reporting verbs and the comments.

1 'Restaurants are very hard to get right.'
2 'We have a lot of confidence.'
3 'You should research the market well.'
4 'Yes, I will give you a loan.'
5 'Why don't you try out your recipes?'
6 'Don't change anything. It's just great as it is!'

When we decided to set up our restaurant as a co-operative, a lot of people ¹warned _____ _____. But we ²replied _____ _____ and great ideas. We spoke to other co-operatives, who ³advised _____ _____. We needed money to get started, and fortunately our bank manager ⁴agreed _____. A friend ⁵suggested _____ by inviting people to a free tasting session. We did this from a stall at a local festival and it was a great success. Some people even ⁶told _____ _____. We officially opened the restaurant a year ago and so far it's going really well.

11 Work in pairs. Exchange texts with your partner. Check your answers. Did you use the same reporting patterns?

11 Resources

BACKGROUND

1 You are going to watch an edited version of a TED Talk by Gavin Pretor-Pinney called *Cloudy with a chance of joy*. Read the text about the speaker and the talk. Then work in pairs and discuss the questions.

1 The verb *to idle* means 'to spend time in pointless or trivial activities'. What activities that you do could be considered as *idling* – crosswords, sudoku, browsing online, … ?

2 What do you think members of the Cloud Appreciation Society do?

3 Do you have a busy daily routine? Do you enjoy that, or would you like to take time out sometimes?

TEDTALKS

GAVIN PRETOR-PINNEY is a science writer. His writing combines science with an appreciation of the natural wonders around us. Pretor-Pinney co-founded *The Idler* magazine, a publication that encourages people to take time out of their busy routines to simply enjoy the world around them. He also founded the Cloud Appreciation Society, an organization devoted to the idle pursuit of cloudwatching.

Gavin Pretor-Pinney's idea worth spreading is that we can all benefit from looking up and admiring the beauty of the clouds over our heads.

A cloud passes over the fields, Suceava Province, Romania

KEY WORDS

2 Read the sentences (1–6). The words in bold are used in the TED Talk. Match the words with their definitions (a–f). Then ask and answer the questions with a partner.

1 What kinds of **obstructions** get in the way of your attempts to relax?
2 Do you know anyone who has a **fondness** for the natural world?
3 What kinds of activities might help someone suffering from **angst**?
4 Have you ever tried **meditation** as a way of relaxing?
5 Would you describe all leisure activities as **egalitarian**?
6 Is there an **antidote** to stressful ways of life?

a a strong feeling of anxiety
b things that stop you making progress
c equal for everyone
d the feeling of being affectionate towards or enjoying something
e something that relieves a negative condition or situation
f the act of quiet thinking or reflection

AUTHENTIC LISTENING SKILLS Vowels: sounds and spelling /aʊ/ and /əʊ/

Sometimes you may not recognize a word you hear because its spoken form is not what you expect from the way it is written. For example, *now* and *sound* both have an /aʊ/ sound; *so* and *though* have an /əʊ/ sound. The more you learn about vowel sounds and spelling, the more you will recognize the words you hear in spoken English and understand the speaker's message.

3a 🎧 58 Look at the Authentic listening skills box. Then listen to the first sentence from the TED Talk. Underline the words with an /aʊ/ sound. Circle the words with an /əʊ/ sound.

'Clouds. Have you ever noticed how much people moan about them?'

3b 🎧 59 Four of these words have an /aʊ/ or an /əʊ/ sound. Which ones? Listen to what Gavin Pretor-Pinney says next and check.

| associations | towards | down | store |
| horizon | other | processing | over |

119

11.1 Cloudy with a chance of joy

TEDTALKS

1 ▶ **11.1** Match the two parts of the sentences to complete what Gavin Pretor-Pinney says. Then watch the edited version of the TED Talk and check your answers.

1 People think of clouds as
2 To tune into the clouds is to
3 These rarer clouds remind us that
4 Sometimes we need

a excuses to do nothing.
b slow down, to calm down.
c the exotic can be found in the everyday.
d things that get in the way.

2 ▶ **11.1** Watch the first part (0.00–3.49) of the talk again. Choose the correct option to complete the sentences.

1 People *notice / don't notice* the beauty of clouds.
2 Gavin Pretor-Pinney shows and describes three clouds.
 a He shows the Grim Reaper *first / second / third*.
 b He shows the Abominable Snowman going to rob a bank *first / second / third*.
 c He shows two cats dancing the salsa *first / second / third*.
3 There are Cloud Appreciation Society members in about *ten / a hundred* countries.

▶ (computer) processing /ˈproʊsɛsɪŋ/ **BR ENG**
▶ (computer) processing /ˈprɑsɛsɪŋ/ **N AM ENG**
▶ harbour **BR ENG**
▶ harbor **N AM ENG**
▶ salsa /ˈsælsə/ **BR ENG**
▶ salsa /ˈsɑlsə/ **N AM ENG**

3 ▶ 11.1 Watch the second part (3.49–7.43) of the talk again. Tick (✓) the types of clouds that you have seen yourself.

 a the cirrus cloud (like brush strokes)
 b lenticularis (like flying saucers)
 c fallstreak holes (like jelly fish tendrils)
 d the Kelvin–Helmholtz cloud (like breaking waves)
 e cumulonimbus storm cloud (produces thunder and lightning)

4 ▶ 11.1 Watch the third part (7.43 to the end) of the talk again. Are these statements accurate paraphrases of what Gavin Pretor-Pinney says?

1 Cloudspotting is important because there's no real point to doing it.
2 Doing nothing is never a useful way to spend time.
3 Feeling that you're in the present moment is beneficial in many ways.
4 We should appreciate the beauty around us in the natural world.

5 Work in pairs. Can you complete the idioms from the talk with the correct word? There's one extra word. What do the idioms in sentences 3 and 4 mean?

| feet | head | horizon | in | sky | under |

1 Someone who's down or depressed is '_____ a cloud'.
2 When there's bad news in store, 'there's a cloud on the _____'.
3 Go and do some 'blue-_____ thinking'.
4 If you live with your '_____ in the clouds' every now and then, it helps you to keep your '_____ on the ground'.

VOCABULARY IN CONTEXT

6 ▶ 11.2 Watch the clips from the TED Talk. Choose the correct meaning of the words.

7 Work in pairs. Discuss the questions.
1 What comes to mind when you think of your English classes?
2 Who or what has got a bad press recently?
3 What kinds of groups might need others to stand up for them?

CRITICAL THINKING Identifying the 'take away' message

8 Every speaker hopes that the listener will take away an important message from their talk. What message do you think Gavin Pretor-Pinney wanted you to take away? Was that the message that you took away?

9 Read these comments* about the TED Talk. Match each comment with the main idea (1–3) the viewer has taken away from the talk.

1 Clouds are a beautiful aspect of nature.
2 Cloudspotting represents a particular view of life.
3 The science of clouds is quite complicated.

Viewers' comments

T Taddeu – I have to say I'd never realized until I saw this talk what wonderful things clouds are!

R Roshan – I'm afraid I didn't understand all of his explanations about how clouds form – it seems to be a very complex process.

L G. Murphy – With respect, I think you're both missing his point. For me, this talk was all about a whole approach to life – being 'in the moment'. Don't you think?

*The comments were created for this activity.

PRESENTATION SKILLS Being enthusiastic

TIPS

When you transmit your enthusiasm for your topic to the audience, they become more involved in your talk, pay more attention and understand more.
• Show excitement by varying the speed and volume of your delivery while still speaking naturally.
• Smile and express the interest you feel in the topic.
• Invite the audience to share your enthusiasm with questions and gestures.
• Use well-chosen visuals that show what there is to enjoy about your topic.

10 ▶ 11.3 Look at the Presentation tips box. Then watch the clips from the TED Talk and say which techniques Gavin Pretor-Pinney uses.

11 Choose something (a place, an activity, a hobby) you know a lot about and enjoy doing. Make brief notes on three things you want to communicate about your topic and practise your mini-presentation. Use at least one of the techniques in the box.

12 Work in groups of three. Take turns to give your presentations. How well do you all use the techniques?

▶ shopping centre BR ENG
▶ shopping mall N AM ENG

▶ diverse /daɪˈvɜːs/ BR ENG
▶ diverse /dəˈvɜːrs/ N AM ENG

▶ tune (in) /tjuːn/ BR ENG
▶ tune (in) /tuːn/ N AM ENG

11.2 Sharing our resources?

OUR GLOBAL APPETITES: ARCTIC COMMODITIES USED BY EVERYBODY, EVERY DAY

The whole region is rich in deposits of natural resources. Ten per cent of the world's fresh water is in Greenland, for example. In addition, the Arctic Ocean supports a large amount of marine life.

All eight countries on the map are members of the Arctic Council, but each government has different policies regarding natural resources.

 **Gold**
Gold is found in every mobile phone and computer.

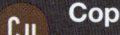 **Copper**
A typical home contains 200 kilograms of copper.

 Oil
There are few products that don't contain some oil-based material. All plastic comes from oil.

 Natural gas
A lot of natural gas is used for the generation of electricity.

 Unexplored oil and gas deposits

VOCABULARY Resources

1 Match the resources in A with the examples in B.

A	B
agricultural	employees
financial	copper
human	money
information	oil
mineral	the Internet
natural	water
non-renewable	wheat

GRAMMAR Articles

2 Look at the infographic. Find:
1 eight countries which form the Arctic Council
2 two metals
3 two energy sources
4 two everyday uses for the commodities shown

3 Read the sentences in the Grammar box. Underline examples of *a/an* + noun, *the* + noun, and nouns with no (zero) article. Then answer the question in the box.

ARTICLES: *A, AN, THE,* ZERO ARTICLE

Canada is a member of an organization of eight Arctic countries.
There are significant amounts of natural resources in the Arctic region.
The unexplored deposits of oil are mostly in Alaska.
Most of the natural gas in the region is in Russia.
Your flat screen TV contains gold.
Synthetic fibres are an oil-based product.

With what type of nouns is *a/an*, *the*, no (zero) article used: countable singular, countable plural or uncountable?

Check your answers on page 160 and do Exercises 1–2.

4 Read the news item from which the articles have been removed. Add nine articles.

> **The race to the Arctic**
>
> UNTIL RECENTLY, it was difficult to access resources of Arctic, which were under thick layer of ice. Now that ice is melting, resource-hungry countries are keen to exploit area. Arctic Council used to be small organization dealing mainly with community issues. Now it has become important focus of attention for these countries. Environmentalists and politicians are also getting involved in intense debates about future of this fragile region.

GRAMMAR Quantifiers

5 Read the sentences in the Grammar box. Find the words in bold in the sentences in the infographic. Answer the question in the box.

> **QUANTIFIERS**
>
> *Every home uses resources on a daily basis.*
> *Very few people live in this part of the world.*
> *There's a large amount of ice in the region.*
> *All natural gas is beneath the earth's surface.*
>
> With what type of nouns are the quantifiers used: countable singular, countable plural or uncountable?
>
> Check your answers on page 160 and do Exercises 3–6.

6 Choose the correct options to complete the comments about different resources.

'Fortunately, not ¹ *every / all* type of energy is non-renewable. Wind and solar power generate electricity. ² *Each / Both* resources are renewable. We need to prepare for the time when there isn't ³ *any / no* oil left.'

'The large ⁴ *amount / number* of meat we eat depends on inefficient farming methods. There are ⁵ *little / several* alternatives to meat that are equally nutritious. There are ⁶ *no / a few* good reasons to keep wasting resources in this way.'

'The most important asset in a company is its staff, but ⁷ *few / a few* big businesses remember that. Often, international companies pay ⁸ *a little / little* attention to the conditions of workers who make their products.'

7 Read about a schoolgirl who became an internet sensation. Complete the paragraph with quantifiers and articles. There is no article in one of the sentences.

a	a few	a huge number of	a lot of
any	both	every	few
no	the		

When Martha Payne was nine years old, she posted ¹_____ photo of her school dinner on her blog ²_____ day to raise money for charity. At first, very ³_____ people saw the photos. Nevertheless, Martha still managed to raise ⁴_____ money – nearly £2,000 – for Mary's Meals, a charity that supplies ⁵_____ school lunches to ⁶_____ children around the world. Then the school banned Martha from taking ⁷_____ photos, so she stopped blogging. ⁸_____ Martha and her school were amazed by what happened next. Within ⁹_____ hours, the story went viral and thousands of people visited Martha's site in the following days. There were ¹⁰_____ reasons for the school to continue the ban, so it was lifted. In total, ¹¹_____ site got three million hits and over £100,000 was raised for Mary's Meals.

SPEAKING How much is too much?

8 **21st CENTURY OUTCOMES**

Complete the quiz with these nouns. Then choose the option that is true for you.

| electricity | food | information | money | paper | things |

> **How much is too much?**
>
> **1** As an English student, I use *a lot of / a small amount of* _____ printing things out.
> **2** I probably waste *no / a little* _____ by not switching things off.
> **3** We often throw *a little / a lot of* _____ away from our fridge each week.
> **4** When I google something, I usually find *lots of / few* useful _____.
> **5** Sometimes at the end of the week, I find that *I've spent all / I haven't spent any* of my _____.
> **6** I recycle *a large number of / a few* _____, like bottles and cans.

9 Work in groups. Compare your answers. Give more information about three of your answers. Do you agree about what are large or small quantities?

I use a packet of paper every two weeks.

21st CENTURY OUTCOMES ENVIRONMENTAL LITERACY Demonstrate knowledge and understanding of the environment

11.3 International movements

READING Life in the slow lane

1 What kind of fast food do you eat, if any? What do you think the term 'slow food' means? Compare your ideas with your classmates.

2 Read the article. Check your ideas from Exercise 1.

3 Read the article again. Match the headings (1–3) with the paragraphs (A–C) in the article.

1 Quality doesn't come cheap
2 Life is a journey, not a destination
3 You are what you eat

4 Work in pairs. Change or rewrite the sentences so that they agree with the information in the article.

1 The slow movement started in the 21st century.
2 The movement believes everything should go at its slowest speed.
3 Slow food promotes the globalization of food production.
4 Terra Madre Day is a Latin American event.
5 Slow travel encourages you to visit popular attractions.
6 You can't embrace slow travel on a package holiday.
7 Slow goods tend not to be of high quality.
8 There are only three types of slow movement at present.

5 Find forms of these verbs in the article. Write the preposition that follows each verb.

1 grow _____ (line 2)
2 focus _____ (line 11)
3 connect _____ (line 26)
4 search _____ (line 29)
5 appeal _____ (line 38)
6 spread _____ (line 46)

6 Complete the sentences with forms of the verbs and prepositions from Exercise 5. Are any of the sentences true for you? Change the underlined words to make true sentences.

1 I enjoy it when the English class _____ grammar.
2 <u>Going vegetarian</u> has always _____ me, but I haven't tried it yet.
3 My initial interest in <u>foreign food</u> has _____ a real passion.
4 The thing I like about <u>learning languages</u> is that it helps you to _____ other people.
5 My friend's family is _____ the country. In my family, we live <u>near each other</u>.
6 I can spend hours online _____ <u>bargains</u>.

7 Work in pairs. List one benefit and one drawback for each of the three movements described in the article. Then compare your ideas with another pair. What do you think about the 'slow' philosophy?

VOCABULARY Quantities

8 Match the captions (1–14) with the pictures (a–n). Which items can you eat or drink?

1 a barrel of oil
2 a bowl of soup
3 a bunch of grapes
4 a carton of eggs
5 a container of goods
6 a crate of beer
7 a packet of biscuits
8 a pad of paper
9 a piece of cake
10 a plate of food
11 a slice of bread
12 a tank of petrol
13 a tin of paint
14 a tube of toothpaste

9 Read the clues and write words from Exercise 8.

1 You need some of these to make sandwiches: _____
2 A student writes on this in class: _____
3 A cup of coffee goes well with this as a morning or afternoon snack: _____
4 The price of this is often an indicator of the world economy: _____
5 Most people use this in the morning and at night: _____
6 If you have a car, you'll know how much this costs: _____
7 You could use a few of these if you're decorating your home: _____
8 Ships transport millions of these around the world every day: _____

Life in the SLOW LANE

Since its beginnings in 1986, the 'slow movement' has grown into a philosophy that people around the world have embraced. These days, there are few aspects of 21st century life that don't have a 'slow' alternative. The movement is a reaction against the idea that faster is always better. It suggests that every activity has its own speed: the one which gives the best quality results.

A The slow food movement started in Italy. It aimed to promote and protect local and traditional foods at a time when industrial food production and globalization were on the rise. Events and activities focus on building links between people, with food at the heart of everything. A typical example took place in Buenos Aires, Argentina one Saturday last December. People came together to visit an urban vegetable garden and then join in a cookery workshop on sustainable Latin American dishes. For each plate of food, bowl of soup or tasty snack which was prepared, all the ingredients came from the garden. This was one of 845 events around the world celebrating 'Terra Madre Day', December 10.

B For many travellers today, the whole idea is to get there as fast as you can. But not every trip is a business trip, when that would be a logical demand. Perhaps there's more enjoyment in finding out more about the communities you're travelling through? Slow travel is about connecting with local people and avoiding all the crowds at the 'must see' attractions that are listed in every guidebook. It's also about looking for the common things that unite us, rather than searching for exotic differences. You don't have to be a student on a gap year to be able to take this approach. Next time you're on a package holiday, don't join in the organized coach tour – buy a ticket and get on a local bus or train. Leave your camera in your hotel room and take the time to look and listen to the sights and sounds around you.

C If you're someone who likes to upgrade their phone each time a new model comes out, then the idea of slow goods might not appeal to you. Slow goods are things built to last a long time. The movement values goods that are made 'on-shore' rather than 'off-shore', by craftspeople rather than factory workers. Small amounts of the product are made, with the emphasis on quality not quantity. Such things may be more expensive, but they won't break down or fall apart within months.

And these are only three examples of a movement which, contrary to its name, is actually spreading around the world rather quickly.

---

a gap year (phrase) a year on ending secondary education when students travel or work before starting college

off-shore (adj) made in a different country from where a company sells its goods

on-shore (adj) made in the same country as where a company sells its goods

SPEAKING Making a difference

10 **21st CENTURY OUTCOMES**

Work in groups of four. Compare what you know about these four organizations.

- World Food Programme
- Greenpeace
- Save the Children
- International Federation of Red Cross and Red Crescent

11 Work in the same groups of four. Decide who is Student A, Student B, Student C and Student D. Read your information on page 164. Then discuss the questions.

1 How much impact have these groups had?
2 Which movement would you support or join?
3 What kind of movement would you start, if you could?

21st CENTURY OUTCOMES **ENVIRONMENTAL LITERACY** Analyse environmental issues and think about solutions

11.4 Come and join us

LISTENING Making enquiries

1. Do you belong to any clubs or societies or go to any classes or courses (apart from your English course)? Which ones?

2. 🎧 60 Listen to three conversations. Answer the questions.

   1. What is the enquiry about?
   2. Does the person get the information they want?

3. 🎧 60 Listen again. Look at the Useful language box and write F (face-to-face) and P (phone) next to the expressions from the conversations. Could these expressions be used in both situations or in only one?

4. Look at the other expressions in the Useful language box. Could they be used in both situations or in only one?

Pronunciation Linking with /r/

5a. 🎧 61 Listen to these words from the conversations in Exercise 2. Is the /r/ sound of the final letter *r* pronounced?

| after | for | your | member | hour | our |

5b. 🎧 62 Listen to the same words in connected speech. In each pair of phrases, notice how the /r/ sound is pronounced when the following word starts with a vowel. Repeat the phrases.

MAKING AND RESPONDING TO ENQUIRIES

Making enquiries

Is this the right place to find out about … ?
Have I got the right number for … ?
Do you deal with … ?
I was wondering if there are any places left on the … ?
Can you write the details/number/name down for me?
Could you send me that in an email, please?
I'd like to talk to the person who handles …
I'm calling/ringing to ask about …

Responding to enquiries

I'll get you the information.
I'm afraid I don't have that information to hand.
Let me check.
Just a second.
If you could hold on just one moment, please.
We've had a few cancellations.
Here are all the details.
Would you like the address of our website?

126

SPEAKING Finding out about a club

6 Work in small groups. Take turns to tell your partners about the club or class you mentioned in Exercise 1. Ask each other questions about it. Would you like to join?

WRITING Short emails

7 Read the four emails. Match the emails that are part of the same exchange. Complete the subject line with an appropriate subject. Which exchange do you think is less formal? Give reasons.

Writing skill Fixed expressions

8a Underline eleven fixed expressions in the emails. Then look at the forms which follow each expression. Add the expressions to these groups.

```
1  … + noun
   In reply to your
   _____     _____
   _____     _____

2  … + -ing
   I'm sorry for
   _____     _____
   _____     _____

3  … + verb clause
   I regret that
   _____     _____
   _____     _____
```

8b Complete the sentences with an appropriate expression from Exercise 8a.

1. _____ we cannot give you a refund on this occasion.
2. _____ answering my enquiry so quickly!
3. _____ causing all this confusion!
4. _____ hearing from you on this matter.
5. _____ the information you requested.
6. _____ to drop me a line if there's anything else I can do for you.
7. _____ you could attend to the matter as soon as possible.
8. _____ getting together with you soon!

9 `21st CENTURY OUTCOMES`

Write a short email to enquire about one of these topics. Use some of the expressions from Exercise 8.

- booking a room for a private function
- group discounts for weekend stays in a hotel
- place availability on a trekking holiday for small groups
- courier charges for sending packages overseas

10 Work in pairs. Exchange emails with your partner. Write a response to the email you receive.

TO: _____ FROM: _____
SUBJECT: _____

Dear Mr Hanif

Thank you for your email about our residential weekend. I'm pleased to say that there are still a few places available. You can fill out the form on our website and pay the deposit online. We look forward to meeting you next month.

Regards

TO: _____ FROM: _____
SUBJECT: _____

Dear Mrs Lea

I am writing with reference to your recent enquiry about the hall. I'm afraid that I am unable to confirm your booking. Our website didn't make it clear that the hall is not available on that date. Please accept my apologies for the mix up.

Yours sincerely

TO: _____ FROM: _____
SUBJECT: _____

Hi Andrea

Thanks for sending me the information about payment. I think you should have this by now, but don't hesitate to get in touch if there are any problems with it. Looking forward to seeing you there!

All the best

TO: _____ FROM: _____
SUBJECT: _____

Dear Mr Ross

I would like to book your Community hall for May 11. Please find attached the completed booking form. I would be grateful if you could confirm the booking at your earliest convenience.

Kind regards

`21st CENTURY OUTCOMES` SOCIAL AND CROSS-CULTURAL SKILLS Conduct yourself in a respectable, professional manner

12 Change

A monk at the Shaolin temple, China

TEDTALKS

MARGARET HEFFERNAN was born in the USA, grew up in the Netherlands and lives in the UK. She began her career at the BBC and later ran a professional organization for film and television producers in the USA. She has been the CEO (Chief Executive Officer) of several companies and is a professor of entrepreneurship, as well as a writer. One of her areas of interest is how organizations work. Surveys of European and American executives have shown that 85 per cent of them are afraid to discuss work-related issues.

Margaret Heffernan's idea worth spreading is that if we truly want the best results at work, we can't be afraid to challenge our colleagues and to dare to disagree with conventional wisdom.

BACKGROUND

1 You are going to watch an edited version of a TED Talk by Margaret Heffernan called *Dare to disagree*. Read the text about the speaker and the talk. Then work in pairs and discuss the questions.

1 Can you name any famous people who have (or had) a reputation for saying unexpected things? Who? What kinds of things do (or did) they say, and why?
2 Have you ever been in a situation where afterwards you regretted either saying something or saying nothing?
3 Many people find it difficult to tell other people that they disagree with them. Why do you think this is?

KEY WORDS

2 Read the sentences (1–6). The words in bold are used in the TED Talk. First guess the meaning of the words. Then match the words with their definitions (a–f).

1 When doctors understood the **epidemiology** of certain cancers, it helped them to find the causes.
2 Most cities have some areas where **affluent** people live and other areas where less well-off people live.
3 Scientists often use data to develop a **model** of how things work: for example, to predict weather patterns.
4 Sometimes a **whistle-blower** can lose their job as a result of the information they make public.
5 Not everyone who has different ideas is a **crank**.
6 It's not easy to **stand up to** people who have more power than you.

a a theory or idea
b the study of patterns and distribution of disease in a population
c someone who reveals or exposes a problem in an organization
d to confront or resist someone in a courageous way
e rich, wealthy
f someone who is considered odd or eccentric because of their opinions

AUTHENTIC LISTENING SKILLS
Grammatical chunks

You don't have to be able to hear and process everything that is said in order to understand a speaker's message. In spoken English, there are 'chunks' of grammatical language that are speeded up and unstressed by the speaker because they don't carry the key meaning. For example, in the sentence 'There are a quarter of a million doctors in the UK' the words *there are* would not be stressed when spoken. As a listener, you can learn to ignore these unstressed chunks and focus on the main content words.

3a 🎧 **63** Look at the Authentic listening skills box. Then listen to the first and second sentences from the TED Talk. Are the underlined chunks stressed or unstressed? Is the message clear without these chunks?

1 In Oxford <u>in the</u> 1950s, <u>there was a</u> fantastic doctor, <u>who was</u> very unusual, named Alice Stewart.
2 And Alice <u>was</u> unusual partly because, of course, <u>she was a</u> woman, <u>which was</u> pretty rare <u>in the</u> 1950s.

3b 🎧 **64** Read the third and fourth sentences. Underline the chunks you think will be unstressed. Then listen and check.

3 And she was brilliant, she was one of the, at the time, the youngest Fellow to be elected to the Royal College of Physicians.
4 She was unusual too because she continued to work after she got married, after she had kids, and even after she got divorced and was a single parent, she continued her medical work.

129

12.1 Dare to disagree

TED TALKS

1 ▶ 12.1 Watch the edited version of the TED Talk. Tick (✓) the areas that Margaret Heffernan mentions.

   a the work of Alice Stewart
   b investigating causes of cancer in children
   c successful working partnerships
   d having the courage to speak out in difficult situations
   e the importance of keeping some information private

2 ▶ 12.1 Watch the first part (0.00 –3.46) of the talk again. Are the sentences true (T) or false (F)?

   1 Alice Stewart chose a difficult area to do research in.
   2 When she analysed the results of her study, they were very confusing.
   3 Nobody at that time suspected that X-rays could be harmful.
   4 Alice Stewart's findings had an immediate effect on medical practices.

3 ▶ 12.1 Watch the second part (3.46–6.38) of the talk again. Choose the correct option to complete the sentences.

   1 Alice Stewart and George Kneale had very *different / similar* personalities.
   2 George Kneale tried to show that Alice Stewart's contentions were *correct / mistaken*.
   3 Margaret Heffernan suggests that it's good to work with people who *agree with / challenge* your ideas.
   4 Alice Stewart *enjoyed / didn't enjoy* conflict with other scientists.

▶ boiled sweets **BR ENG**
▶ hard candy **N AM ENG**

▶ coloured **BR ENG**
▶ colored **N AM ENG**

4 ▶ **12.1** Work in pairs. Watch the third part (6.38 to the end) of the talk again. Answer the questions.

1 Joe thought a medical device his company was developing could be harmful. What did the other people in his company think?
2 Joe worried about discussing his fears with his colleagues. What did he do eventually?
3 In the company, there was conflict and debate about the device. What happened in the end?
4 The University of Delft teaches students to stand up to authority. What does Margaret Heffernan think of this idea?
5 Margaret Heffernan says that we are afraid of the conflict that can come from questioning information. What is her opinion of this fear?

5 Work in small groups. Complete the sentences about Margaret Heffernan's message with four of these words. Then discuss to what extent you agree with her ideas.

| agree | change | disagree |
| leaders | together | understanding |

1 Being open is essential, but, by itself, openness doesn't lead to _____ .
2 Working _____ in 'constructive conflict' takes a lot of energy.
3 When one person speaks out about a problem, usually you find that other people _____ but hadn't wanted to say anything.
4 People who have courage to speak out can be regarded as _____ by their colleagues.

VOCABULARY IN CONTEXT

6 ▶ **12.2** Watch the clips from the TED Talk. Choose the correct meaning of the words.

7 Work in pairs. Complete the sentences in your own words.

1 I remember the first time I had a shot at … . It was easier than I expected.
2 I once lost my … and it was like looking for a needle in a haystack because …
3 I find those TV quiz shows where individuals go head-to-head very …

CRITICAL THINKING Relevant background information

8 Work in pairs. Margaret Heffernan gave a lot of background detail about Alice Stewart and an executive named Joe. Decide why the following background information was relevant to her main message. Use the words in brackets.

1 Alice Stewart's personal life (unconventional)
2 her professional achievements (exceptional)
3 her collaboration with George Kneale (confident)
4 Joe's feelings about his job (afraid)
5 his decision to speak out (courageous)

▶ organization, organisation **BR ENG**
▶ organization **N AM ENG**

9 Work in pairs. Read these comments* about the TED Talk. Discuss how the background information about Alice and Joe added to the viewers' understanding of the talk.

Viewers' comments

S Smith 87 – I was fascinated by Alice Stewart's story. It makes her achievements even more impressive when you know about her personal story.

R RalphG – Large organizations can be so intimidating! I know just how Joe felt. Nobody wants to speak out and rock the boat.

*The comments were created for this activity.

PRESENTATION SKILLS Using pauses

TIPS

Using pauses in your talk is an effective way of emphasizing your main points.

- Pause when you want to draw the audience's attention to your next words.
- Pause at the end of a point to give the audience time to process what you have said.
- Leave longer pauses to allow the audience to reflect and to relate your ideas to their own experiences.

10 ▶ **12.3** Look at the Presentation tips box. Then watch the clips from the TED Talk and use lines to show where Margaret Heffernan pauses. The first line has been added for you.

1 By a rate of two to one, | the children who had died had had mothers who had been X-rayed when pregnant.
2 In fact, she need not have hurried. It was fully 25 years before the British and medical – British and American medical establishments abandoned the practice of X-raying pregnant women.

11 Work in pairs. Think of a surprising news item you have read or heard about recently. Make brief notes on the background to the story and the surprising facts. Practise telling the story with pauses in different places to decide what is most effective.

12 Work with a new partner. Tell each other your stories. Does the story surprise you too? Have you heard about the story before?

12.2 Moments of change

BIG DATA

Big data is data that is more complex than data collected using traditional tools. It can reveal trends and patterns that are difficult to spot.

SOURCES
BIG DATA COMES FROM VARIOUS SOURCES

- PEOPLE INTERACTING ONLINE
- PEOPLE SENDING INFORMATION TO MACHINES
- MACHINES COLLECTING INFORMATION

VOLUME
THE VOLUME OF BIG DATA IS MASSIVE

- 29 MILLION EMAILS EVERY SECOND
- 400 MILLION TWEETS EVERY DAY
- 3 BILLION PEOPLE ONLINE
- MORE THAN 40 EXABYTES OF DATA COLLECTED DAILY
(1 EXABYTE = 1 BILLION GIGABYTES)

CHALLENGES
THE CHALLENGES OF BIG DATA

MANAGEMENT
INTERPRETATION
SOURCES
PROCESSING
PRIVACY
STORAGE
SPEED
COMPLEXITY

GRAMMAR Third conditional

1. Work in pairs. Compare your ideas on possible answers to the questions. Then look at the infographic and check your answers.
   1. What is 'big data'?
   2. Where do we get 'big data' from?
   3. How many digital communications are sent globally each day?

2. 🎧 **65** Listen to part of a radio programme about big data. Complete the sentences with one or two words.
   1. Businesses use big data to _____ themselves more efficiently.
   2. Digital technology keeps track of all kinds of _____ behaviour in real time.
   3. One toothpaste company launched a new _____ that was a disaster.
   4. In Australia, _____ can use big data to avoid accident blackspots.

3. Look at the sentences in the Grammar box. Choose the correct option to complete the rules (1–4).

THIRD CONDITIONAL

If they'd known more about the market, they wouldn't have made that particular product line.

Bird flu would have affected many more people if the health authorities hadn't spotted certain trends.

If they'd had access to big data, would they have marketed the product better?

1. We use the third conditional to refer to *present / past* events.
2. Third conditional sentences refer to events that *happened / didn't happen*.
3. The condition is expressed by *if + past perfect / past simple*.
4. The result is expressed by *would + have + past participle / would + infinitive without to*.

Check your answers on page 162 and do Exercises 1–2.

132

4 Read a story that also involved big numbers. Complete the sentences using the information from the story.

> **The important results of a large-scale study**
> Richard Doll (1912–2005) was a British physiologist who proved the link between smoking and lung cancer. He originally chose to study medicine after he failed his mathematics exams. Doll asked all of the 60,000 doctors registered in the UK to take part in his study, and two thirds agreed. He himself was a smoker, but when he found a link between tobacco and lung cancer, he gave up smoking. At one time, there was some controversy about Doll's working relationship with tobacco companies, but he said he had to work with them because he needed access to their data.

1 If Doll had passed his mathematics exams, he _____ (study)
2 Doll's research wouldn't have been significant if the number of doctors _____ (smaller)
3 If Doll hadn't shown that smoking causes lung cancer, he _____ (smoking)
4 Doll wouldn't have worked with tobacco companies if he _____ (data)

5 Read this story. Then write sentences using the third conditional.

> **The amazing growth of an internet company**
> The social network Facebook was two years old in 2006. The company Yahoo! offered one billion dollars to buy the company even though it wasn't making a profit. However, Mark Zuckerberg said he enjoyed running Facebook. With any money he received, he would just start up a new network. When Facebook eventually became a public company in 2012, it was valued at $104 billion.

1 Yahoo! / buy Facebook / pay one billion dollars
2 Zuckerberg / be a millionaire / sell Facebook in 2006
3 Zuckerberg / sell Facebook in 2006 / start another social networking site
4 Zuckerberg / not make billions of dollars / not wait to sell public shares

GRAMMAR Mixed conditional sentences

6 Read the sentences in the Grammar box. Answer the questions (1–4).

MIXED CONDITIONAL SENTENCES

Mixed third + second conditional

If cyclists **hadn't downloaded** the app, they **wouldn't be able** to use the information.

Mixed second + third conditional

If traditional data **gave** enough information, big data **wouldn't have become** such an important marketing tool.

1 Which tenses are used in each sentence?
2 In each pattern, which tense is in the *if*-clause?
3 Which pattern refers to a past condition with a present result?
4 Which pattern refers to a present condition with a past result?

Check your answers on page 162 and do Exercises 3–4.

7 Work in pairs. Write mixed conditional sentences based on the information in these situations. Are any of the sentences true for you?

1 Social networks are really popular, so I managed to track down my old friends. (mixed second + third pattern)
2 I bought a smartphone and now I can send instant photos to my friends. (mixed third + second)
3 There are price comparison sites online. I used one and saved money on my insurance. (mixed second + third pattern)
4 I signed up to an online bookstore and now I get junk mail from them every day. (mixed third + second pattern)

SPEAKING What if … ?

8 **21st CENTURY OUTCOMES**

Work in groups of three. Decide who is Student A, Student B and Student C. Read your information on page 164 about events from the past. Then imagine and discuss the situation if these things hadn't happened.

1991   Tim Berners-Lee successfully tested what would become the World Wide Web.

If the test had failed, someone would have invented something similar.

If he hadn't invented the Web, we wouldn't know so much about the world.

9 Work in the same groups. Think of key events in these areas and discuss how the world might be different now.

| music | technology | sport |
| economics | science | entertainment |

INFORMATION LITERACY Evaluate information critically and competently

12.3 The benefit of hindsight

READING A letter to my younger self

1 Work in pairs. What kinds of personal qualities do you think would help someone to succeed in these professions?

| actor | athlete | human rights campaigner |
| primatologist | writer | |

2 Read the extracts from the letters. Compare your ideas from Exercise 1 with what the people say about themselves.

3 Read the extracts again. Write the name of the person.

1 He/She wanted to achieve more than previous generations of his/her family. _____
2 He/She describes his/her younger self as anxious and not very sporty. _____
3 He/She thinks he/she could have interacted with people differently. _____
4 He/She doesn't admire the way he/she used to communicate. _____
5 He/She was helped to overcome doubts about his/her abilities by a family member. _____

4 Look at how the expressions (1–8) are used in the extracts. Match these expressions with the expressions that have similar meanings (a–h).

1 back then (line 9)
2 I didn't have a degree (lines 14–15)
3 threw myself into everything (line 27)
4 to the full (line 30)
5 My motto […] is (line 34)
6 Just get on with it (line 46)
7 being […] into (horror movies) (lines 48–49)
8 tend to (line 57)

a are likely to
b I hadn't been to university
c in the past
d liking and enjoying
e my belief can be summed up as
f to the maximum
g started doing something without thinking too much about it
h to join in enthusiastically

5 Work in pairs. Tell your partner three things about what you were like when you were 16. Then discuss the questions.

1 Have you described positive or negative aspects of your younger self?
2 To what extent have those aspects changed?
3 What would you say to your 16-year-old self?

VOCABULARY Personality adjectives (2)

6 Look at the groups of adjectives. Choose the odd one out in each group.

1 argumentative   co-operative   easygoing   pleasant
2 arrogant   insecure   modest   shy
3 bold   brave   courageous   terrified
4 cold   friendly   outgoing   sociable
5 anxious   assertive   independent   self-confident
6 irresponsible   mad   sensible   wild

7 Choose the correct option to complete the sentences. Then say if any of the sentences are true for you.

1 I think you have to be *brave / sensible* to speak on a stage in front of hundreds of people.
2 If I'd been more *irresponsible / outgoing* at school, I would have made friends more easily.
3 I didn't get on with my brother-in-law for years. He was so *argumentative / shy* and I just hate conflict. But he's relaxed since he got older.
4 I knew someone who was brilliant, but she was so *arrogant / cold* about how much better she was than the rest of us.
5 Some of my friends were a bit *easygoing / wild* in their youth, but they never broke any laws.
6 Lots of people feel *anxious / co-operative* when they start a new job, until they get used to how things work.

SPEAKING Never again!

8 **21st CENTURY OUTCOMES**

Work in pairs. Read this story. How would you describe the person's friend?

'A few years ago, when I had very little money, a friend offered to give me a lift to visit my parents. I knew he was a bit irresponsible, but he was my friend. Well, we broke down on the way and it turned out it wasn't actually his car! So we had no insurance or anything. If I'd known, I would have got the bus instead.'

9 Tell your partner about experiences you have had with two people who you used to know, or still know. Describe the people and say if you think they had a positive or a negative influence on you. Would you repeat the experience today?

A LETTER to my younger self

There are people who say you should never look back, while others point out that it can be a positive thing to assess how much you may have changed over the years. We asked some well-known people what they would like to have known when they were 16. This is what they said.

JANE GOODALL
primatologist, the world's leading expert on chimpanzees

If I had been told back then I would be living the kind of life I'm living now, I would have given up. The idea of speaking to audiences would have utterly terrified me. That wasn't the life I wanted to live. When I began my work studying primates, I knew I was different from everyone else in the field. I was female and I didn't have a degree and I had my own ideas about animals. […] But my mother was amazing. She just said, if you really want something worthwhile, never give up.

ROGER BANNISTER
first athlete to run a mile in under four minutes, neurologist

At 16, I was focused on getting to Oxford. No member of my family had studied there. I was impatient to leave school for reasons I'm not sure of now, but I was keen to get on with my medical career. I'd tell my younger self he could and should learn more from his parents. I was rather independent then, though my parents did encourage me. I was always very active and involved in things. I threw myself into everything when I was at school, then when I was at university – president of the sporting club and the students' union. I always felt I must exploit the opportunities my parents hadn't enjoyed to the full.

SHAMI CHAKRABARTI
director of the human rights organization Liberty

If I met my younger self now, I think I'd find her quite precocious, quite argumentative. My motto these days is: everyone's equal, no one's superior. […] And I'd tell that to my younger self – come on, you can be confident without being arrogant. If I didn't work for Liberty now, I'd be sitting in the pub every night complaining about threats to our rights.

PETER CAPALDI
Scottish actor

At his best, I would like the 16-year-old Peter. […] He could be a bit braver. He could be a little bit wilder and not do any harm. He could try seeing more of the world. I'd tell my younger self: worrying that you can't do it is a waste of time. […] Just get on with it. I'd tell him to celebrate being different. […] When I was 16, geeks hadn't been invented, so being tall and skinny, into horror movies and sci-fi, and unable to play football simply made me the go-to guy for the sociopaths.

MEERA SYAL
British author and actor

I'd tell my younger self that social networking is more important than she thinks. I should have been savvier when I was younger. I made friends with the make-up girl and not the director. But the world really does work along tribal lines. People tend to employ their own tribe. […] That occasionally disappoints me, after the body of work I've done.

---

geek (n) someone who is especially knowledgeable about a subject or doesn't fit in socially
go-to guy (n) someone who people always look for in a certain situation
precocious (adj) very able or clever for one's age
primatologist (n) a scientist who studies primates (apes, monkeys, etc.)
savvier (adj) wiser, smarter
sociopath (n) someone who is completely unwilling or unable to behave in a way that is acceptable to society

21st CENTURY OUTCOMES | **INITIATIVE AND SELF-DIRECTION** Reflect critically on past experiences

12.4 Could I have a quick word?

LISTENING Managing change

1 🎧 66 Listen to three conversations in which one person wants the other person to change something they do. Write the number of the conversation.

where?
at college _____
at home _____
at work _____

what?
work later _____
do more work _____
take on some extra tasks _____

response?
busy all day _____
evening commitments _____
moving house _____

2 🎧 66 Listen to the conversations again. Then work in pairs and discuss these questions.

1 What suggestion does the second person make in each case?
2 Do you think the suggestions are reasonable in the circumstances?
3 What would your response to each suggestion be?

Pronunciation Tone and meaning

3a 🎧 67 Meaning is expressed not only by your words but also by your stress and intonation. Listen to sentences that use some of the expressions in the Useful language box. For each sentence, decide if the speaker sounds assertive (AS), aggressive (AG) or ineffective (I).

1 _____   4 _____
2 _____   5 _____
3 _____   6 _____

3b 🎧 67 Listen again and repeat the assertive sentences.

BEING ASSERTIVE

Bringing up a difficult topic

I notice that …
I want to talk about …
We need to talk about …
If you remember, …

Responding to a suggestion you don't like

I appreciate that …
I intend to …
I should explain that …
I understand that …
I'm doing my best to …

Making alternative suggestions

I was hoping …
I wonder if you could … ?
Perhaps we could … ?

SPEAKING Tricky situations

4 **21st CENTURY OUTCOMES**

Work in small groups. Discuss what you could say in these situations in order to get the change you want. Try to use all of the expressions in the Useful language box.

- You want a friend to stop phoning you so late at night.
- You don't have as much money as your friends, so you want to stop going to such expensive places.
- You want your boss to pay you more money.
- You want your teacher to spend more time on grammar activities.

WRITING Letter of complaint

5 Read the email to a car hire company and answer the questions.

1. What four problems does the customer complain about?
2. What four things does the customer think should have happened?
3. What does the customer expect the company to do now?

6 Look at the features of a formal communication (a–f). Underline and label the parts of the email that match the features.

a clear subject line
b formal opening
c formal closing
d clear introductory sentence
e clear factual statement of complaint
f clear statement of action expected

Writing skill Past modals (2)

7a Underline the verbs in these sentences from the email. Which sentences are criticisms, and which refer to possible actions?

> 1 This could have left me without a car …
> 2 Your employee could have provided me with a larger car …
> 3 I believe you should have informed customers with existing bookings about these changes.
> 4 I also feel the refund should have been made into my account immediately.
> 5 Equally, your employee could have handled the matter in a more professional manner.
>
> See page 162 for more information about past modals, and do Exercises 6-7.

7b Complete the customer's comments (1–4) with *should*, *shouldn't*, *could* and *must*. Then match the comments with the functions (a–d).

1. I _____ have looked at the website again, but unfortunately I didn't.
2. The staff member _____ have been so unhelpful.
3. They _____ have known that not contacting customers would cause problems – it's obvious!
4. I _____ have cancelled my booking if I'd known about the changes.

a a criticism
b a deduction
c a possibility
d a regret

FROM: HP_Jones@Jones.co.uk
TO: Customer Service@OntheRoadCars.com
SUBJECT: Complaint: Car Hire Gatwick Airport ref 4159763

Dear Sir / Madam

I am writing to draw your attention to the poor service at the Gatwick Airport office of your company.

In February of this year, I booked a car online for the dates April 11–15, booking reference 4159763. On arriving to pick up the vehicle, I was informed that the credit card used to pre-pay the car hire was not acceptable and I had to provide a different card. This could have left me without a car, but fortunately, I had another card. The staff member I dealt with, Paul, was particularly unhelpful and unable to explain the reasons why he could not accept the original card. It then transpired that there were no cars available in the category I had requested and I was offered a smaller car. This was not adequate for my needs. Your employee could have provided me with a larger car as there was one available, yet he said this was not company policy. It is now ten days since I returned the car and I still have not received the refund which is due for the lower category car.

I now notice that the terms and conditions on your website changed in March. I believe you should have informed customers with existing bookings about these changes. I also feel the refund should have been made into my account immediately. Equally, your employee could have handled the matter in a more professional manner: at no time did he offer an apology.

I would appreciate your co-operation in processing my refund on receipt of this letter and look forward to a clarification of your policy re credit cards and car categories.

Yours faithfully

H P Jones

---

8 Read the situation and write a complaint to the company following the structure of the email in Exercise 5. Use at least one past modal form.

> You were a customer of the same car hire company. You returned the car with a half-full tank of petrol. You now find you have been charged a fee of £100 'refilling charge' as well as the price of the petrol. You were not informed of this policy when you picked up the car.

9 Work in pairs. Exchange letters with your partner. Check that their complaint and the action expected is clear.

21st CENTURY OUTCOMES FLEXIBILITY AND ADAPTABILITY Deal assertively with setbacks and criticism

Review 6 | UNITS 11 AND 12

GiveMeTap

A Simple ideas work best. And GiveMeTap's idea is very simple. Forget bottled water: buy a stainless steel bottle, an app on your phone tells you the places near you that will fill it with free water, and the money from the bottle funds clean-water projects in Africa.

B GiveMeTap gives you a great way to promote your brand while supporting a much-needed charity. You can buy the GiveMeTap bottles with your company's logo and name on them, making ideal gifts for your customers and your employees too. Your company will reduce its plastic waste in your offices and also help to cut down on the amount of plastic that's thrown away. So you're helping your company, the planet and our charity too.

C With GiveMeTap, you get a tap-water refill from participating cafes and shops in the UK, and communities in Ghana, Namibia and Malawi get clean drinking water. Clean water is one of the most effective ways of saving lives. According to UNICEF, illnesses from dirty water are a leading cause of death for children under the age of five, with as many as 1,000 children dying every day around the world.

D GiveMeTap's water pumps and boreholes give access to clean water for more than 6,000 people. It also gives people time: in some areas, women and children spend an average of three hours each day just walking to and from a water source. With water on tap, women have more time to earn money for their families and girls have time to attend school. It's not just about the water.

E Edwin Broni-Mensah is a young man who values solving problems which help change people's lives and environment. While doing a PhD in mathematical finance at the UK University of Manchester, he had already helped set up social enterprises. Edwin had experience of clean-water problems from talking to his extended family in Ghana. GiveMeTap was the third of his business ideas to be successful.

READING

1 Read about GiveMeTap. Match the headings (1–5) with the paragraphs (A–E).

1 A man with a mission
2 Boost your business
3 Change the world
4 Pure and simple
5 Save a life

2 Read the article again. Complete the sentences with one or two words from the text.

1 GiveMeTap wants people to buy reusable water bottles instead of bottled _____.
2 Companies can use GiveMeTap to publicize their _____.
3 One of the biggest killers of young children is _____.
4 Easy access to clean water helps many women to _____.
5 Edwin Broni-Mensah had both the academic skills and the personal _____ to help him start GiveMeTap.

GRAMMAR

3 Complete eight of the sentences about GiveMeTap with these articles and quantifiers. There is no article in one of the sentences.

a few	all	an	each
little	no	the	the

1 A GiveMeTap bottle weighs less than _____ apple.
2 You can help people access clean water with very _____ effort.
3 _____ bottle that is bought funds five years of clean water for one person.
4 _____ bottles come in two sizes: 500 ml and 600 ml.
5 Not all plastic bottles are the same – _____ of them contain a dangerous chemical called BPA.
6 There are _____ toxic chemicals in the GiveMeTap bottles.
7 Using these bottles protects _____ environment from plastic waste.
8 There are already _____ shops outside the big cities which have joined in.
9 _____ the participating shops and cafes are listed on the app.

4 Complete the third conditional and mixed conditional sentences.

1 Edwin Broni-Mensah _____ (not / know) about the water problem if he _____ _____ (not / talk) to his parents about it. (third)
2 How many children _____ (die) if GiveMeTap _____ (not / install) water pumps in their villages? (third)
3 If some communities _____ (not / build) water pumps, they _____ (have to) travel to get water in the dry season. (mixed)
4 If bottled water _____ (not / be) so popular, how much less plastic waste _____ we _____ (create)? (mixed)

VOCABULARY

5 Complete the questions with the correct noun. The first letter is given. Then ask your partner the questions.

1 How many s_____ of bread do you need to make a sandwich?
2 Has the price of a b_____ of oil gone down or up recently?
3 How often do you buy a c_____ of eggs?
4 Do you know how many c_____ of goods are transported around the world every week?
5 What do you drink with a p_____ of cake?
6 How much does a full t_____ of petrol for your car cost (if you have one)?
7 Do you prefer to write on a plain, lined or squared p_____ of paper?
8 Where would you go to buy a t_____ of paint?

6 Choose the correct options to complete the text.

Young people who try to change the world tend to have some things in common. Perhaps their key characteristic is that they are ¹ *arrogant / self-confident* and believe that their ideas are possible. Even the best ideas attract criticism and young activists need to be ² *argumentative / assertive* when they meet resistance. Some of the most successful ideas have come from people who were considered a bit ³ *mad / sociable* initially. When you have an idea to promote, it helps to be ⁴ *anxious / outgoing* rather than ⁵ *independent / shy*. The most successful people are ⁶ *co-operative / sensible* with others and recognize that partnerships are necessary.

DISCUSSION

7 Work in small groups. Discuss the questions.

1 What do you do in your daily life to cut down your use of resources or reduce your impact on the environment?
2 Have you ever done anything to support projects like GiveMeTap? What?
3 Do you think change is more effective when it is on a small or a large scale? Why?

SPEAKING

8 Read the enquiries to a charity, Refugee Aid. Complete the conversations using the prompts.

A: Good morning, Refugee Aid.
B: ¹ *I / ring / ask* about sponsorship activities.
A: OK, well the best way to find out is probably online. ² *like / address / website?*
B: Oh, yes, thanks. That sounds good.

C: Hello there. How can I help you?
D: ³ *like / talk / person / handles* press and media, please.
C: Of course. ⁴ *Let / check* if they're in the office today. ⁵ *Just / second.*
D: Thanks. I'll just take a seat while I wait.

E: Good afternoon, Refugee Aid. Sandra speaking.
F: Hi. ⁶ *Have / right number* for changing the amount of my bank donation?
E: Yes. ⁷ *If / hold on / moment,* please. I'll put you through to the right department.
F: OK, thanks.

G: Good morning.
H: ⁸ *this / right place / find out* about becoming a volunteer with your organization?
G: Yes. What would you like to know?
H: Well, I'm interested in local activities, really.
G: That's great. ⁹ *Here / all / details*. Have a read through this and then I'd be happy to answer any questions you have.

WRITING

9 Read the email and write a response. Include this information:

- not available second weekend
- previous weekend also available
- double or individual rooms?
- half or full board?

FROM: Rosa Greer@trekandfund.com
TO: Leila Brooks
SUBJECT: Conference booking

Dear Ms Brooks

I would like to make a reservation for your hotel's conference facilities for either the weekend of 6th–7th or 13–14th July. I would be grateful if you could email me your rates for a group of 25–30 people with two overnight stays (Friday 5th or 12th and Saturday 6th or 13th).

Regards

Rosa Greer

10 Work in pairs. Exchange emails with your partner. Did you include all the information?

Grammar summary | UNIT 1

PRESENT TENSES: ACTIVE AND PASSIVE

Present simple: active

We use the present simple to talk about:

- routines and habits
  My friend **checks** her emails every hour.
  My sister **doesn't phone** me – she only **sends** texts.
  Do you **update** your online profile regularly?

- facts and general truths
  Most UK adults **connect** to the Internet via broadband.
  Most people under 25 **don't remember** life before social media.
  Does water **damage** a mobile phone?

- permanent or long-term situations
  My brother **lives** at the coast.
  My parents **don't have** a TV.
  Do you **wear** glasses?

We often use adverbs and expressions of frequency (*always, usually, often, every morning, at the weekend*, etc.) with the present simple to talk about how often we do something. Adverbs of frequency usually come before the main verb. When the verb is negative or in the question form, the adverb comes between the auxiliary verb and the main verb. When the verb is *be*, the adverb comes after the verb.
  My wife is Italian and we **often** speak Italian at home. (not *we speak often*)
  My wife is Italian, but we don't **usually** speak Italian at home. (not *we usually don't*)
  Do you **usually** speak Italian at home?
  My wife is a singer and she's **often** away from home on tour. (not *she often is*)

We can use some adverbs of frequency (*usually, often, sometimes*) at the beginning of a sentence for emphasis.
  Sometimes, we speak Italian at home.

Other expressions of frequency usually come at the beginning or at the end of a sentence. We use a comma after the expression at the start of the sentence.
  We start work at eight **every morning**.
  Every morning, we start work at eight.

Present continuous: active

We use the present continuous to talk about:

- temporary situations
  I**'m living** with my parents until I find a new flat.
  I**'m not spending** any money on clothes this month.
  Is your brother **working** at the pool this summer?

- activities in progress at the time of speaking
  My boss **is doing** a Skype interview with the BBC.
  They**'re not printing** anything right now, so you can use the printer.
  Are you **using** your computer at the moment?

- trends and changing habits
  Lots of people **are watching** television shows online instead of on TV now.
  People **aren't eating** as much meat as they did before.
  Are part-time jobs **becoming** more popular?

We often use time expressions with the present continuous: *at the moment, this week*, etc.
  Are you working from home **today**?
  A lot of people are studying Chinese **nowadays**.

▶ Exercise 1

Present simple: passive

Affirmative and negative
  This model of tablet **is** (**not**) **sold** online.
  Camera phones **are** (**not**) **used** to take a lot of photos.

Questions and short answers

Is this model of tablet **sold** online?	Yes, it **is**. No, it **isn't**.
Are camera phones **used** to take a lot of photos?	Yes, they **are**. No, they **aren't**.

We form the present simple passive with the present simple of *be* (*am / is / are*) + past participle of the main verb.

Present continuous: passive

Affirmative and negative
  The email **is** (**not**) **being sent** to all users.
  The videos **are** (**not**) **being filmed** in HD.

Questions and short answers

Is the email **being sent** to all users?	Yes, it **is**. No, it **isn't**.
Are the videos **being filmed** in HD?	Yes, they **are**. No, they **aren't**.

We form the present continuous passive with the present continuous of *be* + past participle of the main verb.

by + agent

We use the passive to focus on the action or object of the action, rather than the person who does the action. The person may be obvious, unknown or not relevant. We can use *by* to specify who or what does the action:
  active: *People are downloading films illegally.*
  passive: *Films* **are being downloaded** *illegally.*
  Films are being downloaded illegally **by people** *in almost every country in the world.*
  Thousands of computers are damaged **by viruses** *every week.*

▶ Exercises 2–6

EXERCISES

1 Complete the conversation with the present simple active and present continuous active form of the verbs.

A: ¹_____ you _____ (watch) anything good on TV at the moment?
B: There's a new detective series on Monday nights, but I ²_____ (not / finish) work until late, so my flatmate ³_____ (record) it for me.
A: Oh yeah, the Danish one about the politician? I ⁴_____ (not / want) to start watching it yet because I ⁵_____ (read) the book. I'm going to watch it online later.
B: Well, don't wait too long. I think each episode only ⁶_____ (stay) online for a week or two.
A: I'm surprised – all the Scandinavian stuff ⁷_____ (get) really popular these days.
B: I know. They ⁸_____ (make) really good programmes. It's good to see something different too.

2 Complete the newspaper article with the present simple passive and present continuous passive form of the verbs.

Cyber-attacks on the increase
Stories of 'cyber-attacks' ¹_____ (report) in the media on a regular basis, but it seems very difficult to discover who is responsible for the attacks. The procedure follows a pattern: the computer records of a large organization ²_____ (hack), files ³_____ (steal) and then some of the information ⁴_____ (post) online. In a growing new trend, private details ⁵_____ (expose) in public, causing embarrassment for the individual concerned. In one recent case where the attacks are continuing, two theories ⁶_____ (investigate). The first is that the hacker is a member of a hacking group; the second is that the cyber-attacks ⁷_____ (carry out) by an ex-employee. The only certainty is that the organization involved needs to review its computer security before more damage ⁸_____ (do).

3 Rewrite the sentences in the active or passive form.

1 They make hundreds of films every year.
_____
2 Is their website updated weekly?
_____
3 In the cinema, films aren't interrupted to show adverts.
_____
4 Someone is downloading a lot of films illegally.
_____
5 They aren't releasing the new 'superhero' film until next week.
_____
6 A popular 'superhero' comic is being rewritten for the cinema.
_____

4 Choose the correct option to complete the sentences.

1 A lot of famous people *don't enjoy / aren't enjoyed* being celebrities.
2 How many celebrities *change / are changed* their original names?
3 Two of my favourite actors *are appearing / are being appeared* on the same show.
4 *Does the video channel check / Is the video channel checked* by anyone?
5 Videos over ten minutes long *don't accept / aren't accepted* on this site.
6 On many websites, personal details *keep / are kept* private.
7 Identity documents *need / are needed* for international travel.
8 Identity theft means somebody else *is using / is being used* your personal details.

5 Complete the text with the verbs. There is one extra verb.

are attracted	is being designed	are started
are trying	aren't required	come up with
don't have	don't make	need

One of the interesting things about internet companies is that they ¹_____ by young people. Often these people ²_____ any business experience. However, they ³_____ lots of creative ideas. An advantage of internet companies is that big investments ⁴_____. This could be why so many young people ⁵_____ to the idea. All they ⁶_____ is a computer, an internet connection and an idea. However, quite a lot of these companies ⁷_____ any money. For every internet millionaire, there are thousands of people who ⁸_____ to find success.

6 Correct the mistake in each sentence.

1 Hi, my name's Monica and I'm living in London. I was born there.
2 How much do you paid in your job?
3 What's the matter? What happens?
4 I'm a teacher and I'm work in a primary school.
5 In my family, we don't watch usually much TV.
6 On my English course, we assess once a term.

Grammar summary | UNIT 2

FUTURE FORMS AND USES

will + infinitive, going to + infinitive

We use both *will* and *going to* to talk about:
- predictions and beliefs about future events or situations. The meaning is very similar and when the prediction is based on the same information, either form can be used. The choice often depends on the speaker's personal preference. It doesn't depend on how sure the speaker is about the prediction.
  *After everything the teacher has said, I think the exam **will be** easy.*
  *After everything the teacher has said, I think the exam **is going to be** easy.*

We also use *will* to talk about:
- a decision or an offer we think of at the time we're speaking
  *I'm hungry – I think I'**ll make** some pasta.*
  *'I can't fill in this form.'   'I'**ll help you** – let me have a look.'*

We also use *going to* to talk about:
- a decision we have already taken about a plan or an intention
  *My colleague is worried about his presentation, so I'**m going to help** him with it tomorrow.*
  *The restaurant is fully booked, so we'**re going to invite** everyone to our house for lunch instead.*
- a prediction about an event which is based on evidence at the moment of speaking
  *Usain Bolt is ahead of everyone else. He'**s going to win** the race.*

We don't use *will* or *going to* after the adverbs of future time *when, until,* etc. We use the present simple even though the action is in the future.
  ***When** I **get** home, I'll call you.*

will be + -ing (future continuous)

Affirmative	Negative
I/You/He/She/It/We/They'**ll be waiting**.	I I/You/He/She/It/We/They **won't be waiting**.

Question	Short answer
Will I/you/ he/she/it/we/they **be waiting**?	Yes, I/you/he/she/it/we/they **will**. No, I/you/he/she/it/we/they **won't**.

We use the future continuous to talk about:
- an activity that will be in progress at a stated time in the future
  *Today's my last day at work. This time next week, I'**ll be driving** across Europe.*
- a prediction about an activity that will be in progress at a time in the future
  *In twenty years' time, they **won't be making** cars that run on petrol.*

We often use time expressions with the future continuous to say when the activity will be in progress or the point when it will stop.
  ***This time tomorrow**, you'll be doing your driving test.*
  *My friend has failed his test five times. He'll be learning to drive **until** he's an old man!*

▶ Exercise 1

will have + past participle (future perfect)

Affirmative	Negative
I/You/He/She/It/We/They'**ll have arrived**.	I/You/He/She/It/We/They **won't have arrived**.

Question	Short answer
Will I/you/he/she/it/we/they **have arrived**?	Yes, I/you/he/she/it/we/they **will**. No, I/you/he/she/it/we/they **won't**.

We use the future perfect to talk about:
- actions that will be completed before a stated time in the future
  *According to the schedule, the interview team **will have chosen** a candidate by the end of the week.*
- predictions about actions completed before a stated time in the future
  *It's only Wednesday – the manager **won't have decided** anything yet.*

▶ Exercises 2–6

142

EXERCISES

1 Complete the conversation with the future continuous form of the verbs.

A: Is everything ready for tomorrow?
B: Yes, it is. This time tomorrow we ¹_____ (open) the doors of our new gallery!
A: ²_____ people _____ (wait) outside when we open? What do you think?
B: I hope so! We've done so much publicity! Now remember, you ³_____ (stand) at the door to give everyone a gift bag.
A: Yes, I know. What about the local press? What time ⁴_____ they _____ (get) here?
B: About half an hour after we open. But I ⁵_____ (not / do) the interview until later on. I need to spend time with the artists first.
A: And the artists ⁶_____ (talk) to people about their work until about nine o'clock, I imagine. I'm really looking forward to it!

2 Complete the sentences with the future perfect form of the verbs.

1 I think we _____ (sell) at least one painting before nine o'clock.
2 By the end of the week, everyone _____ (hear) our news.
3 _____ the new business _____ (make) a profit by the end of its first year?
4 The deadline is Friday, but they _____ (not / do) all the work – it's impossible.
5 How many people _____ we _____ (interview) by the end of the day?
6 I need to talk to Samira, but her meeting _____ (not / finish) yet.

3 Choose the correct option to complete the sentences.

1 A: What *will happen / will be happening* when all the oil runs out?
2 B: I'm sure someone *will invent / will have invented* new sources of energy by then.
3 A: *Will the exam have / Will the exam be having* multiple-choice questions?
4 B: I think *they'll have discussed / they'll be discussing* that tomorrow.
5 A: The manager *will come / will be coming* to the office this afternoon.
6 B: Do you think *she'll have stayed / she'll be staying* long?
7 A: What job *will you do / will you be doing* this time next year?
8 A: I don't think *I'll find / I'll have found* anything by then!

4 Match the two parts to make logical sentences.

1 My brother says he isn't going to have
2 Many people believe that they will achieve
3 The office manager says he'll be hiring
4 These sales figures mean that the new model isn't going to do
5 We're confident that the new offices will be
6 I've seen lots of flats and I'm sure I'll have found
7 Lots of people think they'll be
8 Don't worry! I'm sure that

a some new staff next month.
b everything is going to be OK.
c happier with more money.
d any children before he's 30.
e well this year.
f their personal goals.
g perfect for our business.
h a new place by next week.

5 Complete the text with the verbs. There is one extra verb.

are going to change	is going to cause	is going to enjoy
will affect	will be working	will combine
will fall	will have replaced	won't think

A recent survey predicts that working habits ¹_____ dramatically for young adults. Experts predict that in the next few years the number of full-time jobs ²_____. Some say that part-time positions ³_____ over a third of full-time jobs by the end of the decade. This ⁴_____ men as well as women. In addition, a large proportion of people ⁵_____ for themselves in 2020. Instead of working for one employer, they ⁶_____ different part-time and short-term positions. The survey predicts that, as a result of this, many young adults ⁷_____ about saving for retirement or a pension. It's clear that this situation ⁸_____ problems in the future for some workers.

6 Correct the mistake in each sentence.

1 I don't think the plan is a good idea. I explain.
2 When I'll finish the course, I'm going to celebrate.
3 Will they have finish by lunchtime?
4 I expect that tomorrow's exam is difficult.
5 This time on Monday she'll be start her new job.
6 I'll apply for this job because it looks really interesting.

Grammar summary | UNIT 3

PRESENT PERFECT SIMPLE AND CONTINUOUS

Present perfect simple

We form the present perfect simple with *have/has* + past participle, for example: *changed, listened, made, put, understood.*

We use the present perfect simple to talk about:

- completed actions that have a measurable result in the present. We want to emphasize the result of the activity.
  *UNICEF **has published** three reports on this topic this year.*
  *I**'ve found** five spelling mistakes in your essay.*
- a past action when the specific time is not stated and we want to emphasize the action
  *The new medicine **has saved** thousands of lives.*
- life experiences, when the person is still living
  *Our speaker today **has worked** in his field for over three decades and **has published** several books on economics.*
- an action or a situation in a time that continues up to the moment of speaking
  *The number of people in the UK over the age of 100 **has risen** since last year.*
  *People **haven't believed** the official statistics for years.*
- actions with time expressions such as *today, this morning, this week, this year* when the period of time is not finished at the moment of speaking
  ***Have** you **seen** the news today?*
  *I **haven't spoken** to my sister this week.*
  *We**'ve had** too much work to do this morning.*

We often use the adverbs *already, yet, just* with the present perfect simple to show the connection of the action with the time of speaking.

- to emphasize that an action has happened before the time of speaking
  *It's only 11 am and I've **already** had three meetings.*
- in negative sentences to say that something that was expected hasn't happened
  *Today is our deadline, but we haven't finished the work **yet**.*
- in questions to ask whether something which we are expecting has happened
  *I'm getting a parcel today. Has the post arrived **yet**?*
- to emphasize that something happened recently
  *I'm sorry, Suzanne has **just** left the office. She won't be back until tomorrow morning.*

We use the adverbs *for* and *since* to show the duration of the time period.

- *for* + a period of time
  *Estelle and Jane have known each other **for** about ten years.*
- *since* + a point in time
  *We've had an office in Rome **since** 2012.*

Present perfect continuous

Affirmative	Negative
I/You/We/They **have been working**.	I/You/We/They **haven't been working**.
He/She/It **has been working**.	He/She/It **hasn't been working**.

Question	Short answer
Have I/you/we/they **been working**?	Yes, I/you/we/they **have**. No, I/you/we/they **haven't**.
Has he/she/it **been working**?	Yes, he/she/it **has**. No, he/she/it **hasn't**.

We form the present perfect continuous with *have/has* + *been* + *-ing*.

We use the present perfect continuous to talk about:

- a recent activity when we want to emphasize the process or the duration of the activity. The result of the activity is less important or is not mentioned at all.
  *People **have been spending** a lot of money on luxury items.*
  *I **haven't been watching** that new cookery series on TV.*
  *What **has** Frances **been doing** all morning?*
- an activity that started in the past and may or may not be in progress at the moment of speaking
  *We**'ve been working** especially hard on the report this week and it's finally ready!*
  *We had a lot of interest in the advert at first, but recently people **haven't been calling**.*
  ***Has** anyone **been counting** the number of responses to our advert?*

We don't use stative verbs (*believe, belong, know, seem*, etc.) in the present perfect continuous form. However, we can use *have, mean, think* in the present perfect continuous form.
*My sister **hasn't been having** much success with her job applications.*
*I know you haven't spoken to Ian recently, but **have** you **been meaning** to call him?*
*I**'ve been thinking** about the article I read yesterday. It was really shocking.*

We don't usually use the adverbs *already* and *yet* with the present perfect continuous. We can use adverbs such as *since, this week, recently, just, for the last few days*, etc. to show when the activity started and its duration.
*Have you **just** been using the photocopier? It's out of paper.*
*Matt has been helping on the project **for the last few days**.*

▶ Exercises 1–6

144

EXERCISES

1 Complete the sentences with the present perfect continuous form of the verbs.

1. I _____ (work) at the same company since I left college.
2. The price of oil _____ (fall) for several months.
3. How long _____ your friend _____ (study) English?
4. We _____ (not / make) any progress in our health project.
5. _____ the development agencies _____ (plan) a new programme?
6. The company _____ (not / do) very well recently.

2 Choose the correct option to complete the sentences.

1. *I've visited / I've been visiting* ten countries in the last three months.
2. Is there a problem with email? Your boss *has tried / has been trying* to contact you.
3. The customer *hasn't replied / hasn't been replying* to our email.
4. *Has he saved / Has he been saving* enough money to buy a car yet?
5. Many of the women in the study *have had / have been having* at least three children.
6. I'm afraid we *haven't finished / haven't been finishing* the report.
7. *Have you listened / Have you been listening* to me? This is important!
8. The new director *has run / has been running* several successful companies in her career.

3 Complete the sentences with the present perfect simple and continuous form of the verbs.

1. Sorry I'm late! I _____ (have) lunch with an old friend.
2. _____ the proposal from the design department _____ (arrive)?
3. It's a great film. We _____ (see) it three times.
4. I'm not buying a tablet. The prices _____ (not come) down enough yet.
5. The government _____ (know) about the problem for a while.
6. I'm so tired these days. I _____ (not / sleep) well lately.
7. The charity _____ (help) people around the world for two decades.
8. Experts say the world economy _____ (reach) crisis point.

4 Complete the texts with the present perfect simple and continuous form of the verbs.

Many people around the world ¹_____ (see) a huge improvement in their standard of living since their parents' generation. Consumer products ²_____ (become) more widely available and the price of these products ³_____ (fall) steadily for years.

I'd like to introduce Rita Wilson. I ⁴_____ (know) her for ten years, first as a friend then as a colleague. For the past six years, we ⁵_____ (design) a new clean-water system. It ⁶_____ (be) exceptionally hard, but Rita ⁷_____ always _____ (believe) that we could succeed.

We know that family size in many countries ⁸_____ (go) down for years, but what ⁹_____ that _____ (mean) for the economies of these countries? Economists say that the working population ¹⁰_____ (shrink) too far now and there aren't enough working adults in some countries.

5 Choose the correct option to complete the sentences. Sometimes, both options are possible.

1. My brother has been living in South America *already / since 2011*.
2. My classmates and I have been preparing our presentation *this week / for a few days*.
3. The government has announced changes in taxes *this week / recently*.
4. Oh hi! I've *just / already* been phoning you, but I didn't get an answer.
5. We've been married for a while, but we haven't had any children *yet / recently*.
6. Has the engineer been fixing the computers *all morning / yet*?
7. Hi! What have you been up to *since / yet* I last saw you?
8. My tablet hasn't been working properly *already / recently*.

6 Correct the mistake in each sentence.

1. We're here since ten o'clock this morning.
2. In my opinion, spending habits are changing for many years.
3. I work for this company for about three years.
4. For a long time I've been learning English.
5. How long are you living here?
6. I've just been hearing the news! Congratulations!

Grammar summary | UNIT 4

NARRATIVE TENSES

Past simple

We use the past simple to talk about:

- an event or sequence of events in the past. The past time is stated (*last month*, *ten years ago*, etc.) or is clear from the context.
  I **started** my company five years ago. I **opened** a small office and I **hired** my first employee.

Past continuous

We use the past continuous to talk about:

- activities or states that describe the background to past actions
  My business **was going** really well and I was happy.
- activities or situations that were in progress when another action took place
  The demand for cheap air travel **was growing** when he **started** his company.

We don't generally use *be* in the past continuous.
My business **was going** really well and I was happy.
(not *was being happy*)

Past perfect simple

We form the past perfect simple with *had* + past participle.

We use the past perfect simple to talk about:

- actions that took place at an earlier time than the main event in a narrative, especially when the events are not related in the sequence they happened
  I got to the office and remembered I**'d left** my phone at home.

Past perfect continuous

Affirmative	Negative
I/You/He/She/It/We/They**'d been talking**.	I/You/He/She/It/We/They **hadn't been talking**.

Question	Short answer
Had I/you/he/she/it/we/they **been talking**?	Yes, I/you/he/she/it/we/they **had**. No, I/you/he/she/it/we/they **hadn't**.

We form the past perfect continuous with *had* + *been* + *-ing*.

We use the past perfect continuous to talk about:

- an activity or state in progress before the main event took place
  The company **had been working** on the product for ten years before they decided to market it.

▶ Exercises 1–3

USED TO AND WOULD

used to

Affirmative	Negative
I/You/He/She/It/We/They **used to cry**.	I/You/He/She/It/We/They **didn't use to cry**.

Question	Short answer
Did I/you/he/she/it/we/they **use to cry**?	Yes, I/you/he/she/it/we/they **did**. No, I/you/he/she/it/we/they **didn't**.

We use *used to* + infinitive to talk about:

- habits and states that took place in the past but do not happen or exist now
  When I started the company, I **used to do** everything myself. Now I have ten staff.
  There **used to be** a lot of problems with the internet connection, so we changed provider.

We also use the past simple to talk about past habits and states.

would

Affirmative	Negative
I/You/He/She/It/We/They **would cry**.	I/You/He/She/It/We/They **wouldn't cry**.

Question	Short answer
Would I/you/he/she/it/we/they **cry**?	Yes, I/you/he/she/it/we/they **would**. No, I/you/he/she/it/we/they **wouldn't**.

We use *would* + infinitive to talk about:

- habits that took place in the past but do not happen now
  When I started the company, I **would do** everything myself. Now I have ten staff.

We don't use *would* + infinitive to talk about past states.
There ~~would be~~ **used to be** a lot of problems with the internet connection, so we changed provider.

▶ Exercises 4–6

EXERCISES

1 Complete the sentences with the past perfect continuous form of the verbs.

1. My friend _____ (think) about leaving college, but I persuaded him to stay on.
2. I _____ (not / work) for the company long when I got promoted.
3. They were so pleased with their success because they _____ (not / expect) it.
4. How long _____ you _____ (discuss) the new plans before everyone agreed?
5. _____ the business _____ (lose) money for a long time when it closed?
6. We _____ (not / get) good results, so we tried a new strategy.

2 Choose the correct options to complete the text.

My family business

My grandparents ¹*came / had come* to live in Australia from the UK a year after their wedding. ²*They lived / They'd been living* with my great-grandparents in London and they ³*wanted / were wanting* a better life. After six months in Sydney, ⁴*they opened / they'd been opening* a fish and chip shop even though they ⁵*didn't run / hadn't run* their own business before – my grandfather ⁶*worked / had worked* in a factory in the UK. Two years later, the business ⁷*did / was doing* really well when ⁸*there was / there had been* a fire in the shop. They almost ⁹*lost / were losing* everything. However, my grandmother ¹⁰*was saving / had been saving* money every month and they ¹¹*had / were having* enough to start again. Now the family business is in four cities across Australia.

3 Complete the profile with the correct narrative tense of the verbs.

Frank Capra

Frank Capra was an Italian-American film director. His film career ¹_____ (begin) in the silent-movie era. By 1938, he ²_____ (win) three Oscars. Capra ³_____ (direct) one of the most successful films of all time: *It's a Wonderful Life.* At that time, 1946, he ⁴_____ (work) for his own film studio, Liberty Films. He ⁵_____ (start) it with three other film directors the year before. The four men ⁶_____ (meet) in the American army during the Second World War and they ⁷_____ (make) films together for several years. When they ⁸_____ (leave) the army, they ⁹_____ (not / want) to go to the big Hollywood studios. Liberty Films wasn't a financial success and when the studio ¹⁰_____ (close), they ¹¹_____ (release) only two films.

4 Choose the correct option to complete the sentences. Sometimes, both options are possible.

1. At school, my best friend *used to get / would get* better marks than me.
2. *Did you use to have / Would you have* one of those really big mobile phones?
3. I remember when computer monitors *used to be / would be* enormous.
4. Until I got this job, I *didn't use to spend / wouldn't spend* much money on clothes.
5. When we were students, we *used to take turns / would take turns* to cook.
6. In your last job, *did you use to leave / would you leave* early on Fridays?
7. My best friend *used to be / would be* late for school at least once a week.
8. I *didn't use to understand / wouldn't understand* Italian, but then I learned a few words on holiday there.

5 Complete the sentences with the correct form of *used to* or *would*. Sometimes, both options are possible.

1. When I was a child, we _____ (live) in Italy.
2. In my first job, we _____ (take) a long lunch break every Friday.
3. You look different. _____ you _____ (wear) glasses?
4. When my brother was learning to drive, he _____ (have) lessons twice a day.
5. Before the new manager arrived, I _____ (not / enjoy) my job.
6. Where _____ your family _____ (go) on holiday every summer?
7. I wasn't a good student: I _____ (miss) classes all the time.
8. Everything has changed here. There _____ (be) a big shop on this corner.

6 Correct the mistake in each sentence.

1. I met Jane yesterday and we had talked about the project.
2. Last year, the company has opened a new office.
3. I was very excited when I first start my new job.
4. I use to be a bad student because I never did my homework.
5. What did your boss said to you?
6. The man gave me his business card and was walking away.

147

Grammar summary | UNIT 5

MODALS AND RELATED VERBS: PAST FORMS (1)

can (not) + infinitive without to, to (not) be able to + infinitive: past

We use *could* + infinitive without *to* and *was/were able to* to talk about:

- the possibility of doing something and the ability to do something in a general period of time in the past
  My friend **could speak** five languages before she was sixteen. I **was able to speak** a bit of French, but that was all.

We use *could* + *not* + infinitive without *to* and *was/were* + *not able to* to talk about:

- not succeeding at something in a general period of time in the past or at a specific time in the past
  When we were travelling around Asia, we **couldn't understand** anyone.
  I **wasn't able to finish** my language course last year because I didn't have enough time.

We use *was/were able to*, but not *could* to talk about:

- success in achieving something at a specific time in the past
  The office was closed, but we **were able to contact** them by phone. (not ~~could contact~~)

▶ Exercise 1

must + infinitive without to / have to + infinitive: past

The past form of *must* + infinitive is *had to* + infinitive.

We use *had to* + infinitive to talk about:

- the necessity to do something at a specific time in the past
  The car broke down and we **had to call** the pick-up truck.

We use *didn't have to* + infinitive to talk about:

- the lack of necessity to do something at a specific time in the past
  The office was near the station, so they **didn't have to walk** far.

manage to + infinitive and succeed in + -ing: past

We use *managed to* and *succeeded in* to talk about:

- ability and success in achieving (or not achieving) something at a specific time in the past
  The office was closed, but we **managed to contact** them by phone.
  The meeting went on all day, but we **didn't succeed in reaching** an agreement.

▶ Exercises 2–4

QUESTIONS

Negative questions

The negative form of the verb is contracted in negative questions.
   Don't you **agree**?
   Isn't that a great picture?

We use negative questions to express a variety of feelings, including:

- softening opinions or advice
  Wouldn't it **be** a bit risky to invest all of your money at once?
- showing surprise
  Didn't you **see** the email I sent? I marked it as priority.
- checking information that you think is correct
  Wasn't today the last day for sending in the job application?

Indirect questions

Indirect questions begin with fixed expressions (*I wonder / I was wondering … , Do you know/think … , Could you tell me … , Can I ask you …*, etc.) and the subject–verb order after the fixed expression is affirmative, not interrogative. We use *if* or *whether* in indirect questions which have yes/no answers.
   I wonder if/whether you can help me?

We use indirect questions:

- to be more polite, especially in more formal situations
  Do you know if this process will take long?
  Can I ask you how long this process will take?
- to appear cautious or less direct
  I was wondering when the website will be ready?
  Could you tell me if the website will be ready soon?

Tag questions

Tag questions have two parts, separated by a comma. The first part is an affirmative or negative statement. The second part is the auxiliary verb in the question form. The auxiliary verb in the second part is negative (and contracted) when the first part is affirmative. The auxiliary verb in the second part is affirmative when the first part is negative.
   You**'re going to employ** staff, **aren't** you?
   You **aren't going to run** the business yourself, **are** you?

We use tag questions:

- to confirm or check information
  You**'ll employ** more staff, **won't** you?
- to soften opinions or advice
  You **didn't run** the business yourself, **did** you?

▶ Exercises 5–7

148

EXERCISES

1 Choose the correct option to complete the sentences. Sometimes, both options are possible.

1. The manager left the office early, but we *could talk / were able to talk* to him about the problem.
2. There were some technical problems, but Jack *could give / was able to give* a great presentation.
3. We had a training course, but we *couldn't use / weren't able to use* the new software.
4. *Were you able to find / Could you find* the file you were looking for?
5. Rosa sat her French exam three times and finally she *could pass / was able to pass*.
6. All my friends *could play / were able to play* tennis better than me.

2 Match the two parts to make sentences.

1. Everyone was surprised when Charlie managed to
2. I'm afraid I was so busy I didn't manage to
3. Lin got to the final interview, but she didn't succeed in
4. After many years, Wilson finally succeeded in
5. The team didn't succeed in
6. Thanks to everyone's donations, the charity managed to

a. build a new sports centre.
b. call you back yesterday.
c. complete his first marathon.
d. getting the job.
e. selling many copies of their fitness DVD.
f. winning a match.

3 Write the correct form of the verb.

1. A: Did the electrician come to fix the alarm?
   B: Yes, we finally _____ (succeed / get) in touch with him.
2. A: Did you get an appointment with the doctor?
   B: Yes, they _____ (manage / fit) me in at the end of the day.
3. A: Did you go to the match with Jeanne last week?
   B: No, she _____ (not / able to / take) the day off work.
4. A: _____ you _____ (manage / get) to work on time this morning?
   B: No, the bus strike caused chaos.
5. A: Did your department have a successful year?
   B: Yes, finally we _____ (able to / beat) the sales record.
6. A: Did your team win the championship?
   B: No, we _____ (not / succeed / reach) the finals.

4 Complete the text with the past form of the modal verbs.

Earlier this year our department was overloaded with work, so we ¹_____ (must / think about) new ways of doing things. We held a meeting and everyone ²_____ (be able to / make) suggestions. We ³_____ (succeed in / come up with) a lot of ideas in a very short time. It was a very positive meeting. The management team looked at what we ⁴_____ (can / do) most easily. We ⁵_____ (not / be able to / use) all of the ideas, but in fact we didn't need to. With some small changes to our systems, we ⁶_____ (manage to / deal with) the workload. Fortunately for the budget, we ⁷_____ (not / have to / hire) any extra staff.

5 Rewrite the questions as negative and indirect questions.

1. Do you want to come with us?
   _____
2. Is that Suzanne over there?
   _____
3. Would you prefer to meet on Friday?
   _____
4. How much does it cost? (Can you tell me)
   _____
5. Have you got any free time tomorrow? (I was wondering)
   _____
6. Why doesn't this machine work? (Do you know)
   _____

6 Rewrite the questions as tag questions.

1. Don't you understand?
   _____
2. Is it a fantastic idea?
   _____
3. Have you read the document?
   _____
4. Aren't they coming until later?
   _____
5. Did the plane arrive late again?
   _____
6. Couldn't you give me a hand?
   _____

7 Correct the mistake in each sentence.

1. When I was at school, we must to work in groups quite often.
2. On our trip, we could visit every capital city in South America.
3. I was so tired, but I could make it to the end of the race.
4. I tried to tell you, but I didn't could find you.
5. The team succeeded to win in the final minute.
6. We weren't able finish the race.
7. I wonder what time is it?
8. You didn't phone the office, isn't it?

149

Grammar summary | UNIT 6

ZERO, FIRST AND SECOND CONDITIONALS

Zero conditional

If-clause	Main clause
If + present simple,	present simple

When the sentence begins with *If*, there is a comma after the *if*-clause. The sentence can also begin with the main clause, in which case there is no comma.

We use the zero conditional to talk about:

- situations or facts that are generally true
  If a computer **gets** a virus, you **can get rid of** it with an anti-virus programme.
  You **can get rid of** a virus with an anti-virus programme if your computer **gets** one.

- habits and repeated actions when there's a given condition
  If you **leave** your phone on, the battery **runs out**.
  The battery **runs out** if you **leave** your phone on.

We can use *when* instead of *if* in zero conditional sentences with no change in meaning.
  When a computer **gets** a virus, you **can get rid of** it with an anti-virus programme.
  The battery **runs out when** you **leave** your phone on.

We can also use *unless* to talk about possible actions and situations in the future. *Unless* means 'if not'.
  Computers don't need a large memory **if** they **don't run** large programmes.
  Computers don't need a large memory **unless** they **run** large programmes.

First conditional

If-clause	Main clause
If + present simple,	will + infinitive without *to*

We don't use *when* with the first conditional.

We use the first conditional to talk about:

- something the speaker thinks is likely to happen in the future
  If you **give** me your number, I**'ll call** you later.

We also use the first conditional to talk about:

- possible situations that are generally true
  If prices **go up** a lot, people **will complain**.

We can also use the present perfect, *going to* and the present continuous in first conditional sentences: the present perfect is also used to describe a specific current situation; *going to* and the present continuous are both used to refer to future events.

If-clause	Main clause
If + present perfect,	will + infinitive without *to*
If + present simple,	going to + infinitive
If + present simple,	present continuous

If they**'ve left** their details, we**'ll be** in touch.
If they **get** any news about the flight, they**'re going to tell** us.
If I **get** a bonus this week, I**'m taking** you to lunch on Friday.

▶ Exercise 1

Second conditional

If-clause	Main clause
If + past simple,	would + infinitive without *to*

We use the second conditional to talk about:

- something that is the opposite of the real situation
  If I **had** your number, I**'d be able** to call you. (I don't have your number, so I'm not able to call you.)

- something that the speaker thinks is unlikely to happen in the future
  If I **bought** that tablet, it **would be** useful on trips.

We can choose the first or second conditional according to how likely the action is to happen in the speaker's opinion.
  If I **bought** that tablet, it **would be** useful on trips. (I'm not buying it)
  If I **buy** that tablet, it **will be** useful on trips. (I might buy it)

We can use the contraction of *would* – I'd, you'd, she'd, etc. – in the main clause. When *had* is in the *if*-clause, it is a main verb (not an auxiliary verb) and so is not contracted.
  If ~~I'd~~ **I had** your number, I**'d be able** to call you.

▶ Exercises 2–4

Intensifiers

We use words like *very* and *really* to emphasize the adjective.
  The tickets were **very** cheap.

| amazingly | exceptionally | extremely | incredibly |
| particularly | really | unusually | very |

We don't normally use *very* with strong adjectives (*appalling, awful, disgusted, excellent, fantastic, terrible, useless, wonderful*, etc.). We use other intensifiers.
  The seats were ~~very~~ **absolutely** fantastic.

| absolutely | completely | particularly |
| really | totally | utterly |

We can use *really* with both groups of adjectives.
  The film was **really** good/wonderful.

▶ Exercises 5–7

EXERCISES

1 Read the first part of the sentences. Choose the correct option to complete the sentences. Sometimes, both options are possible.

1 If the technician doesn't fix my computer,
 a I'll talk to the IT manager.
 b I'm going to talk to the IT manager.
2 We won't be able to change the report
 a if Joan has already sent it.
 b if Joan is going to send it.
3 If Elisa hasn't given Scott the data,
 a he'll be able to finish the report.
 b he won't be able to finish the report.
4 If the company changes its name again,
 a a lot of customers have been confused.
 b a lot of customers are going to be confused.
5 I'll help you with your work later
 a if you haven't done it by lunchtime.
 b if you don't do it by lunchtime.
6 If Simon can't come to the presentation on Friday,
 a we're not going to change the time again.
 b we're not changing the time again.

2 Choose the correct option to complete the sentences.

1 If the new phone doesn't offer good value for money, nobody *buys / will buy* one.
2 What will you do if *there are / there were* no seats left on the flight?
3 If you use your credit card to buy things, you *pay / paid* more in the end.
4 *Will / Would* people buy so much stuff if there was no advertising?
5 If I can't have the latest model, I *won't want / don't want* anything.
6 I'd come shopping with you if I *didn't have to / don't have to* work on Saturday.
7 If we valued what we have more, *we'd be / we'll be* happier.
8 The shops *are / will be* really crowded if the sales start today.
9 Where *do you go / would you go* if you could have the holiday of a lifetime?
10 Words *lose / will lose* their meaning when we use them in the wrong way.

3 Complete the conversation with the second conditional.

A: Next Saturday is 'Buy nothing day'. Can you imagine what ¹_____ (happen) if everybody in the country ²_____ (join) in?
B: Well, all the shops ³_____ (be) completely empty.
A: Yeah, what ⁴_____ the shop assistants _____ (do)?
B: Nothing! And they ⁵_____ (not / be able to) go home if the shops ⁶_____ (have to) stay open.
A: But if I ⁷_____ (own) a shop and nobody ⁸_____ (come) in by lunchtime, I ⁹_____ (give) my staff the afternoon off.
B: But what if just one customer ¹⁰_____ (want) to buy something?
A: Well I ¹¹_____ (be) there – I ¹²_____ (not / close) the shop, just in case.
B: It's never going to happen though.
A: I know!

4 Complete the zero, first and second conditional sentences with the correct form of the verb.

1 If Andrew decides to sell his car, I _____ (buy) it from him.
2 If you _____ (sound) enthusiastic about your ideas, people will listen to you.
3 If you _____ (have to) choose the most important thing in your life, what would it be?
4 Most shops let you return products if they _____ (be) faulty.
5 There _____ (not / be) so many arguments if people listened to each other more.
6 What will your colleague do if she _____ (lose) her job?

5 Choose the correct option to complete the sentences.

1 We had a *really / very* fantastic holiday.
2 The hotel was *absolutely / incredibly* good value for money.
3 We were *very / completely* amazed by the Grand Canyon.
4 We saw some *very / totally* interesting things.
5 We had *very / absolutely* perfect weather.
6 The flight took an *extremely / utterly* long time.

6 Choose the correct option to complete the sentences.

1 The coffee was very *fantastic / good*.
2 We had some absolutely *nice / delicious* cake.
3 The portions were very *big / enormous*.
4 The service was extremely *slow / appalling*.
5 The serving area was utterly *awful / untidy*.
6 The staff were completely *friendly / wonderful*.

7 Correct the mistake in each sentence.

1 If I would have enough money, I'd buy a new phone.
2 What you will say if they offer you the job?
3 If I were you, I would to ask for help.
4 If we all will pass the exam, we'll go out for a meal.
5 If you would be younger, you'd have better opportunities at work.
6 We're going to China next year if we'll have enough money.
7 We had an absolutely good weekend in the mountains.
8 The exam was very impossible for me to finish on time.

Grammar summary | UNIT 7

PASSIVES

Form

We form the passive with the verb *be* + the past participle of the main verb. We can use the verb *be* in all tenses and with modal verbs, although the present perfect continuous and past perfect continuous forms of the passive are not used very often. We use *be* in the negative and question form to make negative passive sentences and questions with the passive. The past participle of the main verb does not change form.

Simple tenses
*Hundreds of new products **were developed** last year.*
*Results **aren't** usually **shared** between companies.*
*Where **was** the launch of the new product **held**?*

Continuous tenses
*Solutions **are being designed** continually.*
*The trial **wasn't being supervised** when the problem arose.*
***Were** the subjects in the trial **being monitored** during the trial?*

▶ Exercise 1

Perfect tenses
*Several market research surveys **have been carried out** so far.*
*Unfortunately, the fault **hadn't been noticed** during the testing process.*
***Has** the new product **been tested**?*

▶ Exercise 2

Modals
*When **will** the app **be launched**?*
*The media **can't be told** until next week.*
*Existing needs **must be** clearly **identified**.*
*Results **should be reviewed** by peers in academic settings.*

▶ Exercise 3

Use

We use the passive to focus on what happens: the action or process which takes place. Information about the agent (who or what does the action) doesn't need to appear in the sentence. The passive is often used in formal writing contexts such as academic, business or legal texts and also when describing processes which consist of a series of stages. The choice between the use of the passive or active form of a verb depends on whether we want to emphasize the action (passive) or the agent (active).
***The story was reported** before the press conference.*
***Our economics editor reported** the story before the press conference.*

We often use the passive:
- when the agent is obvious
*The story **was published** in today's newspaper.* (it's obvious that journalists published the story)
- when the agent is not known or not important
*The story **was published** on the Internet.* (the person who published the story is unknown or not as important as the fact of its publication)
- when the agent is clear from the context
*The news story **was** widely **reported**.* (the context of 'news' makes it clear that the press and media reported the story)
- when the agent is general
*Further information on this story **can be found** on our website.* (people in general can find the information)
- when we don't want to say who the agent is
*The story **was revealed** to the press this morning.*

We don't use the passive for verbs without a direct object.
The technician worked all day.
(All day was worked by the technician.)

We can give information about when or where the action takes place using adverbs of time and place.
*The trials were held **last year**.*
*The samples will be given out **in selected supermarkets**.*

▶ Exercise 4

by and *for*

Sometimes information about the agent is relevant or useful to know.

We can give information about who does the action using the preposition *by*.
*The machine **was designed by** a team of engineering students as part of their degree work.*

We can give information about the purpose of the action or why it takes place using the preposition *for*.
*The product **was tested for** faults.*

▶ Exercises 5 and 6

152

EXERCISES

1 Rewrite the sentences in the passive form.

1. An astronaut took a 3D printer to the International Space Station.
   _____
2. When did they invent the computer mouse?
   _____
3. Were doctors using stem cell therapy in the 1990s?
   _____
4. They didn't install fibre optic cables in my area until last year.
   _____
5. Which company is manufacturing driverless cars?
   _____
6. Were they demonstrating electric cars at the exhibition?
   _____

2 Complete the sentences with the passive form of the tenses in brackets.

1. These medicines _____ (prescribe) since 1995. (present perfect)
2. The patients _____ (examine) before taking part in the trial. (past perfect)
3. The group _____ (contact) by the hospital. (present perfect)
4. Only one of the participants _____ (not / speak) to. (present perfect)
5. _____ the results of the tests already _____ (give) to the patient? (past perfect)
6. Where _____ the patient _____ (take)? (present perfect)

3 Complete the sentences with the passive form of the modals.

1. Visitors to the factory _____ (should / accompany) at all times.
2. The new policy _____ (not / will / implement) until next year.
3. Customers _____ (must / notify) in writing about any changes to their contract.
4. When _____ the building checks _____ (will / complete)?
5. The exit _____ (not / should / use) by unauthorised staff.
6. Which department _____ these boxes _____ (should / deliver) to?
7. _____ the invitations _____ (can / send) out today?
8. This email _____ (not / must / see) by anyone outside this department.

4 Choose the best option to follow each sentence. Both are grammatically correct.

1. I love these photos you took on your trip to Venezuela.
   a. What did you use – a camera or your phone?
   b. What was used – a camera or your phone?
2. This is a state-of-the-art factory for new medicines.
   a. They built it last year.
   b. It was built last year.
3. Three ambulances were called to an incident in the town centre last night.
   a. They took several people with minor injuries to hospital.
   b. Several people with minor injuries were taken to hospital.
4. Our new local doctor is very different to the previous one.
   a. She's completely changed the appointments system.
   b. The appointments system has been completely changed.
5. Several health organizations are trialling a new drug for malaria.
   a. They will report their findings next year.
   b. Their findings will be reported next year.
6. The government has proposed changes to the public health service.
   a. They are discussing the proposals this week.
   b. The proposals are being discussed this week.

5 Choose the correct option to complete the sentences.

1. The research department is being funded *by / for* the government.
2. The plants are being investigated *by / for* new medicinal uses.
3. A survey into the use of prosthetics will be carried out *by / for* Professor Ross.
4. New medicines are being trialled *by / for* the most important diseases.
5. The work was carried out *by / for* an outside contractor.
6. Following the man's accident, he was checked *by / for* broken bones.

6 Correct the mistakes in these sentences.

1. The emails were send yesterday.
2. Too many changes are been made too quickly.
3. The faulty device was sold for most shops.
4. The report will publish next week.
5. Many people was questioned in the survey.
6. All of this work has done by our group.

Grammar summary | UNIT 8

VERB PATTERNS WITH -ING AND INFINITIVE

verb + -ing

We always use the -ing form of the verb which follows these verbs. These verbs are never followed by an infinitive. This verb + -ing pattern is used with verbs that include:

avoid	consider	dislike	enjoy	finish
imagine	keep	mind	practise	recommend
regret	risk	suggest		

I **dislike getting** home late from work.
(I **dislike to get** home late from work.)

The negative form of this pattern is *not* + *-ing*:
I **regret not talking** to him before now.
(I **regret not to talk** to him before now.)

verb + to + infinitive

We use *to* + infinitive of the verb which follows these verbs. These verbs are never followed by *-ing*. This verb + *to* + infinitive pattern is used with verbs that include:

agree	aim	arrange	choose	decide
expect	hope	intend	learn	manage
need	plan	prepare	promise	want

She **learned to play** the piano when she was 25.
(She **learned playing** the piano when she was 25.)

The word order in the negative form is *not* + *to* + infinitive:
We **agreed not to discuss** the matter until the meeting.
(We **agreed to not discuss** the matter until the meeting.)

▶ Exercises 1 and 2

verb + object + to + infinitive

We use *to* + infinitive of the verb when it follows these verbs + object.

allow	ask	encourage	expect	force
help	invite	need	persuade	remind
teach	tell	want	would like	

I **persuaded him not to leave** his job.
Shall we **invite Jim to come** with us to the theatre?

verb + object + infinitive

We use the infinitive of the verb without *to* when it follows these verbs + object.

| feel | hear | let | make | notice | see | watch |

We **heard the car hit** the lamppost
I **didn't notice Andy** arrive today. Is he here?

▶ Exercises 3 and 4

verb + -ing / verb + infinitive with similar meanings

These verbs can be followed by either of the patterns without a significant change in the meaning of the sentence.

| begin | continue | hate | like | love | prefer | start |

We **began working** flexitime a couple of years ago.
We **began to work** flexitime a couple of years ago.
I don't like **eating** ice cream in winter.
I don't like **to eat** ice cream in winter.

verb + -ing / verb + infinitive with different meanings

These verbs can be followed by both of the patterns, but there is a change in the meaning of the sentence.

| forget | go on | mean | regret | remember | stop | try |

Did you **remember to buy** bread on your way home? We've run out. (= talking about an action that needs to be done)
Do you **remember buying** these souvenirs in Rome? (= talking about a past activity or a memory)
You didn't like the company, so why **did** you **go on working** there? (= why did you continue / carry on)
After leaving her job, Mary **went on to work** as a volunteer for a charity. (= Mary changed the situation and did something different)
The mistake with the orders **meant phoning** every client personally. (= the result of something)
Sorry. I **meant to phone** you last night, but I forgot. (= an intention)
I **regret saying** John's application was perfect – it wasn't. (= to be sorry about something you did)
I **regret to say** your application wasn't successful on this occasion. (= a way of giving bad news in a formal situation)
I **forgot to go** to my appointment last week. (= talking about an action that needs to be done)
I'll never **forget going** to the beach for the first time. (= talking about a past activity or a memory)
I'm going to **stop having lunch** at my desk. (= I won't eat at my desk anymore)
I'm going to **stop to have lunch** in about half an hour. (= I'll take a break so that I can have lunch)
I've **tried sending** her emails, but she doesn't respond. (= talking about an action that was completed but didn't have a positive result)
I've **tried to send** her an email, but my connection isn't working today. (= talking about an attempt to do something that wasn't completed)

▶ Exercises 5 and 6

EXERCISES

1 Choose the correct option to complete the sentences.

1. I practise *speaking / to speak* French whenever I can.
2. I really enjoy *working / to work* with my colleagues.
3. Did they agree *looking / to look* at the ideas again?
4. I can't imagine *not living / not to live* in this great city.
5. When did your friend decide *giving up / to give up* his job?
6. We expect *reaching / to reach* our targets in all areas.
7. Why would she risk *losing / to lose* her job like that?
8. I dislike *having / to have* to queue for things.

2 Match the parts to make sentences.

1. When I turned 30, I decided
2. Nobody should avoid
3. After a year at home with his kids, he learned
4. I think most of us need
5. We can all consider
6. My sister's planning

a. making small changes to our daily routine.
b. taking responsibility for their own lives.
c. to appreciate his family life more.
d. to spend all her savings on a motorbike.
e. to stop all my bad habits and turn my life around.
f. to think about the balance in our lives.

3 Complete the conversations with the correct form of the verbs.

1. A: Can you remind me _____ (book) a room for the meeting?
   B: Of course. Or would you like me _____ (do) it for you? It's no problem.

2. A: We're going to watch our team _____ (play) football tomorrow.
   B: Do you expect them _____ (win)? The other team is pretty strong.

3. A: I don't think we can force staff _____ (come) in on Saturdays, do you?
   B: No. But I heard Paulina _____ (say) she needed some extra money this month.

4. A: I wonder if the golf club will let us _____ (use) their room for a party?
   B: Probably – they allowed Harry _____ (have) a chess tournament there.

4 Complete the text with the correct form of these verbs. There is one extra verb.

| be | do | find | get | give | give up |
| go off | invite | learn | set | stop | |

I work all day and study in the evening, and recently it's been getting too much. My friend suggested ¹_____ my course, but I don't want ²_____ now. The course is nearly finished and, anyway, I've always enjoyed ³_____ things. In fact, I need ⁴_____ time to revise for the final exams next month. I could ask my boss ⁵_____ me some time off work, but I don't think he'd agree ⁶_____ that. I decided ⁷_____ my alarm clock for 6 am hoping ⁸_____ some work done before breakfast. That was a disaster because I just didn't hear the alarm ⁹_____! Well, it's not long to go now. I don't mind ¹⁰_____ exhausted if I pass everything in the end.

5 Complete the sentences with the logical form of the verbs.

1. A: You seem a lot more relaxed lately.
   B: Yes, I stopped _____ (check) my work mail on my personal phone.
2. A: The place you stayed last weekend looks amazing.
   B: It was. We regretted not _____ (stay) there longer.
3. A: Why did you stop _____ (talk) to that man?
   B: Oh, he goes to my gym. He's a nice guy.
4. A: Did you remember _____ (buy) the tickets for the play next week?
   B: Of course. They're on the kitchen table.
5. A: I was awake for hours last night – I just can't get to sleep.
   B: Have you tried _____ (eat) an apple before you go to bed? Apparently that helps.
6. A: Your sister was really successful at Smith's, wasn't she?
   B: Yes. After her first promotion, she went on _____ (be) CEO eventually.

6 Correct the mistake in each sentence.

1. Sorry, I forgot tell the neighbours about our party!
2. I recommend to you read this book – it's great.
3. Taking a break can help you to avoid get stressed.
4. My company doesn't allow to do flexitime.
5. My friend asked me to not phone him too early.
6. I didn't tell you because I didn't want that you know.

Grammar summary | UNIT 9

RELATIVE CLAUSES

Defining relative clauses

We form defining relative clauses with the relative pronouns *who, that, which, whose, where* and *when*. The defining relative clause gives information about the noun that precedes it in the sentence. The information in a defining relative clause is essential for the sentence to make sense: it identifies exactly what is being referred to.

> These are **the people who** saw the advert.
> **The people who** saw this advert won't forget it.
> That's **the company which** needs the advert.
> **The company which** needs the advert sells footwear and accessories.
> She's **the designer that** came up with the logo.
> **The designer that** came up with the logo is fantastic.

The relative pronouns *who, which* and *that* can be both the subject and the object in a sentence. In the examples above, the relative pronouns are the subject of the defining relative clause and they are followed by a verb. The relative pronouns must be included.

> These are **the people who saw** the advert.
> (~~These are~~ **the people saw** ~~the advert.~~)

When the relative pronoun is followed by a subject + verb, it is the object of the defining relative clause. It can be omitted.

> These are the people **who we showed** the advert to.
> These are the people **we showed** the advert to.

We use defining relative clauses with pronouns as follows:

- *who* to identify people
  The designer who thought of this concept is a genius.
- *which* to identify things
  The idea which the team came up with was great.
- *that* to identify people and things. This is less formal than *who* and *which*.
  The designer that thought of this concept is a genius.
  The idea that the team came up with was great.
- *whose* to talk about possession
  The agency whose advert went viral last year has won an award.
- *where* to identify places
  The building where they held the exhibition was beautiful.
- *when* to identify times
  Monday's **the day when** everyone arrives late.

▶ Exercises 1 and 2

Non-defining relative clauses

Non-defining relative clauses give information about the noun which is not essential to the sentence – the information can be omitted and the sentence will still make sense. We separate a non-defining relative clause from the rest of the sentence with commas.

> The **client, who** makes children's **toys,** is keen to see our ideas.
> These **toys, which** are made by our client**,** are really popular with the under-fives.

A non-defining relative clause can also come at the end of a sentence. In this case, only one comma is used.

> This is our most recent **client, who** makes children's toys.
> Our client makes these **toys, which** are really popular with the under-fives.

The same relative pronouns are used in non-defining relative clauses as in defining relative clauses, with the exception of *that*.

> The **client**, ~~that~~ **who** makes children's toys, is keen to see our ideas.
> Our client makes these **toys**, ~~that~~ **which** are really popular with the under-fives.

▶ Exercise 3

Reduced relative clauses

Reduced relative clauses never include relative pronouns. We form a reduced relative clause by replacing the relative pronoun and using an *-ing* form or past participle.

- We use *-ing* when the relative clause is in the active form.
  Visitors arriving by car can park for free. *(who arrive / who are arriving)*
- We use a past participle when the relative clause is in the passive form.
  Some of **the adverts shown** on TV are terrible. *(which are shown)*

We can only use reduced relative clauses when the relative pronoun would be the subject of the relative clause.

> **Visitors who arrive** by car can park for free. ⟶ **Visitors arriving** by car can park for free.
> Some of **the adverts which are shown** on TV are terrible.
> ⟶ Some of **the adverts shown** on TV are terrible.

▶ Exercises 4–6

156

EXERCISES

1 Complete the sentences with *who, which, whose* or *where*.

1. The talk _____ most impressed me was about creativity.
2. Are you a person _____ always has lots of ideas?
3. The person _____ presentation I liked best was Sunni Brown.
4. Creative problem-solving is a skill _____ can be learned.
5. The town _____ I grew up has changed a lot.
6. What was the name of the teacher _____ taught us how to draw?
7. The step _____ is hardest is the first one.
8. Is this the problem _____ is causing difficulties?

2 Cross out the relative pronouns which are not needed.

1. The artists who I like best never doodle.
2. Most people that object to doodling don't really understand its value.
3. The books which I used in school are covered in doodles.
4. These are the pictures that I drew while I was listening to the lecture.
5. The magazine that published my drawings didn't pay me.
6. The time when I doodled most was in college.
7. Doodling is something which everyone does from time to time.
8. The drawings that Picasso did are worth a fortune.

3 Complete the sentences with a relative pronoun and commas to make non-defining relative clauses.

1. My favourite 20th century artist is Picasso had several different styles.
2. In the 1880s Picasso was born Claude Monet was a successful painter.
3. Central Saint Martins is a famous art college many famous designers studied.
4. Advertising is a relatively new industry is a mix of creativity and sales.
5. My friend loved art at school is now a graphic designer.
6. Holiday adverts appear on TV every winter make you think of summer.
7. I work for TPQ magazine is only published online.
8. I lost my phone has hundreds of my photos on it last week.

4 Rewrite the sentences using a reduced relative clause.

1. The ideas that were suggested by the new team were great.
2. Young artists who are seeking experience are welcome here.
3. The candidates who were interviewed yesterday were excellent.
4. Students who enrol on this course must be over eighteen.
5. Adverts which are paid for in advance get a discount.
6. Clients who need personal attention should make an appointment.
7. Customers who pay a deposit are given priority.
8. The applications which we processed yesterday are on file.

5 Complete the relative clauses in this magazine article with seven of these words. Then add commas where they are needed.

seeing	using	when	where	which
which	which	who	who	whose

Charity adverts

Many charities ¹_____ depend on donations from the public use advertising. Adverts ²_____ make the public more aware of a charity's activities are a good way of raising money. One style of advertising ³_____ has recently become more common is using shocking scenes. Charities ⁴_____ use this style say it is effective. However, many viewers ⁵_____ the latest campaign from a children's charity have complained. The UK Advertising Standards Authority ⁶_____ job it is to monitor adverts surveyed the public. As a result, the Authority is considering changing the time ⁷_____ such adverts can be shown on TV until after 10 pm.

6 Correct the mistake in each sentence.

1. The DVD what you lent me was really interesting.
2. The actor, that was in the Nike advert, is famous now.
3. The people which we spoke to helped us a lot.
4. The film, which director is French, has won an Oscar.
5. I have two jobs where take up all my time.
6. I ate melon, that is quite unusual in winter, at the restaurant.

Grammar summary | UNIT 10

REPORTED SPEECH AND REPORTING VERBS

We use reported speech to report someone's words or thoughts. We can use different verbs to express the message of the original words, which is also called direct speech.

Reported statements

Verb tenses, pronouns, possessive adjectives, and adverbs of time and place change when we report people's words. The most common reporting verb for statements is *say*. After the reporting verb, *that* is optional.

- Present simple becomes past simple. When the situation is still true at the moment of reporting, the present simple doesn't need to change.
  Kate: 'I listen to music on the way to work.'
  Kate said (that) **she listened / she listens** to music on the way to work.

- Past simple usually becomes past perfect, though it may stay as past simple.
  Kate: 'I didn't hear my alarm clock.'
  Kate said (that) **she hadn't heard / she didn't hear her** alarm clock.

- Present continuous becomes past continuous.
  Kate: 'Jack isn't working today.'
  Kate said (that) Jack **wasn't working that day**.

- Past continuous becomes past perfect continuous.
  Kate: 'We were watching a great movie.'
  Kate said (that) **they had been watching** a great movie.

- The modal verbs *might*, *should*, *would* and *could* don't usually change. *Will* becomes *would*. *Must* becomes *had to*.
  Kate: 'We might stay here this weekend.'
  Kate said (that) **they might** stay **there that weekend**.
  Kate: 'I'll phone the office tomorrow.'
  Kate said (that) **she'd** phone the office **the next day**.'

▶ Exercise 1

Reported questions

We don't use auxiliary verbs or question marks when we report questions. The subject–verb order is affirmative, not interrogative. The most common reporting verb for questions is *ask*. We don't use *that* after the reporting verb: we refer to the person the question was directed to.

- We use *if* or *whether* to report yes/no questions.
  Kate: 'Did you hear about the new exam?'
  Kate asked (**me**) **if/whether I'd heard** about the new exam.

- We use the same *wh-* word to report questions with *who*, *where*, *what*, *why*, etc.
  Kate: 'What were you talking about with Jack?'
  Kate asked (**us**) **what we'd been talking** about with Jack.

Pronoun, adjective and adverb changes

When the original words were spoken at a different time/place from when/where they are reported, changes to words referring to people, time and place might need to be made.

Direct speech	→	Reported speech
I	→	he/she
we	→	they
my	→	his/her
our	→	their
now	→	then
today	→	that day
tomorrow	→	the next day
yesterday	→	the day before
last night	→	the night before
here	→	there
this office	→	that office

▶ Exercises 2 and 3

Reporting verbs and patterns

The most common reporting verbs are *say* and *tell*, but there are many other reporting verbs which give more information about the speaker's intention. The most common verb for reporting questions is *ask*. *Say* and *tell* use different patterns. Some other verbs use more than one pattern.

- **verb + *that***
  The student **said that** he hadn't been listening.
  The student: 'I wasn't listening.'
  Verbs that use this pattern include: *admit, agree, deny, explain, realize, say, warn*

- **verb + object + (*not*) *to* + infinitive**
  The speaker **told the audience to think** about their own experiences.
  The speaker: 'Think about your own experiences.'
  Verbs that use this pattern include: *advise, ask, convince, encourage, invite, persuade, remind, tell, warn*

- **verb + object + *that***
  The speaker **told the audience that** she had discovered something amazing.
  The speaker: 'I've discovered something amazing.'
  Verbs that use this pattern include: *advise, persuade, tell, warn*

- **verb + *-ing***
  The saleswoman **recommended buying** the programme.
  The saleswoman: 'You should buy the programme.'
  Verbs that use this pattern include: *admit, advise, deny, mention, propose, recommend, suggest*

- **verb + (*not*) *to* + infinitive**
  James **promised not to interrupt** my speech.
  James: 'I won't interrupt your speech.'
  Verbs that use this pattern include: *agree, offer, promise, refuse, threaten*

▶ Exercises 4–6

EXERCISES

1 Read the original statements. Then complete the reported statements.

1 'I never phone customer helplines.'
He said that he never _____ customer helplines.
2 'We're thinking about making a complaint.'
He said they _____ about making a complaint.
3 'Everything went wrong on the trip.'
He said that everything _____ wrong on the trip.
4 'We didn't have a good time.'
She said that they _____ a good time.
5 'I'll write a letter to Customer Service.'
He said he _____ a letter to Customer Service.
6 'We might request a refund for the full cost of the trip.'
He said they _____ a refund for the full cost of the trip.

2 Read the original questions. Then complete the reported questions.

1 'Do you know the number for Customer Service?'
He asked me _____ the number for Customer Service.
2 'What did you say to the receptionist?'
She asked us _____ to the receptionist.
3 'Will you be at work tomorrow?'
He asked me _____ at work _____.
4 'Where have they decided to go on holiday?'
She asked me _____ on holiday.
5 'Can you finish this work today?'
She asked me _____ the work _____.
6 'How long have you all worked here?'
He asked us _____.

3 Read the conversation. Then report each person's words using *said* and *asked*.

1 Mark: I heard a great song on the radio this morning.
2 Anya: Which station were you listening to?
3 Mark: I don't know its name. I was in a café.
4 Anya: Why didn't you ask one of the waiters?
5 Mark: It was too busy to interrupt them.
6 Anya: You could go back there tomorrow.

1 _____
2 _____
3 _____
4 _____
5 _____
6 _____

4 Complete the sentences with reporting verbs using the correct patterns.

1 The manager _____ (explain / that) they had been very busy that morning.
2 The assistant _____ (suggest / wait) a few minutes longer.
3 The customer _____ (tell / the company / that) he wasn't satisfied.
4 The manager _____ (promise / give) everyone a discount.
5 The receptionist _____ (persuade / the customer / not / complain).
6 The driver _____ (ask / us / stay) in our seats.
7 The customer _____ (deny / start) an argument.
8 The company _____ (realize / that) they had made a mistake.

5 Read the direct speech. Then complete the reported speech with the correct verb. There is one extra verb.

| admitted | advised | agreed | invited |
| offered | recommended | told | |

1 'The best thing is to call a TV engineer.'
The shop assistant _____ calling a TV engineer.
2 'If I were you, I'd go back to the shop.'
A friend _____ us to go back to the shop.
3 'This TV we bought last week doesn't work.'
We _____ the assistant that the TV didn't work.
4 'It's true that our service was not good enough.'
The manager _____ that their service was not good enough.
5 'Yes, of course we'll replace the TV.'
The manager _____ to replace the TV.
6 'We'd be happy to give you some free DVDs.'
The manager _____ to give us some free DVDs.

6 Correct the mistake in each sentence.

1 Our teacher explained us the homework.
2 I asked them where had they been.
3 My friend told that he'd bought a new car.
4 The manager said them that they could have a refund.
5 I asked the woman to not phone me before lunchtime.
6 I recommend that you doing this course.

Grammar summary | UNIT 11

ARTICLES: *A, AN, THE*, ZERO ARTICLE

a, an

The articles *a* and *an* come before singular countable nouns.
*There's **a cloud** on the horizon.*
*Cloudspotting is **an activity** I really enjoy.*

We use *a* and *an* before:
- something we mention for the first time
  *Last weekend I discovered **a café** that sells amazing cakes.*
- something which is one of many
  *If you're going to the shop, could you get me **a packet** of crisps?*

the

The article *the* comes before specific singular or plural countable nouns and specific uncountable nouns.
*People send photos of clouds to **the website**.*
***The photos** people send us are always interesting.*
*I like **the sunshine** in this photo.*

We use *the* before:
- something we have already mentioned
  *I took photos of clouds and later tried to identify **the clouds** on the website.*
- something that is unique
  *There's a cloud on **the horizon**.*
- something which is specific in the given context
  *I love looking at **the photos** people send us.*
- the names of some countries, places and geographical features (oceans, seas, deserts, rivers, mountain ranges)
  the United States of America, the Middle East, the Arctic Ocean, the Mediterranean Sea, the Gobi Desert, the Amazon, the Rockies, etc.

▶ Exercise 1

no (zero) article

There is no article before general plural nouns and uncountable nouns.
*I love **clouds**, but I prefer **sunshine**.*

We use no article before:
- plural things or people in general
  *I don't really understand how **cars** work.*
- an uncountable thing in general
  *I didn't know **oil** had so many uses.*
- the names of most countries, states, cities, lakes, mountains, languages, people and companies
  Australia, Alaska, Frankfurt, Lake Geneva, Kilimanjaro, Russian, Volvo, etc.

▶ Exercise 2

QUANTIFIERS

each, every, the whole

We use these expressions before singular countable nouns. They refer to the totality of individual things or of a single thing. We use: *every* for three or more (not two) things; *each* for two or more things; *the whole* for the total number of things in a defined group or set (a team, a week, etc).
*There's a meeting **each/every** month.*
*Decisions must be agreed by **the whole committee**.*

few, a few, several, both, a large/small number, (not) many

We use these expressions before plural countable nouns. They indicate approximate numbers.
***A large number of** / **A small number of** / **Several of** / **Many of my friends** came to meet me.*

- *both* = two things
  *There's a meeting on Monday and one on Tuesday. I will be at **both meetings**.*
- *a few* = a small number, but with a positive meaning
  *It was a good meeting and we got **a few things** organized.*
- *few* = a small number, but with a negative meaning
  *We talked for ages, but there were **few points** of agreement.*

little, a little, a large/small amount, (not) much

We use these expressions before uncountable nouns. They indicate approximate quantity.
*They found **a large amount of** / **a small amount of oil**.*

- *a little* = a small quantity, but with a positive meaning
  *I can lend you **a little money** if you need some.*
- *little* = a small quantity, but with a negative meaning
  *It's shocking – they work hard for **little money**.*

either, neither, all, any, no, a lot of

- We use *either* and *neither* before singular nouns to talk about two things or options.
  *Monday or Tuesday – **either day** is fine for me.*
  *Monday or Tuesday? **Neither day** is possible for me.*
- We use *either* with a verb in the negative form, or *neither* with a verb in the affirmative form. The meaning is the same.
  *I did**n't** think **either** / I thought **neither** solution was suitable.*
- We use *all, any, no* and *a lot of* before countable nouns and uncountable nouns. *All* indicates an entire group or quantity. *No* indicates a lack of something. *A lot of* indicates a large quantity. We use *any* in questions and negative forms only.
  ***All/No meetings** are held at weekends.*
  ***All/No petrol** sold here is unleaded.*
  *Were there **any meetings**? / There wasn't **any petrol**.*
  *There were **a lot of people**. / There was **a lot of oil**.*

▶ Exercises 3–6

EXERCISES

1 Choose the correct options to complete the conversation.

A: There was ¹ *an / the* article in the Independent yesterday about ² *a / the* price of petrol.
B: Was that ³ *an / the* article by George Montrose? I didn't have time to read it. I had ⁴ *a / the* really busy day.
A: He said that ⁵ *a / the* big oil companies should reduce their prices because globally ⁶ *a / the* demand for oil is falling.
B: Well, it's ⁷ *an / the* interesting idea, but I don't remember ever seeing ⁸ *a / the* decrease in prices at the petrol station!

2 Add *the* where necessary.

Fracking is a process for extracting ¹ _____ oil and ² _____ gas from ³ _____ deposits deep underground. ⁴ _____ process is very controversial because ⁵ _____ impact on ⁶ _____ environment can be very damaging. Two of ⁷ _____ biggest concerns are ⁸ _____ water pollution and ⁹ _____ carbon emissions. In addition, fracking is a very expensive way of extracting ¹⁰ _____ resources like these.

3 Cross out the option which is not possible.

1 I promise that I'll be on time *every / the whole / each* morning.
2 We met *both / all / much* of your employees yesterday.
3 The conference organizers provided *several / a large amount of / little* food.
4 Are there *many / much / a few* emails that need an answer today?
5 He read *the whole / a small amount of / every* report in one morning.
6 I didn't have *many / much / a large amount of* work in my old job, so I got bored easily.
7 The result was a surprise to *all / each / the whole* team.
8 There were *many / much / several* responses to the enquiry.

4 Choose the correct option to complete the sentences.

1 We had *a few / a little* enquiries about the society yesterday.
2 There's very *little / few* time left to take a decision about the product name.
3 Could you pay *a few / a little* attention, please? This point is important.
4 Apparently, *little / few* people went to the meeting.
5 We were disappointed that there was *little / a little* interest in our idea.
6 It's strange that *a few / few* customers took up the special offer.
7 I had *a few / a little* interesting phone calls this morning.
8 It's no surprise that *few / little* customers wanted to pay that price!

5 Complete the conversation with the expressions. There is one extra expression.

| a lot of | all | any | both | either | neither | no |

A: Have you got a gas oven or an electric oven at home?
B: Actually I have ¹ _____. I only have a microwave. I use that for ² _____ my hot food.
A: Don't you actually cook ³ _____ meals?
B: Well, I don't do ⁴ _____ cooking. I'm not really interested in it.
A: I can't imagine having ⁵ _____ oven!
B: Well, you'd be surprised what you can do in a microwave. When I got it, I was considering ⁶ _____ a microwave or a mini-oven. But the microwave is all I need.

6 Correct the mistake in each sentence.

1 I download a lot of music from Internet.
2 I love my new job – I'm analyst for a big oil company.
3 A big challenge for us all is the climate change.
4 I really have few time to finish all my work.
5 I can't choose between the city and the country – I like the both.
6 I listen to English online all days.

Grammar summary | UNIT 12

THIRD CONDITIONAL

If-clause	Main clause
If + past perfect,	*would have* + past participle

The third conditional pattern has two parts: the *if*-clause and the main clause. The *if*-clause is followed by a comma. We can contract both *had* in the *if*-clause and *would* in the main clause to *'d*.
  *If I **had known** you were sleeping, I **would have called** you later.*
  *If I**'d known** you were sleeping, I**'d have called** you later.*

The sentence can also begin with the main clause, in which case there is no comma.
  *I**'d have called** you later if I**'d known** you were sleeping.*

We use the third conditional to talk about events that did not happen. We imagine the event and we imagine the result. The *if*-clause refers to the imagined condition and the main clause refers to the imagined result.
  *If she**'d asked** me, I**'d have helped** her.*
  (She didn't ask me, so I didn't help her.)

Questions with the third conditional are usually made by using the question form of the main clause, not the *if*-clause.
  ***Would** you **have helped** her if she**'d asked** you?*
  *If she**'d asked** you, **would** you **have helped** her?*

▶ Exercises 1 and 2

MIXED CONDITIONAL SENTENCES

Mixed third + second conditional

If-clause	Main clause
If + past perfect,	*would* + infinitive without *to*

We use mixed third + second conditional sentences to talk about a past condition and its result in the present or the future (not the past).
  *If you **hadn't helped** me with this software, **I wouldn't be able to** use it.* (You did help me, so I am able to / will be able to use it.)

Mixed second + third conditional

If-clause	Main clause
If + past simple,	*would have* + past participle

We use mixed second + third conditional sentences to talk about a present condition and its imagined past result.
  *If the fitness app **didn't exist**, I **wouldn't have realized** how unfit I am.* (The app does exist, so I did realize how unfit I was.)

▶ Exercises 3 and 4

wish

We use *wish* to express regrets.

We use *wish* + past simple to talk about something that is the opposite of how we want it. Its use is linked to the use of the second conditional.
  *I wish you **didn't live** such a long way away now.* (You live a long way away now.)
  *Maya wishes I **lived** in the same town as she does.*
  *Does Sonia wish she **lived** closer to you?*

We use *wish* + past perfect to talk about something that is the opposite of how we wanted. Its use is linked to the use of the third conditional.
  *I wish you **hadn't moved** to New York last year.* (You moved to New York last year.)
  *Eduardo wishes I**'d stayed** in London.*
  *Do you wish you **hadn't left** London?*

We don't often say *don't wish* or *didn't wish*. We can say both *I wish I* + past simple and *I wish I* + past perfect.

▶ Exercise 5

PAST MODALS (2)

We can use the modals *could (not)*, *might (not)*, *should (not)* and *must (not)* instead of *would* with *have* + past participle.

- We use *could have* and *might have* + past participle in third conditional patterns to talk about possible actions as a result of imagined past events.
  *If you'd told us our choice wasn't available, we **could have chosen** a different product.*
  *If you'd told us there were other options, we **might have chosen** a different product.*

- We don't use *couldn't have* + past participle with third conditional patterns. We use *couldn't have* to talk about things that were impossible.
  *We **couldn't have chosen** a different product – there were no other options.*

- We use *should have* and *shouldn't have* + past participle to criticize past actions. It can also express regret.
  *If there was no alternative available, you **should have told** us earlier.*
  *I **should have checked** all the details, but I didn't have time.*

- We use *must have* + past participle to express a deduction about a past event.
  *There are no tickets left after only two days – they **must have sold out** really quickly.*

▶ Exercises 6 and 7

162

EXERCISES

1 Choose the logical option to complete these third conditional sentences. Each option is grammatically correct.

1. If Jack hadn't argued with his boss, *he'd have lost / he wouldn't have lost* his job.
2. If *they'd analysed / they hadn't analysed* the data sooner, they'd have found the problem.
3. I wouldn't have left Facebook if *I'd known / I hadn't known* how useful it was.
4. *We'd have made / We wouldn't have made* a mess of it if we'd read the instructions.
5. If *you'd remembered / you hadn't remembered* your password, you wouldn't have been locked out of your account.
6. If scientists hadn't shown the effects of smoking on health, more people *would have died / wouldn't have died*.

2 Read the first sentence. Then write a sentence with the third conditional to give the same information. Begin each sentence with *If*.

1. Jack won a lot of money, so he bought a car.
   _____
2. My friends didn't know I was at home, so they didn't visit me.
   _____
3. I had a day off work because I felt ill.
   _____
4. Everyone passed the exam because it was very easy.
   _____
5. The film was really interesting, so we watched it twice.
   _____
6. You didn't tell me about the article, so I didn't read it.
   _____

3 Match the parts to make mixed conditional sentences.

1. If Alice Stewart hadn't researched childhood cancer,
2. If you had taken the medicine,
3. If I hadn't failed my exams,
4. If it wasn't so difficult to get a job with that company,
5. If Twitter didn't exist,
6. If the company was more well-known,

a. I'd have started working there ages ago.
b. I'd have the job of my dreams today.
c. sales would have been much better.
d. somebody would have invented something similar.
e. we'd still give X-rays to pregnant women.
f. you would feel better by now.

4 Complete the mixed conditional sentences with the correct form of the verb.

1. If I'd invented Youtube, I _____ (be) a millionaire.
2. If you _____ (not / be / always) so forgetful, you would have found the car keys more quickly.
3. If we _____ (not / keep) in touch online, would we know each other now?
4. I _____ (see) more adverts online if I hadn't installed the blocking software.
5. There would be a serious flu epidemic if doctors _____ (not / give) everyone a vaccination.
6. Where _____ you _____ (be) today if you hadn't decided to stay in New York?

5 Read the situations. Then write a sentence (S) or a question (Q) with *wish* to express regret.

1. We're lost because we haven't got a map. (S)
2. If it was Saturday, I'd be at the beach. (Q)
3. I changed my job last month, but it was a mistake. (S)
4. Lois can't apply for the job because she doesn't speak French. (S)
5. Dani says the car he hired was really expensive. (Q)
6. I think the hotel's awful. We should have chosen a different one. (S)

6 Choose the correct option to complete the sentences.

1. It was our mistake. We *might have / should have* given you the correct information.
2. The plane was delayed by four hours. The passengers *might have / must have* been furious.
3. If the train had had wi-fi, I *could have / couldn't have* checked my emails on the journey.
4. I can't believe David missed his flight. He *should have / shouldn't have* stopped for a meal on the way to the airport.
5. Don't worry about getting to the meeting late. You *couldn't have / mightn't have* known the traffic would be bad.
6. If the service had been better, I *might have / must have* thought about using the company again.

7 Correct the mistakes in these sentences.

1. If you would have worked harder, you'd have passed your exam.
2. Tom wouldn't be ill if he would have taken his tablets.
3. I wouldn't have been successful, if you hadn't supported me.
4. If the epidemic had spread, more people would died.
5. If we didn't have bought the tablet, we would have bought a laptop.
6. What you would have done if you had failed the exam?
7. I'm sorry I'm late – I must have phoned you to let you know.
8. I often think I would have chosen a different career.

163

Communication activities

Unit 1.2 Exercise 10, page 13

Consumer: You get most of your entertainment online and on demand. You don't believe in old-fashioned things like DVDs or paper books. For you, the online world is *the* world. Try to limit your use of pirate sites!

Networker: Your professional life would fall apart if you couldn't go online. You use the Internet to stay in touch with colleagues and contacts and/or do a large chunk of your work online too. You're never out of reach, but remember, everyone needs a break now and then.

Dinosaur: You prefer to do things face-to-face and in real time. You get fed up with the way modern life and work depends so much on the Internet. What's wrong with meeting over a cup of real coffee, you ask? Don't get left behind – times have moved on from the 20th century!

Unit 10.3 Exercise 10, page 113
Student A

In the United States, the minimum wage for employees who get tips (such as bartenders and waitresses) is under $3 an hour. They often depend on customers' tips to earn a living wage.

Unit 11.3 Exercise 11, page 125
Student A

WFP: World Food Programme
WFP is the world's largest humanitarian agency fighting hunger. In 2011, the WFP provided 3.6 million tonnes of food to people in 75 countries, including school meals of cups of rice or beans to 23 million school children. As well as providing food, the WFP promotes agricultural production in local communities.

Unit 12.2 Exercise 8, page 133
Student A

1950s The USA and the (then) USSR started programmes to explore space. A whole range of new technology was invented (non-stick pans, freeze-dried food, solar cells, etc.).
1980 CNN, the US TV news network, was founded.

Unit 10.3 Exercise 10, page 113
Student B

In the United States, the service charge may be added to the bill, but you're not legally required to pay it. It is, however, considered unacceptable to deduct the amount from what you pay.

Unit 11.3 Exercise 11, page 125
Student B

Greenpeace
The first ever Greenpeace campaign was in 1971, against nuclear weapons testing. Since then, Greenpeace has worked to stop the killing of whales for food and has supported the United Nations convention on better management of the world's fish resources.

Unit 12.2 Exercise 8, page 133
Student B

1962 The Decca record company said there was no future in guitar groups and didn't give the Beatles a contract.
2003 The human genome was finally decoded.

Unit 10.3 Exercise 10, page 113
Student C

In the United States, if you don't tip, the restaurant manager or employee is likely to ask you why you didn't. If the service was bad, you should explain this. Just saying you object on principle isn't an appropriate response.

Unit 11.3 Exercise 11, page 125
Student C

Save the Children
Between 2006 and 2009, Save the Children's *Rewrite the Future* campaign helped 1.4 million more children go to school. In 1979, it launched the Stop Polio Campaign as part of an attempt to get rid of polio worldwide. Since its beginnings in 1919, it has supported children in all countries in times of conflict, hunger and natural disaster.

Unit 12.2 Exercise 8, page 133
Student C

1977 The first *Star Wars* film was released.
2014 A contestant on a TV quiz show in the USA failed to win a million dollars because he pronounced the word 'Achilles' wrongly.

Unit 11.3 Exercise 11, page 125
Student D

IFRC: International Federation of Red Cross and Red Crescent Societies
After the 2004 Indian Ocean Tsunami, the IFRC gave humanitarian support to more than 4.3 million people; 57,000 new homes were built; 700,000 people were given access to improved water supplies; and 63,000 families received cash, training or equipment to help them rebuild their lives. The IFRC is the world's largest humanitarian organization, providing assistance without discrimination as to nationality, race, religious beliefs, class or political opinions.

Audioscripts

Unit 1

🎧 1

1. At four oh four the next day, we gave out four hundred and four dollars in cash.
2. But these things [404 pages] are everywhere. They're on sites big, they're on sites small.
3. The 404 page is that. It's that broken experience on the Web. It's effectively the default page when you ask for something and a website can't find it.
4. You can type in an url and put in a 404 and these [webpages] will pop.

🎧 2

P = Presenter

P: Every day, millions of videos are uploaded to the Internet, but very few of them go viral. If you think that it's impossible to predict what kind of videos go viral, you might be right. But the phenomenon of viral videos is fast-growing. And more people than ever are posting videos online. The whole phenomenon is being studied closely, because there's a lot of money to be made if you can reach an audience of millions with your video. But the key to a viral video isn't how it's spread – it's the content. The mechanism for the spread of viral videos is clear and it's quite different to traditional mass media. Millions of people watch mass media every day and they all see a broadcast at the same time, whereas online videos are seen by a much smaller number at first, and then they are shared with the viewers' contacts. They can be seen multiple times and at any time the user chooses. A viral video is ultimately viewed by a huge, global audience. A lot of people who started out posting videos as a hobby now host adverts on their sites and so they've turned their hobby into a source of income. Later on in the programme, we'll be talking to three people who have done exactly that. But first, the business news headlines.

🎧 3

1a You can get that music as a download quite cheaply.
1b Do you know how to download music files?
2a How often do you use online shopping sites?
2b When I go online, I usually check my emails first.
3a I never update my Facebook status. Do you?
3b I don't know how to install this software update.
4a With this app, you can upload photos really quickly.
4b What's the difference between an upload and an attachment?

🎧 4

Conversation 1

P = Paul, R = Rowan

P: Do you mind if I join you?
R: No, not at all.
P: I'm Paul, TGB Systems. How are you finding the conference?
R: It's pretty good so far. I'm Rowan, by the way. I'm with Alliance Graphics.
P: Pleased to meet you. Alliance Graphics … you're based in Edinburgh?
R: Yes, that's right, but we're opening up a couple of new offices in other cities too.
P: So things are going well, then?
R: Actually, yes. And that's why I'm here really, at this conference. It's got a lot to offer us right now.

Conversation 2

J = Joan, N = Nikolai

J: Hello. I'm Joan, I live on Rowan Street.
N: Hi, nice to meet you.
J: I believe you live near Marco? Is that right?
N: Yes, we're next-door neighbours. We moved in last year, number 25. I'm Nikolai.
J: Ah yes, Nikolai. Marco and I used to work together on the neighbourhood committee.
N: Really? I didn't know he'd been on the committee. What was that like?
J: Oh, you know – interesting but time-consuming. So how do you like living here?
N: Oh it's great. We're really happy here.

Conversation 3

R = Roger, E = Elise

R: Hi.
E: Hello. I don't think we've met. I'm one of BKG's regional co-ordinators, Elise Binoche.
R: My pleasure. I'm Roger Kennedy, Global Digital Strategies Director at Lynne Robson Jones.
E: Digital Strategies? What kind of things does that involve?
R: Well, I work primarily in web technologies. I handle viral marketing and social media for our international clients.
E: That sounds interesting. Viral marketing is a really exciting thing to be involved in, I guess.
R: It is. It's fun too.

🎧 5

1. You're based in Edinburgh?
2. So things are going well, then?
3. I believe you live near Marco?
4. How do you like living here?
5. Digital Strategies?

🎧 6

1. You're based in Edinburgh?
2. So things are going well, then?
3. I believe you live near Marco?
4. Digital Strategies?

Unit 2

🎧 7

1. Everyone, please think of your biggest personal goal.
2. For real – you can take a second.
3. You've got to feel this to learn it.
4. Take a few seconds and think of your personal biggest goal, OK?

🎧 8

1. Well, bad news: you should have kept your mouth shut, because that good feeling now will make you less likely to do it.
2. So, let's look at the proof. 1926, Kurt Lewin, founder of social psychology, called this 'substitution'.

165

3   It goes like this: 163 people across four separate tests – everyone wrote down their personal goal.
4   So, if this is true, what can we do? Well, you could resist the temptation to announce your goal.

🎧 9

Conversation 1

P = Presenter, G = Giselle

P: Giselle, you're our youngest contestant. How old are you?
G: I'm nine.
P: That's very young to be a chef.
G: I know, but my family own a restaurant and I've been there since I was like two years old ... and I'm crazy about cooking. I'm going to run my own restaurant, with my mom.
P: OK! Now Giselle, are you going to make it to the final of Junior Chef?
G: Totally!
P: Good job! And what will you have learned by then, do you think?
G: Some new skills, I guess. Some tricks of the trade ... and hopefully I'll learn enough to be a judge on Junior Chef one day.

Conversation 2

P = Presenter, J = Jared

P: So Jared, are you looking forward to today's challenge? What will you be making for us today?
J: It's a kind of ravioli with seafood, it's my own recipe.
P: Sound delicious. So Jared, you are twelve years old, right? Where do you think you'll be in ten years' time? Do you see yourself in college, maybe?
J: College, I don't know ... I want to be famous, a really famous chef. I think I'll have made my name by 22.
P: With your seafood ravioli as your signature dish?
J: Absolutely!

Conversation 3

P = Presenter, M = Maisie

P: Maisie, that looks awesome! Now, what's your food dream?
M: I want to have a chain of restaurants.
P: A chain?
M: Yeah, I hope I'll have opened at least four or five places before I'm 21.
P: Right! So how are you feeling about today's challenge?
M: I'm cool. It's basically pasta and I do a lot of pasta dishes at home.
P: So you're pretty confident?
M: I am. Somebody will be going home at the end of today's show, but it's not going to be me.

🎧 11

J = Jill, A = Andy

J: Hi, Andy. It's Jill. Do you have a moment? I was just wondering if you could check my application for that job I told you about? The closing date for applications is next week. So it's a bit urgent.
A: Yeah, of course. Do you want to email it to me and I'll have a look through it?
J: That would be great. I'm sending it through to you now.
A: And then do you want to meet up and talk about it? And we could prepare you for the interview too.
J: OK, then. I'd really appreciate that! When are you free? I'm not doing anything all week, so any time is good for me.
A: Let me look at my schedule ... I'm working late on Tuesday and Wednesday, but I should be able to get away early on Thursday.
J: Let's say Thursday at six, then. I'll come round to your place, if that's OK with you.
A: Yeah, that's fine with me. When are the interviews, by the way?
J: Just a moment, let me check ... they're on two days – the 12th and 15th of next month.
A: Right, so you'll need to do a bit of research and bring some information about the company with you on Thursday.
J: Yeah, I can do that. And will you send the checked form back to me?
A: Yes, either that or I'll print it out and bring it with me.
J: Right, see you on Thursday, then. Thanks again.

🎧 12

1   I was just wondering if you could check my application?
2   And we could prepare you for the interview too.
3   Any time is good for me.
4   I'll come round to your place, if that's OK with you.

Unit 3

🎧 14

1   I still remember the day in school when our teacher told us that the world population had become three billion people, and that was in 1960.
2   And I'm going to talk now about how world population has changed from that year and into the future.
3   And that's what I'm going to show you, because since 1960 what has happened in the world up to 2010 is that a staggering four billion people have been added to the world population. Just look how many. The world population has doubled since I went to school.

🎧 **15** Trends in household expenditure have not shown great changes over the past ten years. The biggest chunk of household spending goes on housing and utilities, and this has jumped from 22 per cent to 26 per cent. Equally, transport costs have increased by four per cent. These numbers are not surprising, as fuel costs have been rising steadily over the ten-year period. As fast foods have become more and more popular, our spending on them has tripled. We've also been buying more health products – are we compensating for our poor eating habits? Unusually, given that clothes prices have been falling year-on-year, we still spend the same amount on clothes.

🎧 16

Message 1

L = Louisa

L: Hi there, Elaine. This is Louisa Redhill getting back to you about the licence for live music. I've got all the information you asked for – could you call me back before Friday as our office is closed all next week? Thanks.

Message 2
M = Matt

M: Hi, Elaine. Matt here. I'm just getting back to you about the meeting with the bank manager that we talked about. It's confirmed for Wednesday 4th August at half past nine. Will you be able to make it? Let me know.

Message 3
A = Aziz

A: Good morning, this is a message for Elaine. This is Aziz from ATZ Cars. I'm calling about using your venue for a company event, the weekend of 2nd and 3rd June. Could you email me your prices at Aziz at ATZ dot com, please? That's A for apple, Z for zebra, I for Italy, Z for zebra at ATZ dot com.

Message 4
N = Nelson

N: Hi, Elaine. It's Nelson. I'm returning your call but … err … it looks like I've missed you. I can't make it on Friday, I'm afraid. Also, the report on the market research we did in February and March is ready, and I'll email it to you. I'm out of the office for the rest of the week, but if you've got any questions, you can get in touch with me on 645 698 421.

Unit 4

🎧 **19** Why do so many people reach success and then fail? One of the big reasons is, we think success is a one-way street. So we do everything that leads up to success, but then we get there. We figure we've made it, we sit back in our comfort zone, and we actually stop doing everything that made us successful. And it doesn't take long to go downhill. And I can tell you this happens, because it happened to me.

🎧 **20**

P = Presenter, G = Gina

P: Welcome to the programme, Gina. Many listeners will know you as the founder of the children's charity Places for Kids, which has worked with over 10,000 vulnerable young people in London. You've just been named as one of the 100 most powerful women in the UK. How does that feel?
G: Very odd, to be honest! I don't feel completely comfortable with the idea of power.
P: But your voice is listened to, certainly in the field of children's rights and education. Your charity is very large and successful.
G: I hope that it's successful in the sense that we make a difference. Size itself is not important.
P: How did your charity work begin?
G: I suppose you have to go right back to my childhood. We used to live in India – that's where my family is from originally. And so when we came to London and I went to school, I felt different.
P: Was that a difficult time?
G: It was, yes. Because the other girls wouldn't talk to me. Children can be very cruel. There used to be a girl called Alisha, and she would put my toys in strange places. It's hard to understand.
P: And I think you used to be dyslexic too?
G: Well, I still am dyslexic. I can't send texts or use a computer even now. I think I used to make it worse because I needed glasses, but I didn't use to wear them. So I really couldn't even see properly.
P: But somehow, you survived those experiences.
G: I did. And that was a success story. I got through those difficulties and from them I learned how I could help children.
P: So tell me more about how Places for Kids works …

🎧 **22**

J = Jason, T = Tamara, A = Andy

J: OK, so let's move on now to looking at last summer's Open Day. I think we all agree that it was a great success and we made a good profit on the day, but we still need to talk about how to avoid some of the things that went wrong.
T: Well, we can't do anything about the weather, unfortunately!
J: No, I know. And it hadn't rained for weeks before that day! Oh well. Why don't we think about setting up another covered area?
T: OK, let's look into that. I can do that. But I think the most important thing we need to sort out is the problem with the food. Two people said they'd got food poisoning from the burger stall.
J: Well, that may or may not be true.
T: It doesn't matter – it's a risk we can't afford to take. We should be careful here.
A: I couldn't agree more: that's our priority. We ought to check all the caterers more carefully and see what their certification is, and of course, I don't think we should have that burger stall back.
T: I heard that they went out of business! We made a big mistake getting them in the first place.
J: I think you're right. Actually, I don't think we need to have a burger stall.
T: I'm not sure I'm with you on that. Burgers are really popular and everyone expects them at this kind of thing.
A: OK, so we need to find a new burger stall and also we need to check the whole list of caterers and their certificates. I'll do that. What else?
J: Well, by the end of the day all the litter bins were overflowing and it looked terrible.
T: And I think that's connected to another point – we didn't really have enough volunteer helpers, did we? How about putting something out on Twitter to get more volunteers?
A: I like the sound of that. We got loads of coverage last year, so obviously it's a good way of getting a message out.
T: And we could consider other ways of getting more followers on Twitter. I can have a look into that.
J: Yes, that's a good idea. Let's talk more about that next time.
T: It's a shame we ran out of T-shirts. We'd better get more printed this time.
A: OK … or I could look at the prices first. They were quite a big cost and I think it's better to sell out than to be left with unsold T-shirts.
T: Yes, I think you're right, actually. That's a good point.
J: Now, the other major thing was the children that got hurt …

Unit 5

🎧 24

1. Nowadays people are sitting 9.3 hours a day, which is more than we're sleeping,
2. Sitting is so incredibly prevalent, we don't even question how much we're doing it,
3. Of course there's health consequences to this, scary ones, besides the waist.
4. 'I have to walk my dogs tomorrow. Could you come then?'

🎧 26

A: We don't normally think of tennis as being a particularly risky or dangerous sport, and yet looking back over the last few years, almost all the top players seem to have been injured at some time. Was it always like this?

B: No, I don't think so. There are several reasons why professional tennis is so demanding these days. One is simply the huge number of tournaments there are. In the past, players could rest between big matches, but nowadays players don't get time to get over injuries. Like Juan Martin del Potro – he hurt his hip early in 2011 and he wasn't able to recover until the 2011 season ended. He said that he'd considered retiring several times and it was only the encouragement of his friends that kept him going.

A: Ah yes! I remember Novak Djokovic saying something similar in 2013. He had an ankle injury and said he managed to keep going with his teammates' support, despite the pain. But not everyone has been so lucky, have they? It was a tragedy that Rafael Nadal couldn't defend his Wimbledon title in 2009 because of recurring problems with his left knee.

B: Nadal suffers a lot. He had to miss the US Open in 2014 because of a wrist injury too. It's interesting that he doesn't like to blame injury when he loses, though. Remember Steve Darcis? He succeeded in beating Nadal in a first-round match in 2013, but unfortunately it left him with a damaged shoulder.

A: Yes, he dropped out injured before the second round.

B: And what about Andy Murray? When he was younger, he could play five-set matches easily, but I think his back injury has changed things.

A: Oh yes … he had to have surgery on his back and it's definitely affected his stamina.

B: But what about age? Do you think that's a factor too?

🎧 27

P = Presenter, R = Ryan

P: So, Ryan, you're going to tell us about your amazing 'smart' cushion that should help us keep fit at our desks, aren't you?

R: Yes, I am. Basically it monitors your body and sends a message to your phone when to take a break and move around.

P: Where did the idea come from?

R: From my final-year project at college, actually. I was working on something completely different but spending so long in front of the computer that I could feel the effect on my body – and I'm only 22!

P: So tell us about how you got the money to develop your idea into an actual product. Who funded you? Did you go to a bank?

R: No, we didn't. My partner suggested asking my parents for a loan, but I didn't want to. Actually, we worried that it would be hard to find investors, but it wasn't. We managed to raise about £60,000 which all came from Kickstarter, and that was about three times our target!

P: That's impressive! So, can we buy this wonderful cushion in the shops?

R: Not yet. We're still developing it and we haven't got a name yet. People keep telling us a brand name is really important, so we're giving it as much thought as we can.

P: Well, Ryan, good luck and I for one can't wait to get myself one of your cushions.

🎧 28

P = Presenter, R = Ryan

1. **P:** So, Ryan, you're going to tell us about your amazing 'smart' cushion that should help us keep fit at our desks, aren't you?
   R: Yes, I am.
2. **P:** Where did the idea come from?
   R: From my final-year project at college.
3. **P:** Did you go to a bank?
   R: No, we didn't.
4. **R:** My partner suggested asking my parents for a loan, but I didn't want to.
5. **R:** Actually, we worried that it would be hard to find investors, but it wasn't.
6. **R:** People keep telling us a brand name is really important, so we're giving it as much thought as we can.

Unit 6

🎧 29

How many times have you used the word 'awesome' today? Once? Twice? Seventeen times? Do you remember what you were describing when you used the word? No, I didn't think so, because it's come down to this, people: you're using the word incorrectly, and tonight I hope to show you how to put the 'awe' back in 'awesome'.

🎧 30

Recently, I was dining at an outdoor café, and the server came up to our table, and asked us if we had dined there before, and I said, 'Yes, yes, we have.' And she said, 'Awesome'. And I thought, 'Really? Awesome or just merely good that we decided to visit your restaurant again?'

🎧 31

Conversation 1

S = Shopper, A = Assistant

S: It's so hard to decide, really. My old laptop is five years old, and it's really slow.

A: Well, if laptops slow down like that, there's not much you can do to fix them.

S: I guess not. But I'm wondering about a tablet. It's more in my price range.

A: Ahah! Well, let me show you these particular laptops first. They're excellent value for money because they're last year's models. And we've got a great deal on at the moment – if you decide to buy before the end of the month, we'll extend the guarantee for two years.

S: Oh, that's interesting. So can I have a look at this one?
A: Of course. It's already switched on, so feel free.
S: Thanks. It's quite heavy, isn't it? And I'm just not sure that I can afford to spend that much. If it wasn't so pricey, I'd be really tempted.
A: Well, I can show you some tablets if that's more what you're looking for.
S: Yes, I think so.

Conversation 2

S = Shopper, F = Friend

S: Oh, look at this drill! It's great, and it's just what I need.
F: Really? Look how much it costs! Didn't you want to buy a new toolbox?
S: But this is a really good-quality brand. It's fantastic value for money.
F: Well, I suppose so. But if you got that drill, how often would you use it, really? And what about those other tools you wanted? You wouldn't be able to afford them if you got this drill.
S: Yes, I would. I could put everything on my credit card.
F: Haven't you reached the limit on that?
S: Well, if I've gone over my limit already, it won't make any difference.
F: Listen, we've been in this place for hours. If you don't make up your mind soon, I'm going to get a coffee.
S: OK, I'll take it.
F: Oh no …

32

A = Assistant, C = Customer

A: Good morning. How can I help you today?
C: Hello there. I've got some queries about my phone bill and I was wondering if you could explain why my bill is usually higher than I expect.
A: OK, let's have a look at your contract details, just bear with me a moment. Right, yes, you're on the basic tariff which has a set charge per unit, when probably you should be on the unlimited tariff.
C: And what's the difference between those two tariffs?
A: OK, so if you just take a look at this sheet … if you're on the unlimited tariff – that's this one here.
C: So if I changed to unlimited, would that be more economical?
A: Possibly yes, if your phone use stays as it is now. Let me put it another way: you would pay more, but you would also get more minutes, more free calls and more data use.
C: Did you say I would pay more?
A: Yes, that's correct. You would pay more than your current contract, but less than the additional charges you pay at the moment.
C: And what was my current contract again?
A: As I said, you're on the basic tariff at the moment. But really that's not the most logical tariff for you because you use your phone so much.
C: OK. Well if it's going to be cheaper in the long run to upgrade to the unlimited rate, then I suppose I'll do that.

Review 3 (Units 5 and 6)

35

I = Interviewer, J = Jamila

I: Jamila, tell us how you got involved with the FAR Academy and their skateboard company.
J: Well, I run a club for kids who have problems at school. Most of them left traditional education some time ago because they couldn't fit in. So I'm always looking for ways to get these kids interested in learning, and sport is one of the things that often gives us good results. Our first skateboard workshop was a good example of that.
I: How did it work in practice?
J: Basically, the kids built their own skateboards over a series of sessions. None of them had any of the skills they needed at the beginning, but almost all of them managed to make a skateboard.
I: And what did they learn from that?
J: It was easy to combine the project with some of the traditional school subjects like science or design. At the same time, the fact that the kids were able to commit to coming to workshops over a period of time was a huge step forward for many of them. When they realize that they can do this, it gives them confidence for the future.
I: How are the workshops funded?
J: Well, the skateboard company is a charity which is funded by sponsors, donations and partnerships. They are supported by local councils, corporate partners and individuals. They also work with volunteers – if I had more time, I'd probably become a volunteer myself. I've always loved skateboarding!
I: Why is the company so important to you?
J: I think it's because it brings people together in a very relaxed way – and that's something which this company promotes too. They helped us to organize a community action day and we were able to improve an old skateboard park in our area. Skateboarding is an activity that anyone can do. You don't have to pay a lot to join a club, and you can do it anywhere. It keeps you fit, and you can make some great friends.

Unit 7

37

Conversation 1

TS = Ticket seller, C = Customer

TS: … and here are your tickets. Did you know that you can now get e-tickets for all our local bus journeys?
C: No, I didn't. How does that work?
TS: Just go to our website and choose the kind of ticket you want, and they'll be downloaded to your phone.
C: And will I have to download an app to use them?
TS: Yes, but there are several apps you can choose from. Our tickets work with them all.
C: What about paying for them? How would I do that?
TS: All the main cards are accepted and there's no extra charge for paying by card.
C: Well, it sounds simple enough. Maybe I'll have a go next time.

Conversation 2

C = Customer, BE = Bank employee

C: Excuse me, I wonder if you could help. How do I pay my electricity bill with the self-service machine?
BE: Yes, of course. Let me show you how to do it. OK, so after you've put in your card and your PIN number, choose 'make a payment' on the touch screen.
C: Right. And what do I need to do now?
BE: Now you key in your account number – the one from the bill – and the amount to be paid.
C: OK. And how will I know if it's been paid correctly?
BE: You can print out a receipt by choosing that option on the screen, or you can see your account details. It's updated immediately.
C: Thanks for all your help.

Conversation 3

C = Customer, SA = Shop assistant

C: I shop here quite regularly, so I'm interested in getting your store credit card.
SA: Yes, I can do that for you. If you have your bank details with you, it's easy to arrange today.
C: OK, could I just ask a couple of questions about how it works? When would the money be taken from my account?
SA: The payments are monthly, on the first day of the month, and you can see all the details on your credit card statement.
C: How often are the statements sent out?
SA: They're also monthly.
C: And where do they go? To my home address?
SA: No, they're sent by email.
C: And is there a minimum amount I need to spend?

Unit 8

🎧 **43**

P = Presenter, E = Business editor

P: We've got our business editor in the studio with us today. So Edwina, what has caught your eye in the business news this week?
E: Well, I've been reading about Max Schireson, who's featured in several magazines following his viral blog post.
P: Tell us more.
E: The blog has gone viral because Schireson decided to give up his job as the CEO of a big database company and spend more time with his family. Quite an unusual step for a career businessman.
P: That certainly sounds like a brave thing to do for a CEO. Doesn't he risk limiting his career opportunities in the future?
E: Maybe – not everyone thinks it's a wise choice. But apparently he doesn't miss travelling continually back and forwards from New York to San Francisco and doesn't regret slowing down his career.
P: What was the reaction of his colleagues?
E: Well, it turns out that he hasn't actually left the company altogether: he's still the vice-chairman, so his colleagues encouraged him to do what he felt was right for him.
P: So what benefits has this change brought him?
E: Well, he says he now works a 'normal' full-time schedule instead of a 'crazy' one. This means he now enjoys being involved in the day-to-day care of his three kids and he says he loves helping them with their homework.
P: OK. And what else does he say? Does he recommend following in his footsteps if you're a working parent too?
E: Not exactly. He says he realizes that he's in a privileged position and that it's easier for him than for most parents. What he says is that everyone needs to find the right balance for themselves.
P: And if you're lucky enough to be able to change the way you work …
E: Exactly!

🎧 **44**

C = Carla, S = Steve

C: I haven't had a day off for six months! I need a break! I want to go somewhere new, exciting and not too expensive.
S: Oh, Carla! You don't want much, then!
C: I know, but there's a long weekend coming up and it would be a shame not to make the most of it.
S: Well, you could fly to Rome or Budapest or somewhere on one of those budget city breaks.
C: Yeah, that's a possibility. Although I'd prefer not to deal with airports on a long weekend.
S: OK, you don't want to go abroad. So what are the alternatives? London? There's always something going on there.
C: That's very true, Steve. On the other hand, I've been to London so many times … I'd rather do something new than visit the same old places.
S: And as you said, you have to think about the expense – London's not cheap you know, Carla. Perhaps you'd be better off looking at another option.
C: Yes, but what?
S: Have you thought about an activity weekend? You know, going kayaking or rock climbing? That kind of thing is exciting. And not only that, you'd be doing something totally new.
C: Hmm. I can see your point. But, Steve, I haven't done any sports for years.
S: There are loads of weekends like that for people like you. The only problem would be choosing which one to do.
C: Well, I'd better make my mind up soon if I want to book something.

Unit 9

🎧 **47** So I just want to tell you my story. I spend a lot of time teaching adults how to use visual language and doodling in the workplace.

🎧 **49**

I = Interviewer, C = Chris

I: Chris, you've been in the advertising industry for twenty years now, first as a graphic designer, then you were the art director for one of the biggest advertising agencies in Australia, responsible for adverts seen by millions. Now you run your own business as a consultant.
C: That's right.

I: So you're the best person to explain to us just how the creative process works in advertising. Do you use a different approach according to who the client is?

C: Not really, no. The basic process is the same whether it's a product like soap powder or an NGO like Oxfam. We start with the big picture. That's the basic idea that describes what we're going to do – say, a TV ad to boost sales. And connected to this, we need to know what the overall goal is – something which tells us what the organization wants to achieve. This could be raising their public profile, for example. Then you need to look at the competitors operating in the same areas. It would be disastrous to make an ad that was the same as your client's main business competitor! And then what you really need to know before you can start to come up with ideas is the people who you want to reach with the message – in other words, the target audience.

I: So this is all the background information you need before you can start to think about ideas.

C: Yes, basically. Then we aim for two main things, one is visual and the other is words. So the visuals could be a single photo or video. That's the part of the process that I most enjoy. I just love finding interesting visual ways of representing ideas. And then you need some words too. The slogan, which is a phrase or a sentence, should be short and memorable.

I: And I suppose what a lot of people listening are really interested in is where the ideas come from. How do you come up with them?

🎧 50

N = Nina, G = Greg, J = Joanna

N: OK, welcome everyone. As you know, we're here to talk about the launch of the Series 7 game. Basically we need to agree on a date and a time when Series 7 will go on sale. Greg, what are your thoughts on the date?

G: Well, we obviously want to make the most of the Christmas market, so I think mid-December is best. How about you, Nina?

N: Middle of December – yes, I agree.

J: If I could say something here. I think mid-December might be a little late. I think the beginning of December would be better.

G: It depends what kind of campaign we are going to run, really. I mean, are we thinking about a midnight release with a big build-up?

N: Joanna, would you like to say anything about that?

J: Erm, well there aren't any signs that the public is getting tired of big spectacular launches. So I think opening the stores for a midnight release is still an interesting idea. It creates a lot of excitement around the product.

N: Let me just say that we've got a smaller budget for advertising this year, so we really need to come up with ways of making the launch date memorable.

G: So that would suggest a midnight launch is still a great idea.

🎧 51

1a Greg, what are your thoughts on the date?
1b Greg, what are your thoughts on the date?
2a Joanna, would you like to say anything about that?
2b Joanna, would you like to say anything about that?

Unit 10

🎧 52
We use some pretty cool techniques to do this. One of them is pattern recognition. So in a cocktail party like this, if I say, 'David, Sara, pay attention,' some of you just sat up. We recognize patterns to distinguish noise from signal, and especially our name.

🎧 53
1 differencing is another technique we use
2 filters take us from all sound down to what we pay attention to

🎧 54

J = James, F = Francois

J: Hi, could I speak to Francois Bartolone, please? This is James Rutter.
F: Speaking. Hello, Mr Rutter. Is everything all right with the house?
J: Well, actually it isn't. There's no kettle. How are we going to boil water? What are we supposed to make tea with?
F: Hmm, there's a microwave in the kitchen. Is it broken?
J: A microwave? That's no good for making tea. Are you crazy? The house isn't properly equipped.
F: Well, I'm sorry that you feel that way …
J: Look, we're on holiday. We need to relax. I really think we deserve some sort of a refund.
F: A refund? I don't think so!

🎧 55

N = Neil, P = Pat, R = Rory

N: OK. Well if there's nothing else to add, let's move on to item 2, the helpline. Pat?
P: Yes. Thanks, Neil. OK. Well as you know, at the moment the customer helpline is an 0845 number.
R: And is that a premium-rate line, Pat?
P: It is, yeah. The latest feedback shows that people are really unhappy about this, probably since they're using mobiles more.
N: Yeah …
R: Hmm …
P: I really think the best solution is to change to a free-phone number.
N: You're absolutely right. We'll have to think about this sooner or later. Most of our competitors are moving across to free phones.
R: So, what you're saying is that you think we need to do this too? OK then, why don't I take a look at this? It will mean an additional cost to us, but it's worth looking into. I'll get back to you next week.
N: Great, Rory, thanks. Any other business? … No? OK, thanks. By the way, next month the office is being redecorated, so we'll have to meet somewhere else. I'll email you, so remember to keep an eye out for that.

🎧 56

1	oh	6	OK
2	oh	7	hmm
3	uhuh	8	hmm
4	uhuh	9	yeah
5	OK	10	yeah

Review 5 (Units 9 and 10)

57
P = Presenter, E = Business editor

P: Today we're having a closer look at the world of co-operative businesses. These are businesses which are owned and run by people who are equal members of the co-op. Members are involved in the way the co-op is run and they also share the profits of the business. In the UK, there are over 6,000 businesses set up as co-ops, and they cover the whole range of products and services from supermarkets to web designers. One typical co-op is Alpha Communication, based in the north of England. Our business editor Edwina Jones visited them recently.

E: The marketing sector isn't one that most people associate with co-ops, but Alpha is one of many communications companies operating on co-operative principles. They're a really dynamic group of three designers, two writers and an accountant. The team are all equal owners – directors – of the company. Once they have been paid and all the business costs have been covered, the surplus earnings are returned to the company. The benefit of this approach is that they can grow the business and create more employment opportunities locally.

P: And what about the benefits for the co-op members themselves?

E: Well, on a personal level, job-satisfaction levels are reported as being much higher among people working in a co-op. One of the directors explained to me that Alpha has been in operation for 25 years now and that the creative team has changed several times over the years. However, she said that the co-op's core values haven't changed in this time. The company is guided by the values of co-operation, honesty, equality, fairness and respect. And these values are often shared by Alpha's clients.

P: That's interesting. What kind of clients do they work with?

E: In many cases they are voluntary or community organizations, social enterprise and of course other co-operatives. While I was there, two of the designers offered to show me a social-media campaign they were developing for a local Fairtrade partnership. As they said, the Internet didn't exist when Alpha began, but now online work is the largest part of their business. They do still work on market research, videos, brand development and traditional print materials, of course.

P: It's not the usual image we have of marketing and advertising, is it, Edwina?

Unit 11

59
They get a bad rap. If you think about it, the English language has written into it negative associations towards the clouds. Someone who's down or depressed, they're under a cloud. And when there's bad news in store, there's a cloud on the horizon. I saw an article the other day. It was about problems with computer processing over the Internet. 'A cloud over the cloud,' was the headline.

60
A = Assistant, B = Enquirer

Conversation 1
A: Good morning.
B: Hi there. Is this the right place to find out about the job club?
A: Yeah, sure. You mean help with job applications and interviews, that sort of thing?
B: Yes, a friend told me they run sessions here.
A: We do, yes. Have a seat, please, and I'll get you the information. Just a second.
B: OK, thanks.
…
A: Right, here are all the details. The next sessions are after the holidays. Can I help you with anything else?
B: No thanks. I'll have a read through this first. Thanks for your help.

Conversation 2
A: Can I help you?
B: Yeah, hi. I was wondering if there are any places left on the jewellery-making course? It's this one here, JF2.2 …
A: Let me check. OK, yes, it was full, but we've had a few cancellations at the last minute.
B: Oh, good!
A: So that's the advanced course, for people with some experience of working with gold and silver.
B: Yeah, that's the one.
A: OK, we'll need proof of payment of 50 per cent of the course fee before confirming your place.
B: Can you write the details down for me?
A: It's OK, it's all here in this leaflet.

Conversation 3
A: Hello, Matfield Leisure Centre.
B: Hi, I'm ringing to ask about the judo classes on Thursday evenings. Could you tell me how much they cost?
A: The judo classes for adults?
B: Yes, that's right. On Thursdays.
A: If you could hold on just one moment, please. … There are different rates depending on whether you're already a member of the Centre, what payment plan you'd follow or if you want to pay by the hour. Would you like the address of our website? That's probably the best way to find what you need.
B: Oh, I see. No, it's OK. I can probably find it myself, thank you.

62

1a	after the holidays	4a	a member since last year
1b	after a week	4b	a member of the club
2a	it's for you	5a	one hour for each class
2b	it's for adults	5b	one hour at a time
3a	What's your name?	6a	that's our website
3b	What's your address?	6b	that's our office

Unit 12

65

P = Presenter, J = Journalist

P: If you spend any time at all online, whether you are actually shopping or just looking for information about a new camera, listening to music or streaming videos, then you will almost certainly have noticed that, increasingly, the Internet makes suggestions to you about books you might like to read next, films you might like to watch or products you might want to buy. How does this happen? Well, it's just one example of how businesses are using something called 'big data' to market themselves more efficiently. So what is this thing called big data? How's it different from simple 'data'? That's what we're going to be looking at in today's programme with the help of business journalist Samira Jones. Samira?

J: Hi, well, essentially big data is data that we can now access because of our digital world – it's a huge volume of information that can be extremely complex to analyse using traditional methods. To give a simple example, whereas traditionally a company had to design a market research survey and actually ask customers for responses, these days digital technology keeps track of all kinds of customer behaviour, and in real time. And this information shows trends and changes in behaviour that a company might not have thought about including in their market research. Basically, if traditional data gave enough information, big data wouldn't have become such an important marketing tool.

P: So, let's take the case of a particular toothpaste company that launched a new food line, which was a complete disaster. If they'd had access to big data, would they have marketed the product better? Is that the idea?

J: Yes, in theory, that's one way big data could work. Or perhaps if they'd known more about the market, they wouldn't have made that particular product line. But it's not only in business that big data is useful. It has all kinds of implications. Take the area of health and disease, and one of the big health epidemics of recent times, bird flu. It would have affected many more people if the health authorities hadn't spotted certain trends in the way it was spreading. Even an illness as common as flu can show up quickly because people do online searches for flu medicines. According to one report, a flu epidemic in the USA was predicted ten days before it reached its peak. If the online searches hadn't been tracked, this prediction wouldn't have been possible.

P: And what about for us as individuals? How can big data help us to make decisions in our daily lives?

J: Well, there's an interesting example in Australia. Cycling is becoming more and more popular there, and a lot of cyclists use an app to track all of their journeys. This data provides a useful map of accident blackspots – places where the most accidents happen – so you can change your route if you want to and avoid those spots. It works because so many cyclists downloaded the app. If they hadn't, they wouldn't be able to use the information.

66

Conversation 1

A: So, basically we've had a good month and you have met your targets, well done. The last thing I want to talk about is opening times. If you remember, we carried out extensive market research last month. It's clear that our customers want us to be open later in the evenings and that will affect you.

B: I understand that we have to respond to what customers want, of course. At the moment, this could create some difficulty for me as I have a lot of commitments in the evenings. I wonder if you could look at whether some of my colleagues have more flexibility?

Conversation 2

C: Dan, could I have a quick word? I notice that I haven't had any work from you for a while. You know that this term you're expected to do one assignment a week.

D: Ah, yes. I'm doing my best to keep up with the course. I have a lot on right now. I should explain that I'm in the middle of moving house. It's only a temporary problem, really. I intend to get back on track in the next couple of weeks. I was hoping you could give me some extra time?

Conversation 3

E: Look, we have to do something about the state of this flat. Now that we're all out at work all day, nobody does any housework at all!

F: OK, you're right, we need to talk about it. The thing is, I really haven't got time.

E: I appreciate that, but I'm in the same position. And you don't work in the mornings, so ….

F: That's true, but I'm still busy. Perhaps we could get a cleaner for a few hours a week? It would really make a difference. And it wouldn't cost much if we shared the cost between us.

67

1 I want to talk about how we spend our money.
2 I appreciate that you find this difficult.
3 I intend to make some changes around here.
4 I'm doing my best to keep everyone happy.
5 I was hoping you could do some extra work.
6 Perhaps we could discuss this some time next week?

TED Talk transcripts

The transcripts use British English for all the talks, irrespective of the nationality of the speaker.

Any grammatical inaccuracies in the talks have been left uncorrected in the transcripts.

Unit 1 404, the story of a page not found

0.13 So what I want to try to do is tell a quick story about a 404 page and a lesson that was learned as a result of it. But to start it probably helps to have an understanding of what a 404 page actually is.

0.27 The 404 page is that. It's that broken experience on the Web. It's effectively the default page when you ask a website for something and it can't find it. And it serves you the 404 page. It's inherently a feeling of being broken when you go through it. And I just want you to think a little bit about, remember for yourself, it's annoying when you hit this thing. Because it's the feeling of a broken relationship.

0.55 But these things are everywhere. They're on sites big, they're on sites small. This is a global experience.

1.01 What a 404 page tells you is that you fell through the cracks. And that's not a good experience when you're used to experiences like this. You can get on your Kinect and you can have unicorns dancing and rainbows spraying out of your mobile phone. A 404 page is not what you're looking for. You get that, and it's like a slap in the face.

1.28 So where this comes into play and why this is important is I head up a technology incubator, and we had eight startups sitting around there. And those startups are focused on what they are, not what they're not, until one day Athletepath, which is a website that focuses on services for extreme athletes, found this video.

1.46 (*Video*) Guy: Joey!

1.51 Crowd: Whoa!

1.55 Renny Gleeson: They took that video and they embedded it in their 404 page and it was like a light bulb went off for everybody in the place. Because finally there was a page that actually felt like what it felt like to hit a 404.

2.07 (*Laughter*)

2.08 (*Applause*)

2.11 So this turned into a contest. Dailypath that offers inspiration put inspiration on their 404 page. Stayhound, which helps you find pet sitters through your social network, commiserated with your pet. Each one of them found this. It turned into a 24-hour contest. At 4.04 the next day, we gave out $404 in cash. And what they learned was that those little things, done right, actually matter, and that well-designed moments can build brands. So you take a look out in the real world, and the fun thing is you can actually hack these yourself. You can type in an URL and put in 404 and these will pop. This is one that commiserates with you. This is one that blames you. This is one that I loved. This is an error page, but what if this error page was also an opportunity?

2.54 So it was a moment in time where all of these startups had to sit and think and got really excited about what they could be. Because back to the whole relationship issue, what they figured out through this exercise was that a simple mistake can tell me what you're not, or it can remind me of why I should love you.

3.12 Thank you.

3.14 (*Applause*)

Unit 2 Keep your goals to yourself

0.14 Everyone, please think of your biggest personal goal. For real – you can take a second. You've got to feel this to learn it. Take a few seconds and think of your personal biggest goal, OK? Imagine deciding right now that you're going to do it. Imagine telling someone that you meet today what you're going to do. Imagine their congratulations and their high image of you. Doesn't it feel good to say it out loud? Don't you feel one step closer already, like it's already becoming part of your identity?

0.43 Well, bad news: you should have kept your mouth shut, because that good feeling now will make you less likely to do it. Repeated psychology tests have proven that telling someone your goal makes it less likely to happen. Any time you have a goal, there are some steps that need to be done, some work that needs to be done in order to achieve it. Ideally, you would not be satisfied until you had actually done the work. But when you tell someone your goal and they acknowledge it, psychologists have found that it's called a 'social reality'. The mind is kind of tricked into feeling that it's already done. And then, because you felt that satisfaction, you're less motivated to do the actual hard work necessary. (*Laughter*) So this goes against the conventional wisdom that we should tell our friends our goals, right – so they hold us to it.

1.28 So, let's look at the proof. 1926, Kurt Lewin, founder of social psychology, called this 'substitution'. 1933, Vera Mahler found, when it was acknowledged by others, it felt real in the mind. 1982, Peter Gollwitzer wrote a whole book about this and in 2009, he did some new tests that were published.

1.47 It goes like this: 163 people across four separate tests – everyone wrote down their personal goal. Then half of them announced their commitment to this goal to the room, and half didn't. Then everyone was given 45 minutes of work that would directly lead them towards their goal, but they were told that they could stop at any time. Now, those who kept their mouths shut worked the entire 45 minutes, on average, and when asked afterwards, said that they felt that they had a long way to go still to achieve their goal. But those who had announced it quit after only 33 minutes, on average, and when asked afterwards, said that they felt much closer to achieving their goal.

2.26 So, if this is true, what can we do? Well, you could resist the temptation to announce your goal. You can delay the gratification that the social acknowledgement brings, and you can understand that your mind mistakes the talking for the doing. But if you do need to talk about something, you can state it in a way that gives you no satisfaction, such as, 'I really want to run this marathon, so I need to train five times a week and kick my ass if I don't, OK?'

2.55 So audience, next time you're tempted to tell someone your goal, what will you say? (*Silence*) Exactly, well done.

3.03 (*Applause*)

Unit 3 Global population growth, box by box

0.14 I still remember the day in school when our teacher told us that the world population had become three billion people, and that was in 1960. And I'm going to talk now about how world population has changed from that year and into the future, but I will not use digital technology, as I've done during my first five TED Talks. Instead, I have progressed, and I am, today, launching a brand new analogue teaching technology that I picked up from IKEA: this box.

0.50 This box contains one billion people. And our teacher told us that the industrialized world, 1960, had one billion people. In the developing world, she said, they had two billion people. And they lived away then. There was a big gap between the one billion in the industrialized world and the two billion in the developing world. In the industrialized world, people were healthy, educated, rich, and they had small families. And their aspiration was to buy a car. And in 1960, all Swedes were saving to try to buy a Volvo like this. This was the economic level at which Sweden was. But in contrast to this, in the developing world, far away, the aspiration of the average family there was to have food for the day. They were saving to be able to buy a pair of shoes. There was an enormous gap in the world when I grew up. And this gap between the West and the rest has created a mindset of the world, which we still use linguistically when we talk about 'the West' and 'the Developing World'. But the world has changed, and it's overdue to upgrade that mindset and that taxonomy of the world, and to understand it.

2.13 And that's what I'm going to show you, because since 1960 what has happened in the world up to 2010 is that a staggering four billion people have been added to the world population. Just look how many. The world population has doubled since I went to school. And of course, there's been economic growth in the West. A lot of companies have happened to grow the economy, so the Western population moved over to here. And now their aspiration is not only to have a car. Now they want to have a holiday on a very remote destination and they want to fly. So this is where they are today. And the most successful of the developing countries here, they have moved on, you know, and they have become emerging economies, we call them. They are now buying cars. And what happened a month ago was that the Chinese company, Geely, they acquired the Volvo company, and then finally the Swedes understood that something big had happened in the world. (*Laughter*)

3.18 So there they are. And the tragedy is that the two billion over here that is struggling for food and shoes, they are still almost as poor as they were 50 years ago. The new thing is that we have the biggest pile of billions, the three billions here, which are also becoming emerging economies, because they are quite healthy, relatively well-educated, and they already also have two to three children per woman, as those have. And their aspiration now is, of course, to buy a bicycle, and then later on they would like to have a motorbike also. But this is the world we have today, no longer any gap. But the distance from the poorest here, the very poorest, to the very richest over here is wider than ever. But there is a continuous world from walking, biking, driving, flying – there are people on all levels, and most people tend to be somewhere in the middle. This is the new world we have today in 2010.

4.25 Here I have on the screen my country bubbles. Every bubble is a country. The size is population. The colours show the continent. The yellow on there is the Americas; dark blue is Africa; brown is Europe; green is the Middle East and this light blue is South Asia. That's India and this is China. Size is population. Here I have children per woman: two children, four children, six children, eight children – big families, small families. The year is 1960. And down here, child survival, the percentage of children surviving childhood up to starting school: 60 per cent, 70 per cent, 80 per cent, 90, and almost 100 per cent, as we have today in the wealthiest and healthiest countries. But look, this is the world my teacher talked about in 1960: one billion Western world here – high child-survival, small families – and all the rest, the rainbow of developing countries, with very large families and poor child survival.

5.25 What has happened? I start the world. Here we go. Can you see, as the years pass by, child survival is increasing? They get soap, hygiene, education, vaccination, penicillin and then family planning. Family size is decreasing. They get up to 90-per-cent child survival, then families decrease, and most of the Arab countries in the Middle East is falling down there. Look, Bangladesh catching up with India. The whole emerging economy world joins the Western world with good child survival and small family size, but we still have the poorest billion. Can you see the poorest billion, those boxes I had over here? They are still up here. And they still have a child survival of only 70 to 80 per cent, meaning that if you have six children born, there will be at least four who survive to the next generation. And the population will double in one generation.

6.18 So the only way of really getting world population to stop is to continue to improve child survival to 90 per cent. That's why investments by Gates Foundation, UNICEF and aid organizations, together with national government in the poorest countries, are so good: because they are actually helping us to reach a sustainable population size of the world. We can stop at nine billion if we do the right things. Child survival is the new green. It's only by child survival that we will stop population growth. And will it happen? Well, I'm not an optimist, neither am I a pessimist. I'm a very serious 'possibilist'. It's a new category where we take emotion apart, and we just work analytically with the world. It can be done. We can have a much more just world. With green technology and with investments to alleviate poverty, and global governance, the world can become like this.

7.20 And look at the position of the old West. Remember when this blue box was all alone, leading the world, living its own life. This will not happen. The role of the old West in the new world is to become the foundation of the modern world – nothing more, nothing less. But it's a very important role. Do it well and get used to it.

7.44 Thank you very much.

7.46 (*Applause*)

Unit 4 Success is a continuous journey

0.14 Why do so many people reach success and then fail? One of the big reasons is, we think success is a one-way street. So we do everything that leads up to success, but then we get there. We figure we've made it, we sit back in our comfort zone, and we actually stop doing everything that made us successful. And it doesn't take long to go downhill. And I can tell you this happens, because it happened to me.

0.38 Reaching success, I worked hard, I pushed myself. But then I stopped, because I figured, 'Oh, you know, I've made it. I can just sit back and relax.'

0.46 Reaching success, I always tried to improve and do good work. But then I stopped, because I figured, 'Hey, I'm good enough. I don't need to improve any more.'

0.55 Reaching success, I was pretty good at coming up with good ideas. Because I did all these simple things that lead to ideas. But then I stopped, because I figured I was this hot-shot guy and I shouldn't have to work at ideas, they should just come like magic. And the only thing that came was creative block. I couldn't come up with any ideas.

1.13 Reaching success, I always focused on clients and projects, and ignored the money. Then all this money started pouring in. And I got distracted by it. And suddenly I was on the phone to my stockbroker and my real estate agent, when I should have been talking to my clients.

1:27 And reaching success, I always did what I loved. But then I got into stuff I didn't love, like management. I am the world's worst manager, but I figured I should be doing it, because I was, after all, the president of the company.

1.39 Well, soon a black cloud formed over my head and here I was, outwardly very successful, but inwardly very depressed. But I'm a guy; I knew how to fix it. I bought a fast car. (*Laughter*) It didn't help. I was faster but just as depressed.

1.59 So I went to my doctor. I said, 'Doc, I can buy anything I want. But I'm not happy. I'm depressed. It's true what they say, and I didn't believe it until it happened to me. But money can't buy happiness.' He said, 'No. But it can buy Prozac.' And he put me on anti-depressants. And yeah, the black cloud faded a little bit, but so did all the work, because I was just floating along. I couldn't care less if clients ever called. (*Laughter*)

2.28 And clients didn't call. (*Laughter*) Because they could see I was no longer serving them, I was only serving myself. So they took their money and their projects to others who would serve them better.

2.39 Well, it didn't take long for business to drop like a rock. My partner and I, Thom, we had to let all our employees go. It was down to just the two of us, and we were about to go under. And that was great. Because with no employees, there was nobody for me to manage.

2.54 So I went back to doing the projects I loved. I had fun again, I worked harder and, to cut a long story short, did all the things that took me back up to success. But it wasn't a quick trip. It took seven years.

3.08 But in the end, business grew bigger than ever. And when I went back to following these eight principles, the black cloud over my head disappeared altogether. And I woke up one day and I said, 'I don't need Prozac anymore.' And I threw it away and haven't needed it since.

3.23 I learned that success isn't a one-way street. It doesn't look like this; it really looks more like this. It's a continuous journey. And if we want to avoid 'success-to-failure-syndrome', we just keep following these eight principles, because that is not only how we achieve success, it's how we sustain it. So here is to your continued success. Thank you very much. (*Applause*)

Unit 5 Got a meeting? Take a walk.

0.15 What you're doing, right now, at this very moment, is killing you. More than cars or the Internet or even that little mobile device we keep talking about, the technology you're using the most almost every day is this, your tush. Nowadays people are sitting 9.3 hours a day, which is more than we're sleeping, at 7.7 hours. Sitting is so incredibly prevalent, we don't even question how much we're doing it, and because everyone else is doing it, it doesn't even occur to us that it's not OK. In that way, sitting has become the smoking of our generation.

0.55 Of course there's health consequences to this, scary ones, besides the waist. Things like breast cancer and colon cancer are directly tied to our lack of physical activity. Ten per cent in fact, on both of those. Six per cent for heart disease, seven per cent for type 2 diabetes, which is what my father died of. Now, any of those stats should convince each of us to get off our duff more, but if you're anything like me, it won't.

1.22 What did get me moving was a social interaction. Someone invited me to a meeting, but couldn't manage to fit me in to a regular sort of conference room meeting, and said, 'I have to walk my dogs tomorrow. Could you come then?' It seemed kind of odd to do, and actually, that first meeting, I remember thinking, 'I have to be the one to ask the next question,' because I knew I was going to huff and puff during this conversation. And yet, I've taken that idea and made it my own. So instead of going to coffee meetings or fluorescent-lit conference room meetings, I ask people to go on a walking meeting, to the tune of 20 to 30 miles a week. It's changed my life.

2.03 But before that, what actually happened was, I used to think about it as, you could take care of your health, or you could take care of obligations, and one always came at the cost of the other. So now, several hundred of these walking meetings later, I've learned a few things.

2.19 First, there's this amazing thing about actually getting out of the box that leads to out-of-the-box thinking. Whether it's nature or the exercise itself, it certainly works.

2.30 And second, and probably the more reflective one, is just about how much each of us can hold problems in opposition when they're really not that way. And if we're

	going to solve problems and look at the world really differently, whether it's in governance or business or environmental issues, job creation, maybe we can think about how to reframe those problems as having both things be true. Because it was when that happened with this walk-and-talk idea that things became doable and sustainable and viable.
3.00	So I started this talk talking about the tush, so I'll end with the bottom line, which is, walk and talk. Walk the talk. You'll be surprised at how fresh air drives fresh thinking, and in the way that you do, you'll bring into your life an entirely new set of ideas.
3.18	Thank you.
3.19	(Applause)

Unit 6 Please, please, people. Let's put the 'awe' back in 'awesome'

0.14	How many times have you used the word 'awesome' today? Once? Twice? Seventeen times? Do you remember what you were describing when you used the word? No, I didn't think so, because it's come down to this, people: you're using the word incorrectly, and tonight I hope to show you how to put the 'awe' back in 'awesome'.
0.34	Recently, I was dining at an outdoor café, and the server came up to our table, and asked us if we had dined there before, and I said, 'Yes, yes, we have.' And she said, 'Awesome.' And I thought, 'Really? Awesome or just merely good that we decided to visit your restaurant again?'
0.55	The other day, one of my co-workers asked me if I could save that file as a PDF, and I said, 'Well, of course,' and he said, 'Awesome.' Seriously, can saving anything as a PDF be awesome?
1.13	Sadly, the frequent overuse of the word 'awesome' has now replaced words like 'great' and 'thank you'. So Webster's dictionary defines the word 'awesome' as fear mingled with admiration or reverence, a feeling produced by something majestic. Now, with that in mind, was your Quiznos sandwich awesome? How about that parking space? Was that awesome? Or that game the other day? Was that awesome? The answer is no, no and no. A sandwich can be delicious, that parking space can be nearby, and that game can be a blowout, but not everything can be awesome. (Laughter)
1.57	So when you use the word 'awesome' to describe the most mundane of things, you're taking away the very power of the word. This author says, 'Snowy days or finding money in your pants is awesome.' (Laughter) Um, no, it is not, and we need to raise the bar for this poor schmuck. (Laughter)
2.21	So in other words, if you have everything, you value nothing. It's a lot like drinking from a firehose like this jackass right here. There's no dynamic, there's no highs or lows, if everything is awesome.
2.35	Ladies and gentlemen, here are ten things that are truly awesome.
2.39	Imagine, if you will, having to schlep everything on your back. Wouldn't this be easier for me if I could roll this home? Yes, so I think I'll invent the wheel. The wheel, ladies and gentlemen. Is the wheel awesome? Say it with me. Yes, the wheel is awesome!
2.58	The Great Pyramids were the tallest man-made structure in the world for 4,000 years. Pharaoh had his slaves move millions of blocks just to this site to erect a big freaking headstone. Were the Great Pyramids awesome? Yes, the pyramids were awesome.
3.16	The Grand Canyon. Come on. It's almost 80 million years old. Is the Grand Canyon awesome? Yes, the Grand Canyon is.
3.24	Louis Daguerre invented photography in 1829, and earlier today, when you whipped out your smartphone and you took a shot of your awesome sandwich, and you know who you are – (Laughter) – wasn't that easier than exposing the image to copper plates coated with iodized silver? I mean, come on. Is photography awesome? Yes, photography is awesome.
3.48	D-Day, June 6, 1944, the Allied invasion of Normandy, the largest amphibious invasion in world history. Was D-Day awesome? Yes, it was awesome.
4.00	Did you eat food today? Did you eat? Then you can thank the honeybee, that's the one, because if crops aren't pollinated, we can't grow food, and then we're all going to die. Bees are awesome. Are you kidding me?
4.15	Landing on the moon! Come on! Apollo 11. Are you kidding me? Sixty-six years after the Wright Brothers took off from Kitty Hawk, North Carolina, Neil Armstrong was 240,000 miles away. That's like from here to the moon. (Laughter) That's one small step for man, one giant leap for awesome! You're damn right, it was.
4.42	Woodstock, 1969: Rolling Stone Magazine said this changed the history of rock and roll. Was Woodstock awesome? Yes, it was awesome.
4.52	Sharks! They're at the top of the food chain. Sharks have multiple rows of teeth that grow in their jaw and they move forward like a conveyor belt. Some sharks can lose 30,000 teeth in their lifetime. Does awesome inspire fear? Oh, hell yeah, sharks are awesome!
5.12	The Internet was born in 1982 and it instantly took over global communication. The Internet is awesome.
5.22	And finally, finally some of you can't wait to come up and tell me how awesome my PowerPoint was. I will save you the time. It was not awesome, but it was true, and I hope it was entertaining, and out of all the audiences I've ever had, y'all are the most recent. Thank you and good night.
5.40	(Applause)

Unit 7 The sore problem of prosthetic limbs

0.13	I was born and raised in Sierra Leone, a small and very beautiful country in West Africa, a country rich both in physical resources and creative talent.
0.27	However, Sierra Leone is infamous for a decade-long rebel war in the '90s when entire villages were burnt down. An estimated 8,000 men, women and children had their arms and legs amputated during this time. As my family and I ran for safety when I was about twelve from one of those attacks, I resolved that I would do everything I could to

ensure that my own children would not go through the same experiences we had. They would, in fact, be part of a Sierra Leone where war and amputation were no longer a strategy for gaining power.

1.07 As I watched people who I knew, loved ones, recover from this devastation, one thing that deeply troubled me was that many of the amputees in the country would not use their prostheses. The reason, I would come to find out, was that their prosthetic sockets were painful because they did not fit well. The prosthetic socket is the part in which the amputee inserts their residual limb, and which connects to the prosthetic ankle. Even in the developed world, it takes a period of three weeks to often years for a patient to get a comfortable socket, if ever. Prosthetists still use conventional processes like moulding and casting to create single-material prosthetic sockets. Such sockets often leave intolerable amounts of pressure on the limbs of the patient, leaving them with pressure sores and blisters. It does not matter how powerful your prosthetic ankle is. If your prosthetic socket is uncomfortable, you will not use your leg, and that is just simply unacceptable in our age.

2.20 So one day, when I met Professor Hugh Herr about two and a half years ago, and he asked me if I knew how to solve this problem, I said, 'No, not yet, but I would love to figure it out.' And so, for my PhD at the MIT Media Lab, I designed custom prosthetic sockets quickly and cheaply that are more comfortable than conventional prostheses. I used magnetic resonance imaging to capture the actual shape of the patient's anatomy, then use finite element modelling to better predict the internal stresses and strains on the normal forces, and then create a prosthetic socket for manufacture. We use a 3D printer to create a multi-material prosthetic socket which relieves pressure where needed on the anatomy of the patient. In short, we're using data to make novel sockets quickly and cheaply. In a recent trial we just wrapped up at the Media Lab, one of our patients, a US veteran who has been an amputee for about 20 years and worn dozens of legs, said of one of our printed parts, 'It's so soft, it's like walking on pillows.' (*Laughter*)

3.45 Disability in our age should not prevent anyone from living meaningful lives. My hope and desire is that the tools and processes we develop in our research group can be used to bring highly functional prostheses to those who need them. For me, a place to begin healing the souls of those affected by war and disease is by creating comfortable and affordable interfaces for their bodies. Whether it's in Sierra Leone or in Boston, I hope this not only restores but indeed transforms their sense of human potential.

4.29 Thank you very much.

4.31 (*Applause*)

Unit 8 How to make work–life balance work

0.14 What I thought I would do is I would start with a simple request. I'd like all of you to pause for a moment, you wretched weaklings, and take stock of your miserable existence. (*Laughter*)

0.31 Now that was the advice that St. Benedict gave his rather startled followers in the fifth century. It was the advice that I decided to follow myself when I turned 40. Up until that moment, I had been that classic corporate warrior – I was eating too much, I was drinking too much, I was working too hard and I was neglecting the family. And I decided that I would try and turn my life around. In particular, I decided I would try to address the thorny issue of work–life balance. So I stepped back from the workforce, and I spent a year at home with my wife and four young children. But all I learned about work–life balance from that year was that I found it quite easy to balance work and life when I didn't have any work. (*Laughter*) Not a very useful skill, especially when the money runs out.

1.30 So I went back to work, and I've spent these seven years since struggling with, studying and writing about work–life balance. And I have four observations I'd like to share with you today. The first is: if society's to make any progress on this issue, we need an honest debate. But the trouble is so many people talk so much rubbish about work–life balance. All the discussions about flexitime or dress-down Fridays or paternity leave only serve to mask the core issue, which is that certain job and career choices are fundamentally incompatible with being meaningfully engaged on a day-to-day basis with a young family. Now the first step in solving any problem is acknowledging the reality of the situation you're in. And the reality of the society that we're in is there are thousands and thousands of people out there leading lives of quiet, screaming desperation, where they work long, hard hours at jobs they hate to enable them to buy things they don't need to impress people they don't like. (*Laughter*) (*Applause*) It's my contention that going to work on Friday in jeans and [a] T-shirt isn't really getting to the nub of the issue.

3.02 (*Laughter*)

3.06 The second observation I'd like to make is we need to face the truth that governments and corporations aren't going to solve this issue for us. We should stop looking outside. It's up to us as individuals to take control and responsibility for the type of lives that we want to lead. If you don't design your life, someone else will design it for you, and you may just not like their idea of balance. On the one hand, putting childcare facilities in the workplace is wonderful and enlightened. On the other hand, it's a nightmare – it just means you spend more time at the bloody office. We have to be responsible for setting and enforcing the boundaries that we want in our life.

3.57 The third observation is we have to be careful with the time frame that we choose upon which to judge our balance. We need to be realistic. You can't do it all in one day. We need to elongate the time frame upon which we judge the balance in our life, but we need to elongate it without falling into the trap of the 'I'll have a life when I retire, when my kids have left home, when my wife has divorced me, my health is failing, I've got no mates or interests left.' (*Laughter*) A day is too short; 'after I retire' is too long. There's got to be a middle way.

4.42 A fourth observation: we need to approach balance in a balanced way. A friend came to see me last year – and she doesn't mind me telling this story – a friend came to see me last year and said, 'Nigel, I've read your book. And I realize that my life is completely out of balance. It's totally dominated by work. I work ten hours a day; I commute two hours a day. All of my relationships have failed. There's nothing in my life apart from my work. So I've decided to get a grip and sort it out. So I joined a gym.' (*Laughter*) Now I don't mean to mock, but being a fit ten-hour-a-day office rat isn't more balanced; it's more fit. (*Laughter*) Lovely though physical exercise may be, there are other parts to life – there's the intellectual side; there's the emotional side; there's the spiritual side. And to be balanced, I believe we have to attend to all of those areas – not just do 50 stomach crunches.

5.51   I truly understand how that can be daunting. But an incident that happened a couple of years ago gave me a new perspective. My wife, who is somewhere in the audience today, called me up at the office and said, 'Nigel, you need to pick our youngest son' – Harry – 'up from school.' Because she had to be somewhere else with the other three children for that evening. So I left work an hour early that afternoon and picked Harry up at the school gates. We walked down to the local park, messed around on the swings, played some silly games. I then walked him up the hill to the local café, and we shared a pizza for tea, then walked down the hill to our home, and I gave him his bath and put him in his Batman pyjamas. I then read him a chapter of Roald Dahl's *James and the Giant Peach*. I then put him to bed, tucked him in, gave him a kiss on his forehead and said, 'Goodnight, mate,' and walked out of his bedroom. As I was walking out of his bedroom, he said, 'Dad?' I went, 'Yes, mate?' He went, 'Dad, this has been the best day of my life, ever.' I hadn't done anything, hadn't taken him to Disney World or bought him a Playstation.

7.07   Now my point is the small things matter. Being more balanced doesn't mean dramatic upheaval in your life. With the smallest investment in the right places, you can radically transform the quality of your relationships and the quality of your life. Moreover, I think, it can transform society. Because if enough people do it, we can change society's definition of success away from the moronically simplistic notion that the person with the most money when he dies wins, to a more thoughtful and balanced definition of what a life well lived looks like. And that, I think, is an idea worth spreading.

7.54   (*Applause*)

Unit 9 Doodlers, unite!

0.13   So I just want to tell you my story. I spend a lot of time teaching adults how to use visual language and doodling in the workplace. And naturally, I encounter a lot of resistance, because it's sort of considered to be anti-intellectual and counter to serious learning. But I have a problem with that belief, because I know that doodling has a profound impact on the way that we can process information and the way that we can solve problems.

0.39   So I was curious about why there was a disconnect between the way our society perceives doodling and the way that the reality is. So I discovered some very interesting things. For example, there is no such thing as a flattering definition of a doodle. In the 17th century, a doodle was a simpleton or a fool – as in Yankee Doodle. In the 18th century, it became a verb, and it meant to swindle or ridicule or to make fun of someone. In the 19th century, it was a corrupt politician. And today, we have what is perhaps our most offensive definition, at least to me, which is the following: to doodle officially means to dawdle, to dilly dally, to monkey around, to make meaningless marks, to do something of little value, substance or import, and – my personal favourite — to do nothing. No wonder people are averse to doodling at work.

1.32   Additionally, I've heard horror stories from people whose teachers scolded them, of course, for doodling in classrooms. And they have bosses who scold them for doodling in the boardroom. There is a powerful cultural norm against doodling in settings in which we are supposed to learn something. And unfortunately, the press tends to reinforce this norm when they're reporting on a doodling scene – of an important person at a confirmation hearing and the like – they typically use words like 'discovered' or 'caught' or 'found out', as if there's some sort of criminal act being committed.

2.02   And additionally, there is a psychological aversion to doodling – thank you, Freud. In the 1930s, Freud told us all that you could analyse people's psyches based on their doodles. This is not accurate.

2.15   And here is the real deal. Here's what I believe. I think that our culture is so intensely focused on verbal information that we're almost blinded to the value of doodling. And I'm not comfortable with that. And so because of that belief that I think needs to be burst, I'm here to send us all hurtling back to the truth. And here's the truth: doodling is an incredibly powerful tool, and it is a tool that we need to remember and to relearn.

2.40   So here's a new definition for doodling. Doodling is really to make spontaneous marks to help yourself think. That is why millions of people doodle. Here's another interesting truth about the doodle: people who doodle when they're exposed to verbal information retain more of that information than their non-doodling counterparts. We think doodling is something you do when you lose focus, but in reality, it is a pre-emptive measure to stop you from losing focus. Additionally, it has a profound effect on creative problem-solving and deep information processing.

3.14   There are four ways that learners intake information so that they can make decisions. They are visual, auditory, reading and writing, and kinaesthetic. Now in order for us to really chew on information and do something with it, we have to engage at least two of those modalities, or we have to engage one of those modalities coupled with an emotional experience. The incredible contribution of the doodle is that it engages all four learning modalities simultaneously with the possibility of an emotional experience. That is a pretty solid contribution for a behaviour equated with doing nothing.

3.50   This is so nerdy, but this made me cry when I discovered this. So they did anthropological research into the unfolding of artistic activity in children, and they found that, across space and time, all children exhibit the same evolution in visual logic as they grow. In other words, they have a shared and growing complexity in visual language that happens in a predictable order. And I think that is incredible. I think that means doodling is native to us and we simply are denying ourselves that instinct. And finally, a lot a people aren't privy to this, but the doodle is a precursor to some of our greatest cultural assets. This is but one: this is Frank Gehry the architect's precursor to the Guggenheim in Abu Dhabi.

4.31 So here is my point: under no circumstances should doodling be eradicated from a classroom or a boardroom or even the war room. On the contrary, doodling should be leveraged in precisely those situations where information density is very high and the need for processing that information is very high. And I will go you one further. Because doodling is so universally accessible and it is not intimidating as an art form, it can be leveraged as a portal through which we move people into higher levels of visual literacy. My friends, the doodle has never been the nemesis of intellectual thought. In reality, it is one of its greatest allies.

5.10 Thank you. (*Applause*)

Unit 10 5 ways to listen better

0.13 We are losing our listening. We spend roughly 60 per cent of our communication time listening, but we're not very good at it. We retain just 25 per cent of what we hear. Now not you, not this talk, but that is generally true. Let's define listening as making meaning from sound. It's a mental process, and it's a process of extraction.

0.36 We use some pretty cool techniques to do this. One of them is pattern recognition. (*Crowd noise*) So in a cocktail party like this, if I say, 'David, Sara, pay attention,' some of you just sat up. We recognize patterns to distinguish noise from signal, and especially our name. Differencing is another technique we use. If I left this pink noise on for more than a couple of minutes, you would literally cease to hear it. We listen to differences, we discount sounds that remain the same.

1.05 And then there is a whole range of filters. These filters take us from all sound down to what we pay attention to. Most people are entirely unconscious of these filters. But they actually create our reality in a way, because they tell us what we're paying attention to right now. Give you one example of that: intention is very important in sound, in listening. When I married my wife, I promised her that I would listen to her every day as if for the first time. Now that's something I fall short of on a daily basis. (*Laughter*) But it's a great intention to have in a relationship.

1.43 But that's not all. Sound places us in space and in time. If you close your eyes right now in this room, you're aware of the size of the room from the reverberation and the bouncing of the sound off the surfaces. And you're aware of how many people are around you because of the micro-noises you're receiving. And sound places us in time as well, because sound always has time embedded in it. In fact, I would suggest that our listening is the main way that we experience the flow of time from past to future. So, 'Sonority is time and meaning' – a great quote.

2.17 I said at the beginning, we're losing our listening. Why did I say that? Well there are a lot of reasons for this. First of all, we invented ways of recording – first writing, then audio recording and now video recording as well. The premium on accurate and careful listening has simply disappeared. Secondly, the world is now so noisy, (*Noise*) with this cacophony going on visually and auditorily, it's just hard to listen; it's tiring to listen. Many people take refuge in headphones, but they turn big, public spaces like this, shared soundscapes, into millions of tiny, little personal sound bubbles. In this scenario, nobody's listening to anybody.

3.00 We're becoming impatient. We don't want oratory anymore, we want sound bites. And the art of conversation is being replaced – dangerously, I think – by personal broadcasting. I don't know how much listening there is in this conversation, which is sadly very common, especially in the UK. We're becoming desensitized. Our media have to scream at us with these kinds of headlines in order to get our attention. And that means it's harder for us to pay attention to the quiet, the subtle, the understated.

3.33 This is a serious problem that we're losing our listening. This is not trivial. Because listening is our access to understanding. Conscious listening always creates understanding. I'd like to share with you five simple exercises, tools you can take away with you, to improve your own conscious listening. Would you like that?

3.57 (*Audience: yes*) Good.

3.59 The first one is silence. Just three minutes a day of silence is a wonderful exercise to reset your ears and to recalibrate so that you can hear the quiet again. If you can't get absolute silence, go for quiet, that's absolutely fine.

4.13 Second, I call this the mixer. (*Noise*) So even if you're in a noisy environment like this – and we all spend a lot of time in places like this – listen in the coffee bar to how many channels of sound can I hear? How many individual channels in that mix am I listening to? You can do it in a beautiful place as well, like a lake. How many birds am I hearing? Where are they? Where are those ripples? It's a great exercise for improving the quality of your listening.

4.41 Third, this exercise I call savouring, and this is a beautiful exercise. It's about enjoying mundane sounds. This, for example, is my tumble dryer. (*Dryer*) It's a waltz. One, two, three. One, two, three. One, two, three. I love it. Or just try this one on for size. (*Coffee grinder*) Wow! So mundane sounds can be really interesting if you pay attention. I call that the hidden choir. It's around us all the time.

5.16 The next exercise is probably the most important of all of these, if you just take one thing away. This is listening positions – the idea that you can move your listening position to what's appropriate to what you're listening to. This is playing with those filters. Do you remember, I gave you those filters at the beginning. It's starting to play with them as levers, to get conscious about them and to move to different places. These are just some of the listening positions, or scales of listening positions, that you can use. There are many. Have fun with that. It's very exciting.

5.47 And finally, an acronym. You can use this in listening, in communication. If you're in any one of those roles – and I think that probably is everybody who's listening to this talk – the acronym is RASA, which is the Sanskrit word for juice

	or essence. And RASA stands for: Receive, which means pay attention to the person; Appreciate, making little noises like 'hmm', 'oh', 'OK'; Summarize, the word 'so' is very important in communication; and Ask, ask questions afterward.
6.18	Now sound is my passion, it's my life. I wrote a whole book about it. So I live to listen. That's too much to ask from most people. But I believe that every human being needs to listen consciously in order to live fully – connected in space and in time to the physical world around us, connected in understanding to each other, not to mention spiritually connected, because every spiritual path I know of has listening and contemplation at its heart.
6.47	So I invite you to connect with me, connect with each other, take this mission out and let's get listening taught in schools, and transform the world in one generation to a conscious listening world – a world of connection, a world of understanding and a world of peace.
7.01	Thank you for listening to me today.
7.03	(Applause)

Unit 11 Cloudy with a chance of joy

0.14	Clouds. Have you ever noticed how much people moan about them? They get a bad rap. If you think about it, the English language has written into it negative associations towards the clouds. Someone who's down or depressed, they're under a cloud. And when there's bad news in store, there's a cloud on the horizon. I saw an article the other day. It was about problems with computer processing over the Internet. 'A cloud over the cloud,' was the headline.
0.47	It seems like they're everyone's default doom-and-gloom metaphor. But I think they're beautiful, don't you? It's just that their beauty is missed because they're so omnipresent, so, I don't know, commonplace, that people don't notice them. They don't notice the beauty, but they don't even notice the clouds unless they get in the way of the sun. And so people think of clouds as things that get in the way. They think of them as the annoying, frustrating obstructions, and then they rush off and do some blue-sky thinking.
1.22	(Laughter)
1.24	But most people, when you stop to ask them, will admit to harbouring a strange sort of fondness for clouds. It's like a nostalgic fondness, and they make them think of their youth. Who here can't remember thinking, well, looking and finding shapes in the clouds when they were kids? You know, when you were masters of daydreaming?
1.51	Aristophanes, the ancient Greek playwright, he described the clouds as the patron goddesses of idle fellows two and a half thousand years ago, and you can see what he means. It's just that these days, us adults seem reluctant to allow ourselves the indulgence of just allowing our imaginations to drift along in the breeze, and I think that's a pity. I think we should perhaps do a bit more of it. I think we should be a bit more willing, perhaps, to look at the beautiful sight of the sunlight bursting out from behind the clouds and go, 'Wait a minute, that's two cats dancing the salsa!'
2.31	(Laughter) (Applause)
2.33	Or seeing the big, white, puffy one up there over the shopping centre looks like the Abominable Snowman going to rob a bank.
2.44	(Laughter)
2.47	Perhaps you're having a moment of existential angst. You know, you're thinking about your own mortality. And there, on the horizon, it's the Grim Reaper.
3.01	But one thing I do know is this: the bad press that clouds get is totally unfair. I think we should stand up for them, which is why, a few years ago, I started the Cloud Appreciation Society. Tens of thousands of members now in almost 100 countries around the world. And all these photographs that I'm showing, they were sent in by members. And the society exists to remind people of this: clouds are not something to moan about. Far from it. They are, in fact, the most diverse, evocative, poetic aspect of nature. I think, if you live with your head in the clouds every now and then, it helps you keep your feet on the ground. And I want to show you why, with the help of some of my favourite types of clouds.
3.49	Let's start with this one. It's the cirrus cloud, named after the Latin for a lock of hair. It's composed entirely of ice crystals cascading from the upper reaches of the troposphere, and as these ice crystals fall, they pass through different layers with different winds and they speed up and slow down, giving the cloud these brush-stroked appearances, these brush-stroke forms known as fall streaks. And these winds up there can be very, very fierce. They can be 200 miles an hour, 300 miles an hour. These clouds are bombing along, but from all the way down here, they appear to be moving gracefully, slowly, like most clouds. And so to tune into the clouds is to slow down, to calm down. It's like a bit of everyday meditation.
4.31	Those are common clouds. What about rarer ones, like the lenticularis, the UFO-shaped lenticularis cloud? These clouds form in the region of mountains. When the wind passes, rises to pass over the mountain, it can take on a wave-like path in the lee of the peak, with these clouds hovering at the crest of these invisible standing waves of air, these flying saucer-like forms, and some of the early black-and-white UFO photos are in fact lenticularis clouds. It's true.
5.00	A little rarer are the fallstreak holes. All right? This is when a layer is made up of very, very cold water droplets, and in one region they start to freeze, and this freezing sets off a chain reaction which spreads outwards with the ice crystals cascading and falling down below, giving the appearance of jellyfish tendrils down below.
5.19	Rarer still, the Kelvin–Helmholtz cloud. Not a very snappy name. Needs a rebrand. This looks like a series of breaking waves, and it's caused by shearing winds – the wind above the cloud layer and below the cloud layer differ significantly, and in the middle, in between, you get this undulating of the air, and if the difference in those speeds is just right, the tops of the undulations curl over in these beautiful breaking wave-like vortices.
5.48	All right. Those are rarer clouds than the cirrus, but they're not that rare. If you look up, and you pay attention to the sky, you'll see them sooner or later, maybe not quite as

dramatic as these, but you'll see them. And you'll see them around where you live. Clouds are the most egalitarian of nature's displays, because we all have a good, fantastic view of the sky. And these clouds, these rarer clouds, remind us that the exotic can be found in the everyday. Nothing is more nourishing, more stimulating to an active, inquiring mind than being surprised, being amazed. It's why we're all here at TED, right? But you don't need to rush off away from the familiar, across the world to be surprised. You just need to step outside, pay attention to what's so commonplace, so everyday, so mundane that everybody else misses it.

6.42 One cloud that people rarely miss is this one: the cumulonimbus storm cloud. It's what produces thunder and lightning and hail. These clouds spread out at the top in this enormous anvil fashion, stretching ten miles up into the atmosphere. They are an expression of the majestic architecture of our atmosphere. But from down below, they are the embodiment of the powerful, elemental force and power that drives our atmosphere. To be there is to be connected in the driving rain and the hail, to feel connected to our atmosphere. It's to be reminded that we are creatures that inhabit this ocean of air. We don't live beneath the sky. We live within it. And that connection, that visceral connection to our atmosphere feels to me like an antidote. It's an antidote to the growing tendency we have to feel that we can really ever experience life by watching it on a computer screen, you know, when we're in a wi-fi zone.

7.43 But the one cloud that best expresses why cloudspotting is more valuable today than ever is this one, the cumulus cloud. Right? It forms on a sunny day. If you close your eyes and think of a cloud, it's probably one of these that comes to mind. All those cloud shapes at the beginning, those were cumulus clouds. The sharp, crisp outlines of this formation make it the best one for finding shapes in. And it reminds us of the aimless nature of cloudspotting, what an aimless activity it is. You're not going to change the world by lying on your back and gazing up at the sky, are you? It's pointless. It's a pointless activity, which is precisely why it's so important.

8.31 The digital world conspires to make us feel eternally busy, perpetually busy. You know, when you're not dealing with the traditional pressures of earning a living and putting food on the table, raising a family, writing thank-you letters, you have to now contend with answering a mountain of unanswered emails, updating a Facebook page, feeding your Twitter feed. And cloudspotting legitimizes doing nothing.

9.01 (Laughter)

9.03 And sometimes we need –

9.05 (Applause)

9.12 Sometimes we need excuses to do nothing. We need to be reminded by these patron goddesses of idle fellows that slowing down and being in the present, not thinking about what you've got to do and what you should have done, but just being here, letting your imagination lift from the everyday concerns down here and just being in the present, it's good for you, and it's good for the way you feel. It's good for your ideas. It's good for your creativity. It's good for your soul.

9.48 So keep looking up, marvel at the ephemeral beauty, and always remember to live life with your head in the clouds.

9.58 Thank you very much.

9.59 (Applause)

Unit 12 Dare to disagree

0.13 In Oxford in the 1950s, there was a fantastic doctor, who was very unusual, named Alice Stewart. And Alice was unusual partly because, of course, she was a woman, which was pretty rare in the 1950s. And she was brilliant, she was one of the, at the time, the youngest Fellow to be elected to the Royal College of Physicians. She was unusual too because she continued to work after she got married, after she had kids, and even after she got divorced and was a single parent, she continued her medical work.

0.46 And she was unusual because she was really interested in a new science, the emerging field of epidemiology, the study of patterns in disease. But like every scientist, she appreciated that to make her mark, what she needed to do was find a hard problem and solve it. The hard problem that Alice chose was the rising incidence of childhood cancers. Most disease is correlated with poverty, but in the case of childhood cancers, the children who were dying seemed mostly to come from affluent families. So, what, she wanted to know, could explain this anomaly?

1.25 Now, Alice had trouble getting funding for her research. In the end, she got just 1,000 pounds from the Lady Tata Memorial prize. And that meant she knew she only had one shot at collecting her data. Now, she had no idea what to look for. This really was a needle in a haystack sort of search, so she asked everything she could think of. Had the children eaten boiled sweets? Had they consumed coloured drinks? Did they eat fish and chips? Did they have indoor or outdoor plumbing? What time of life had they started school?

1.56 And when her carbon-copied questionnaire started to come back, one thing and one thing only jumped out with the statistical clarity of a kind that most scientists can only dream of. By a rate of two to one, the children who had died had had mothers who had been X-rayed when pregnant. Now that finding flew in the face of conventional wisdom. Conventional wisdom held that everything was safe up to a point, a threshold. It flew in the face of conventional wisdom, which was huge enthusiasm for the cool new technology of that age, which was the X-ray machine. And it flew in the face of doctors' idea of themselves, which was as people who helped patients, they didn't harm them.

2.49 Nevertheless, Alice Stewart rushed to publish her preliminary findings in The Lancet in 1956. People got very excited, there was talk of the Nobel Prize, and Alice really was in a big hurry to try to study all the cases of childhood cancer she could find before they disappeared. In fact, she need not have hurried. It was fully 25 years before the British and medical – British and American medical establishments abandoned the practice of X-raying

	pregnant women. The data was out there, it was open, it was freely available, but nobody wanted to know. A child a week was dying, but nothing changed. Openness alone can't drive change.
3.46	So for 25 years Alice Stewart had a very big fight on her hands. So, how did she know that she was right? Well, she had a fantastic model for thinking. She worked with a statistician named George Kneale, and George was pretty much everything that Alice wasn't. So, Alice was very outgoing and sociable, and George was a recluse. Alice was very warm, very empathetic with her patients. George frankly preferred numbers to people. But he said this fantastic thing about their working relationship. He said, 'My job is to prove Dr Stewart wrong.' He actively sought disconfirmation: different ways of looking at her models, at her statistics, different ways of crunching the data in order to disprove her. He saw his job as creating conflict around her theories. Because it was only by not being able to prove that she was wrong, that George could give Alice the confidence she needed to know that she was right.
4.57	It's a fantastic model of collaboration – thinking partners who aren't echo chambers. I wonder how many of us have, or dare to have, such collaborators? Alice and George were very good at conflict. They saw it as thinking.
5.23	So what does that kind of constructive conflict require? Well, first of all, it requires that we find people who are very different from ourselves. That means we have to resist the neurobiological drive, which means that we really prefer people mostly like ourselves, and it means we have to seek out people with different backgrounds, different disciplines, different ways of thinking and different experience, and find ways to engage with them. That requires a lot of patience and a lot of energy.
5.59	And the more I've thought about this, the more I think, really, that that's a kind of love. Because you simply won't commit that kind of energy and time if you don't really care. And it also means that we have to be prepared to change our minds. Alice's daughter told me that every time Alice went head-to-head with a fellow scientist, they made her think and think and think again. 'My mother,' she said, 'My mother didn't enjoy a fight, but she was really good at them.'
6.38	So how do we develop the skills that we need? Because it does take skill and practice too. If we aren't going to be afraid of conflict, we have to see it as thinking, and then we have to get really good at it. So, recently, I worked with an executive named Joe, and Joe worked for a medical device company. And Joe was very worried about the device that he was working on. He thought that it was too complicated and he thought that its complexity created margins of error that could really hurt people. He was afraid of doing damage to the patients he was trying to help. But when he looked around his organization, nobody else seemed to be at all worried. So, he didn't really want to say anything. After all, maybe they knew something he didn't. Maybe he'd look stupid. But he kept worrying about it, and he worried about it so much that he got to the point where he thought the only thing he could do was leave a job he loved.
7.45	In the end, Joe and I found a way for him to raise his concerns. And what happened then is what almost always happens in this situation. It turned out everybody had exactly the same questions and doubts. So now Joe had allies. They could think together. And yes, there was a lot of conflict and debate and argument, but that allowed everyone around the table to be creative, to solve the problem, and to change the device.
8.20	Joe was what a lot of people might think of as a whistle-blower, except that like almost all whistle-blowers, he wasn't a crank at all, he was passionately devoted to the organization and the higher purposes that that organization served. But he had been so afraid of conflict, until finally he became more afraid of the silence. And when he dared to speak, he discovered much more inside himself and much more give in the system than he had ever imagined. And his colleagues don't think of him as a crank. They think of him as a leader.
9.05	So, how do we have these conversations more easily and more often? Well, the University of Delft requires that its PhD students have to submit five statements that they're prepared to defend. It doesn't really matter what the statements are about, what matters is that the candidates are willing and able to stand up to authority. I think it's a fantastic system, but I think leaving it to PhD candidates is far too few people, and way too late in life. I think we need to be teaching these skills to kids and adults at every stage of their development, if we want to have thinking organizations and a thinking society.
9.52	The fact is that most of the biggest catastrophes that we've witnessed rarely come from information that is secret or hidden. It comes from information that is freely available and out there, but that we are willfully blind to, because we can't handle, don't want to handle, the conflict that it provokes. But when we dare to break that silence, or when we dare to see, and we create conflict, we enable ourselves and the people around us to do our very best thinking.
10.34	Open information is fantastic, open networks are essential. But the truth won't set us free until we develop the skills and the habit and the talent and the moral courage to use it. Openness isn't the end. It's the beginning.
10.56	(Applause)

NATIONAL GEOGRAPHIC LEARNING

Keynote Upper Intermediate Student's Book with the Spark platform
Helen Stephenson

Publisher: Gavin McLean

Publishing Consultant: Karen Spiller

Development Editor: Liz Driscoll

Editorial Manager: Alison Burt

Head of Strategic Marketing ELT: Charlotte Ellis

Senior Content Project Manager: Nick Ventullo

Manufacturing Manager: Eyvett Davis

Cover design: Brenda Carmichael

Text design: Keith Shaw

Compositor: MPS North America LLC

National Geographic Liaison: Leila Hishmeh

Audio: Tom Dick and Debbie Productions Ltd

DVD: Tom Dick and Debbie Productions Ltd

Cover Photo Caption: View of speaker Nilofer Merchant from the very top of the house at TED2013 - The Young The Wise The Undiscovered, Long Beach, California. February 25 - March 1, 2013. Photo: © Michael Brands/TED.

© 2016 National Geographic Learning, a Cengage Learning Company

ALL RIGHTS RESERVED. No part of this work covered by the copyright herein may be reproduced or distributed in any form or by any means, except as permitted by U.S. copyright law, without the prior written permission of the copyright owner.

"National Geographic", "National Geographic Society" and the Yellow Border Design are registered trademarks of the National Geographic Society ® Marcas Registradas

> For product information and technology assistance, contact us at
> **Cengage Learning Customer & Sales Support, cengage.com/contact**
> For permission to use material from this text or product,
> submit all requests online at **cengage.com/permissions**
> Further permissions questions can be emailed to
> **permissionrequest@cengage.com**

ISBN-13: 979-8-214-33432-5

National Geographic Learning
Cheriton House, North Way,
Andover, Hampshire, SP10 5BE
United Kingdom

National Geographic Learning, a Cengage Learning Company, has a mission to bring the world to the classroom and the classroom to life. With our English language programs, students learn about their world by experiencing it. Through our partnerships with National Geographic and TED Talks, they develop the language and skills they need to be successful global citizens and leaders.

Locate your local office at **international.cengage.com/region**

Visit National Geographic Learning online at **ELTNGL.com**
Visit our corporate website at **www.cengage.com**

CREDITS

The publishers would like to thank TED Staff for their insightful feedback and expert guidance, allowing us to achieve our dual aims of maintaining the integrity of these inspirational TED Talks, while maximising their potential for teaching English.

The publisher would like to thank all the reviewers who took part in the piloting and development of the material.

Although every effort has been made to contact copyright holders before publication, this has not always been possible. If contacted, the publisher will undertake to rectify any errors or omissions at the earliest opportunity.

The publishers would like to thank the following for permission to use copyright material:

Text: 135 The Big Issue for text adapted from 'Letter to my younger self', The Big Issue, http://www.bigissue.com/features/letter-my-younger-self. Reproduced with permission.

Cover: © Michael Brands/TED.

Photos: 6 (tl, tr, bl) © James Duncan Davidson/TED; 6 (ml) © Robert Leslie/TED; 6 (mr) © TED Conferences, LLC; 6 (br) © Ryan Lash/TED; 7 (tl) © Ryan Lash/TED; 7 (tr) © Nils Jorgensen/REX/Newscom; 7 (ml, mr, bl, br) © James Duncan Davidson/TED; 8 © Robb Kendrick/National Geographic Creative; 9 © James Duncan Davidson/TED; 10 © James Duncan Davidson/TED; 11 © Bloomua/Shutterstock.com; 15 (l) © ryabinina/Shutterstock.com; 15 (r) © Yuri_Arcurs/Getty Images; 16 © Cultura Creative (RF)/Alamy; 18 © Gerd Ludwig/National Geographic Creative; 19 © James Duncan Davidson/TED; 20 © James Duncan Davidson/TED; 21 © PhotoAlto/Laurence Mouton/Getty Images; 23 © Echo/Getty Images; 25 © Luis Alvarez/Getty Images; 26 © Jason Alden/Bloomberg/Getty Images; 28 © Disability Images/Alamy; 30–31 © Leon Chew; 30 © Robert Leslie/TED; 32 © Robert Leslie/TED; 33 (l) © luoman/iStockphoto; 33 (ml) © Givaga/Shutterstock.com; 33 (mr) © natrot/Shutterstock.com; 33 (r) © bestv/Shutterstock.com; 38 (t) © Thomas Barwick/Getty Images; 38 (b) © Ariel Skelley/Getty Images; 39 © Blend Images/Shutterstock.com; 40–41 © Christopher Gregory/The New York Times/Redux Pictures; 40 © Rob Waymen; 42 (all) © TED Conferences, LLC; 43 (l) © Ian Shaw/Alamy; 43 (r) © Marc Romanelli/Getty Images; 44 (tl) © Dusko Despotovic/Sygma/Corbis; 44 (tm) © Popperfoto/Getty Images; 44 (tr) © epa european pressphoto agency b.v./Alamy; 44 (bl) © Adrian Sherratt/Alamy; 44 (bm) © Francois Guillot/AFP/Getty Images; 44 (br) © Omar Torres/AFP/Getty Images; 45 © Bruce Glikas/FilmMagic/Getty Images; 47 © Hill Street Studios/Getty Images; 48 © The Republican-Herald, Jacqueline Dormer/AP Photo; 50 © Krochet Kids Intl.; 52–53 © Mike Tittel/Cultura/Aurora Photos; 52 © James Duncan Davidson/TED; 54 © James Duncan Davidson/TED; 55 (t) © Vector/Shutterstock.com; 55 (m) © sonia.eps/Shutterstock.com; 55 (b) © 123render/Getty Images; 57 © Delly Carr/Sportshoot; 59 © John Martin/Alamy; 60 © wavebreakmedia/Shutterstock.com; 61 © The Canadian Press, Phil Skinner/AP Photo; 62–63 © Danny MacAskill; 62 © Ryan Lash/TED; 64 © Ryan Lash/TED; 66 (tl) © Grzegorz Petrykowski/Shutterstock.com; 66 (tr) © cobalt88/Shutterstock.com; 66 (bl) © Denys Prykhodov/Shutterstock.com; 66 (br) © Aleksandra Pikalova/Shutterstock.com; 67 © wavebreakmedia/Shutterstock.com; 69 © Gavin Gough/Getty Images; 70 © Lionel Bonaventure/AFP/Getty Images; 71 (tl) © jethuynh/Shutterstock.com; 71 (tr) © sosha/Shutterstock.com; 71 (b) © Paul Fleet/Alamy; 72 © FooARage; 73 © By Ian Miles-Flashpoint Pictures/Alamy; 74 © Aurora Photos/Alamy; 75 © Ryan Lash/TED; 76 © Ryan Lash/TED; 79 (left col: l) © Alexander Raths/Shutterstock.com; 79 (left col: r) © Kendall/D2G2 Group; 79 (right col: tl) © David Paul Morris/Bloomberg/Getty Images; 79 (right col: tr) © Zoran Milich/Getty Images; 79 (right col: bl) © Phil Degginger/Alamy; 79 (right col: br) © Rex Features/AP Images; 81 © JGI/Jamie Grill/Getty Images; 82 © Matthew Chattle/Alamy; 84 © Dawn Kish/National Geographic Creative; 85 © Nils Jorgensen/REX/Newscom; 86 (all) © TED Conferences, LLC; 87 © Cultura Creative (RF)/Alamy; 91 © andresr/Getty Images; 92 © Hero Images/Getty Images; 94 © AP Photo/Roswell Daily Record, Bill Moffitt; 96 © Charlie Pérez/Demotix/Corbis; 97 © James Duncan Davidson/TED; 98 © James Duncan Davidson/TED; 103 © chatchai surakram/Alamy; 104 © epa european pressphoto agency b.v./Alamy; 105 © MoMo Productions/Getty Images; 106–107 © Quang Tran; 106 © James Duncan Davidson/TED; 108 © James Duncan Davidson/TED; 111 (l) © Twitter; 111 (r) © maxim ibragimov/Shutterstock.com; 113 © Manuela Weschke/Getty Images; 114 © ullstein bild/Getty Images; 116 © Hero Images/Getty Images; 118–119 © Gabriel Marian/National Geographic Creative; 118 © James Duncan Davidson/TED; 120 © James Duncan Davidson/TED; 121 Courtesy of Helen Stephenson; 123 © Rex Features/AP Images; 125 © David Gee/Alamy; 126 © Claudia Wiens/Alamy; 128 © XPACIFICA/National Geographic Creative; 129 © James Duncan Davidson/TED; 130 © James Duncan Davidson/TED; 135 © Adrian Brown/Bloomberg/Getty Images; 136 © Ute Grabowsky/Photothek/Getty Images; 138 © Sanum Jain.

Illustrations and Infographics: 12, 22, 34, 44, 56, 66, 78, 88, 89, 100, 103, 109, 110, 122, 132 emc design; 36, 37, 124 MPS North America LLC.

Infographics: 22 Source: PewResearchCenter: Global Gender Gaps – Women Like Their Lives Better (October 29, 2003); 34 Source: IMF, World Economic Outlook; 122 Source: RIA Novosti ©2010; 132 Sources: comScore, Radicati Group, Twitter, Asigra

Printed in Greece by Bakis SA
Print Number: 03 Print Year: 2025